FIVE AT 10

Also by Diana Farr

Gilbert Cannan: A Georgian Prodigy

Five at 10

Prime Ministers' Consorts Since 1957

DIANA FARR

ANDRE DEUTSCH

First published 1985 by
André Deutsch Limited
105 Great Russell Street
London WC1

British Library Cataloguing in Publication Data

Farr, Diana
    Five at 10: prime ministers' consorts since 1957.
    1. Prime ministers' wives — Great Britain —
    Biography 2. Women prime ministers' husbands —
    Great Britain—Biography
    I. Title
    941.085'092'2   DA590

    ISBN 0-233-97733-3

Typeset by Inforum Ltd, Portsmouth
Printed in Great Britain by
The St Edmundsbury Press, Bury St Edmunds, Suffolk

To Jerry Epstein

*who thought of the book
and encouraged me with unfailing enthusiasm
to write it*

CONTENTS

━━━

LIST OF ILLUSTRATIONS

ACKNOWLEDGEMENTS

First I thank most warmly the subjects of this book with the exception, of course, of the late Lady Dorothy Macmillan. It is not always pleasant to be selected for a biography, and I particularly appreciate the time given to me by Lady Home of the Hirsel (who once jokily described herself as one of my 'victims'), Lady Wilson of Rievaulx and Mrs James Callaghan. All three generously granted me interviews and checked their own profiles. I am also deeply indebted to the Duke of Devonshire for talking to me about his aunt, for allowing me to quote from his grandfather's diaries and for reading, with the Duchess's assistance, my piece on Lady Dorothy. I am very grateful to Mr Derek Howe, of Conservative Central Office, who provided vital information and checked the profile of Denis Thatcher, to whom he turned for advice and confirmation when he felt it necessary.

I also express my appreciation for kind suggestions, corrections and comments made by Mr James Callaghan and Lord Home. Mr Charles Regan's meticulous reading of the book has been invaluable. His expert and experienced eye picked up inaccuracies which escaped many of us. My thanks go also to Mr Jerry Epstein whose guidance and unflagging enthusiasm have sustained me throughout, especially during those moments of crisis which beset every biographer.

Many people from different walks of life have generously assisted me with memories, anecdotes, information and hospitality. Without them the book would not have been possible. Some wish to remain anonymous, but I am delighted to record my most sincere thanks to the following: Lady Catherine Amery, Dr Eric Anderson (head master of Eton), Miss E. Barchard, Lord Barnett of Heywood and Royton, Mrs Georgina Battiscombe, Miss Rosemary Bishop, Lord Boothby, Mrs Alan Bullock, Mrs Ursula Boyer, Mr Ted Cathie, Mr Christopher Chataway, Mr D.C. Crane, Mr and Mrs S. Collingwood, Miss Jean F. Darge, Lady Falkender, Mr G.W. Fenn, Miss Peggy Field, Mr T.J. Gillighan, Mrs G.E. Hatcher, Lady Hickman, Mr Anthony Holden, Lady Hornsby-Smith, Mrs Roshan Horobin, Lord Houghton of Sowerby, Mrs Laurette Hudson, Mrs Margaret Jay, Lord Kissin of Camden, Mr R.G.B. Milchem, Miss Anthea Montgomery, Mrs Harry Moon, Mr Edward Moore, Mrs M.J. Mould, Mrs Shirley Mowbray, Lord Paget of

---

Northampton, Miss Peggy Read, Major General D.H.G. Rice, Mr Andrew Roth, Brigadier J.S. Ryder, Mr Nicholas Scott MP, Mr Ray Sollett, Mrs Margot Strickland, Mr G.C. Sutcliffe, Mr Anthony Swainson, Mrs Annette Warren, Mr John Wells and Mr Keith Wilson.

In addition, I wish to thank for their specialist advice: Mrs Griselda Bear and Miss Anne House of Canada House, London, Mr Peter Day of the Devonshire Collections, Chatsworth, Mr William Reid of the National Army Museum, and their staff. I also acknowledge most gratefully the willing co-operation and help I received from the staff at the British Library Newspaper Library, Chiswick Public Library, the Imperial War Museum, the London Library, and the Public Records Office.

Finally, I thank Mrs Pamela Hewitt who typed the book so good naturedly, my husband, Dennis, for his wise counsel and my children, Benedict and Joanna for their patience and good humour.

The author wishes to thank her subjects for supplying photographs. Other illustrations are reproduced by permission as follows: Central Press (1. far right; 4. bottom right, bottom left; 8. top); Keystone Press (3. top, centre left, centre right; 7. top); Srdja Djukanovic (8. centre, bottom); Associated Press (1. centre); Rex Features (7. bottom – credit Herbie Knott); *The Times* (6. top left).

Extracts from Mary Wilson's poems reproduced by kind permission of Mary Wilson and Hutchinson Ltd.

Author's note
In these profiles I have used the names by which I believe my subjects are best known to the general public.

PROLOGUE

Some years ago when my husband was director of the City of Birmingham Museums and Art Gallery, I became accustomed to being in a small way the wife of a public figure. Although I was happy enough, it was a position which did not entirely suit my temperament, since I am not, I think, without a certain egocentricity and a touch of ill-placed pride. Certainly I never became entirely reconciled to being introduced as 'the director's wife'. I was not jealous but I wanted to be recognised for myself as well and had never intended when I married to be judged on my husband's achievements rather than my own personality. At times I felt that I was simply an appendage and this set me thinking about the wives of important men. Mary Wilson I knew wanted to be recognised as a poet. But what of the others? For almost a decade I had stood in the receiving line of the Art Gallery's annual ball, my fingers squeezed sometimes almost unbearably by three hundred or more hand-shakes. But, I reflected, this was only yearly, while our prime ministers' consorts were constantly on parade. How did *they* survive? Had they also wanted to make their own way in their own right? Had they suspected for a moment the magnitude of their partner's future when they stood at the altar promising love until 'death us do part'?

These thoughts came back with added force when this book was suggested to me, with the extra dimension presented by a male spouse; mild interest quickly sparked into avid enthusiasm. Very soon the work presented me with unusual and fascinating problems, putting me in touch with a host of intriguing people.

Biographers, as all the literary world knows, are beggars. We live on the idiosyncrasies, charity and lives of others. Our progress and success depend largely on the generosity and loquaciousness of our subjects and their friends. We write letters and make telephone calls asking favours, seeking the truth while trying never to be dull.

When you write about those connected with the leaders of our nation you find that the Official Secrets Act has closed the mouths of

I

many of their servants and aides, and that a free and sometimes vociferous press has tempered tongues and taught your subjects unequivocal discretion. More than anyone, they know that an unwise word may be tomorrow's headline.

'For many years I have kept my head below the parapet,' wrote Denis Thatcher in his flamboyant hand, charmingly refusing me an interview.

'Yes, it's a nice flat with that lovely view across Horse Guards,' said Lady Home, though clearly she must have found the official residence cramped compared with the great Border houses in which she has lived.

While Lady Wilson, once hounded more than most by newspaper men, said firmly, as she poured delicious coffee into porcelain cups, that she would gladly talk about her childhood, but not about 'my time as prime minister's wife. My father . . .'

So, like a magpie, I have collected where I can the anecdote, the comment, the newspaper report, to add a little sparkle to the straight biographical detail. I have combed many books by or on the great political figures of the day. My brief has been to describe within a given time how life prepared five very different people to face the privileges and responsibilities of being a prime minister's consort. The outcome, I must stress, is not an academic work, although I have tried throughout to be fair and accurate, but simply five stories for the general reader, linked by a common factor.

In Britain we are fortunate, because the semi-retired spouses of the great normally answer letters sent by friendly and literate outsiders. Although none wished to be the subject of a biography, Lady Home, Lady Wilson and Mrs James Callaghan all agreed to see me.

I travelled to Scotland to The Hirsel where the Homes gave me lunch and help, without ever allowing me to feel like an intruder. On my return the next day to study their scrapbooks, I lay on the carpet, as is my custom, to turn the pages of these large red and green volumes.

'She likes it there,' explained Lady Home, putting a tray with tea beside me on the floor, as her husband wandered through, stopping to water the flowers and plants that are his special care.

Lunching with me at the Tate Gallery, Lady Home was at notable pains to choose the cheapest item on the menu, while I was only too aware that others might have grabbed the opportunity to order the best.

Also generous to an author she had never met, her friend Georgina Battiscombe, the biographer, offered me lunch and spirited talk in her Windsor flat, although she was in the throes of finishing her own book on the Spencers.

These are some of the pleasures of a writer's life, but illuminating and enjoyable though such meetings are, there is a capricious element in recollections which cannot be ignored. Apart from Lady Dorothy Macmillan my subjects and many of their friends were all in, or nearly in, their seventies or eighties and inevitably their memories sometimes played them tricks. On the surface at least we remember what we want to remember, occasionally subconsciously editing accounts to our own advantage, and, as old age approaches, the experiences of childhood are usually clearer than those of our middle years, but even these, as every biographer knows, can be suspect when it comes to dates and detail. In addition I was faced with my subjects' peculiarly British habit of playing down their successes.

It was therefore doubly essential that I should turn particularly to earlier interviews, given at the height of the subject's political life, for a sense of immediacy and greater accuracy. For, because the existence of a prime minister's consort becomes suddenly so full, those years at the top are the most likely to be blurred or telescoped with the passage of time. That is, of course, why diaries are to every writer such a godsend, with scrapbooks a good second best.

I am indeed grateful to the ninth Duke of Devonshire for his daily records, short and mundane though they sometimes are, not least because they pinpoint certain moments in his family life. You cannot argue with an entry which says 'Today we sailed from Southampton.'

Throughout my researches I have attempted to check the authenticity of newspaper reports and other sources of information. Inevitably because no two people see each other in exactly the same light there have been conflicting opinions and stories. It has therefore been my job to sift the evidence and make the final judgements. I have said from the first that this is to be a good-natured book and so it may be that occasionally when in doubt I have been too benign, but I have been struck by the basic kindness of my subjects.

The fear of being a nuisance is a personal drawback which has always ensured that I could never be a journalist, but Audrey Callaghan, more than anyone, has gone out of her way to counter this handicap, despite her own aversion to talking about herself — an emotion shared by Lady Home. During the hours spent talking in the Callaghans' one-bedroom, purpose-built flat in Kennington and in the more spacious rooms, and garden, of their Sussex farmhouse, she became a valued friend. And yet she has remained in some respects the hardest of the five to describe; paradoxically, Denis Thatcher's vivid, four-page letter refusing an interview revealed more personal traits than an hour's talk with Audrey.

Lady Wilson has given so many interviews over the years that she has learned, on top of discretion, to avoid the funny story, a habit completely at variance with reports of the high-spirited accounts of life at Number 10 she gave to friends at the time. After reading the first published interview I found later pieces followed a similar pattern. Talking to her I sometimes felt that her ears were pricked for the question framed to provoke an answer leading to unpleasant innuendo or scandalous suggestions staring at her from a printed page. Experience and libel cases have taught her to build fences round her deeper feelings. Strangers are suspect, biographers unpredictable, but in spite of past traumas and present fears, she was always willing, when she could, to see me or to talk to me over the telephone, so long as I discussed her as a poet and woman in her own right, rather than as her husband's wife. So, for her profile I have turned often to her friends and acquaintances for help, as well as to standard works, listed in the bibliography, such as the *Crossman Diaries*, whose accuracy, it must be said, she sometimes disputes.

My research on Lady Dorothy has taken me to Chatsworth, Bolton Abbey, Holker Hall, Hardwick Hall and Birch Grove, because whenever possible I have seen the houses in which my subjects lived. I have knocked on many a cottage door in Yorkshire and Derbyshire, roasted in tiny rooms heated to the eighties for their octogenarian occupiers, and stood in biting winds talking through windows to retired servants who once knew the Macmillans. One meeting often led to another, but sometimes, after driving danger-ously fast down twisty Yorkshire lanes, I arrived too late; the person I needed was dead or ill or about to take a long journey, and time would not allow me to go back, so that in a sense each profile has been shaped in this book by the information I have found within a given period, for with every biography there comes the time when the detective work must stop and the writing begin.

For Denis Thatcher special patience and persistence has been essential. Two impeccable sources who wish to remain anonymous have provided many basic facts; some unknown, I believe, except to his family and closest friends, which have led to wider fields. I started work on him in the classic way with a birth certificate, moving on to street registers, delighting or dismaying house owners with the news that Denis once ran up and down their stairs and played in their gardens. I have turned mainly to public records and war diaries for details of his military service. I have verified reports on his first marriage by sending information gleaned from various sources to his first wife for comment. One afternoon was wasted on a wild goose chase, when taken in by an April fool's joke in the *Tatler* — of all places — I searched in vain for a son purported to be of that union, who was described as a director of a Chiswick company dealing in spare parts for cars.

I have taken pains not to trivialise, while including incidents which may appear at first glance trivial, when I believe they throw light on character or personality.

A well-meaning friend's suggestion that my subjects' lives might not be intrinsically interesting touched on precisely one of those intriguing questions that I wanted to pursue. Do the powerful choose in youth interesting spouses? Or do they fear a mate's talents, egoism or ambition competing with their own? Are they actually so politically minded that they select a partner with their future career in mind? Or do they, like lesser beings, simply fall in love and marry? Is there indeed any uniform answer to this question, some characteristic or overriding concern common to them all? But, my detractor insisted, I was writing about the second best. 'Who cares where they went to school or whether they wanted their spouse to reach the top?' Thus she ignored the appeal of those books about the first ladies of America which have so captured the American imagination; stories of women, who, like our own prime ministers' spouses, have it in their power to bring down their partners, if not the administration: women whose private lives have already been more open to public scrutiny than their British counterparts', probably largely because of slacker United States' libel and slander laws. They are stars; they are rich; their clothes set fashion; their faces smile from magazine covers, yet almost every iota of their existence continues to be combed by members of the media for new and sometimes trivial information.

As president's wife each one has to some degree played the part of a member of our royal family, whose existence satisfies those who live through the activities of the great and the glamorous, people who might otherwise expect more from our ministers' consorts. Because we have the Queen and her family the subjects of my book have been able to slip occasionally into the shadows, to act the shy pea hen a step behind her more fabulous mate, in a manner not afforded to, or perhaps wanted by, a Jackie Kennedy or Nancy Reagan. Yet who can dispute my subjects' unique place in their partners' lives; their capacity to damage or diminish?

A climate of opinion which can bring political ruin to John Profumo or perhaps jeopardise the career of a Cecil Parkinson as a result of marital infidelity, however fleeting or regretted, ensures that nowadays those in Britain who hold the highest public office must combine with their partners to present an outwardly united marital front. In addition the consort may be expected to provide the base camp, to which the climber returns for comfort and renewal before the final ascent, the voice that says 'You can do it,' the stimulation that sets the adrenalin flowing again when all seems lost. Who can say how much further Lord Butler might have advanced in his political career had his beloved first wife not fallen ill and died at so crucial a moment? Would Neil Kinnock have become leader of the Labour Party without the back-up and inspiration of his intelligent wife?

In so many ways a leading politician's partner can, often unconsciously, change the fate of nations — a nudge in the right or wrong direction, well-meant, sometimes ill-judged advice, sexual rejection, a breakfast quarrel are just a few examples. Such influences are rarely chronicled (although here, paradoxically, the Earl of Stockton is more generous than most eminent husbands). And it is my hope that these profiles may illuminate the lives of those who struggle with the loneliness and stress of a politician's life at one remove, keeping their marriages intact, suppressing their own egoism and desires, to serve, sometimes reluctantly, a spouse and a system.

LADY DOROTHY MACMILLAN

'You can't beat breeding,' remarked one of Lady Dorothy's admirers, but Macmillan's wife never quite resembled the public's idea of a duke's daughter; she possessed a noble nose, of course, and direct blue eyes, but not the elegance, the touch of grandeur, nor the long a's that many people associate with the English nobility. And yet the stamp of the Devonshires undoubtedly was there; the innate characteristics of those who have been at the top for generations. It was not possible that anyone could live at Chatsworth, the Devonshires' country seat, and remain untouched. She was born grand and, with the perversity of human nature or a natural humbleness, she turned away from grandeur, and like her father preferred the earthier aspects of life.

In middle and later years she took on the appearance of an ill-dressed housekeeper or, perhaps, a sensible and hale farmer's wife, for there was always more than a touch of the outdoor woman about her. She strode rather than walked, liked horses although she did not ride, and excelled at gardening, an abiding pleasure which also provided an escape from the griefs and perplexities of life, a therapy which had sustained her father, too, through many tribulations. Impervious to flattery, unimpressed by affectation, she was a woman who would when possible reduce every problem to a practical level and, was, therefore, a fine counterweight to Britain's most intellectual prime minister since Asquith.

Lady Dorothy Evelyn Cavendish was born on July 28th 1900, eight years before her father became the ninth Duke of Devonshire, a title inherited from his uncle, Spencer Compton, who died childless. Her early years were spent at her birthplace, Holker Hall, a Cumbrian mansion, close to Grange-over-Sands, at Cark-in-Cartmel, where the land is green and fertile and the air laced with the salty tang of the sea. Here the Cavendish children lived in the Georgian wing with their nurse and nursery servants while their parents occupied the grander west wing, which had been rebuilt in Elizabethan style after a fire in 1871. Holker Hall, whose influence on the child Dorothy was profound partly because she stayed there longest, and partly because her mother was happiest there, is much homelier than Chatsworth, not only because it is much smaller, but also because its three different styles of architecture have created three different entities whose dimensions keep within limits a child can absorb without feeling diminished. Its gardens were ideal for hide and seek, sardines and all those other games so much enjoyed by Victorian and Edwardian children. There were superb and rare shrubs and trees, and roses, roses everywhere all summer and autumn, and the magic of water, its eddies and its stillness, and the sharp silver flow of the fountain, catching the changing light. As soon as Dorothy's eyes could focus she would have seen the veined leaves, the spiked fruit and the foliage of the sombre conifers and later the reds and golds, russets and browns, the royal colours of dying October leaves; she would have smelled too, the smoky bonfires, overriding the sweeter scents of autumn flowers; and all this she would help to re-create in later years in the green acres that surrounded the Macmillans' house Birch Grove.

Dorothy's temperament was closer to the Duke's than the Duchess's; her tastes were his tastes and to look at his life is to come nearer to understanding hers.

If a girl's attitude towards the male sex is shaped by her father's feelings towards her, Dorothy was particularly well endowed, for the Duke, although unimaginative, adored children and was constantly kind and loving towards his daughters.

'Felt very miserable, especially leaving the babies,' he wrote in his diary in 1899 before departing with his wife for a trip to North America and Canada, 'I shall never have been away from them so long before;' and the pain of family partings is a refrain that runs right through the thirty notebooks in which he recorded in everyday words without embellishments the daily happenings in his life. Each child was a blessing; each grandchild a cause of joy.

On Saturday, July 28th 1900 he wrote that he woke about eight o'clock and added, with his usual gift for understatement: 'Evie not feeling very comfortable. Baby was born about 1.40 p.m. — a fine girl. Mother was here. Lady Lansdowne arrived soon after.'

On August 2nd he was complaining again. 'Children left early for Buxton. Very dull without them.'

Eight years later the wrench was leaving Holker after his uncle's death. Regretfully he read the lesson in the parish church for the last time on April 28th. 'Terribly sad to think it is all over now,' he wrote, as though it were the end of an era.

He was now the father of six, Edward William Spencer, his heir, Maud Louisa Emma, Blanche Catherine, Dorothy Evelyn, Rachel and Charles Arthur Francis. Anne, the last, was to be born in 1909.

Meanwhile they spent the autumn and long cold winter at Hardwick Hall, an Elizabethan mansion near Mansfield in Derbyshire, while the eighteenth-century drains of Chatsworth were modernised and electricity installed; a time graphically described by Lady Maud in a short piece that dispels any idea that these aristocratic children were in any way spoiled or indulged. Clearly much of their upbringing was planned on the premise that 'the devil finds things for idle hands to do'. And Dorothy Macmillan's consistent activity in the years to come must have largely sprung from her parents' close adherence to that belief.

All the Devonshires' children lived on the top floor, ninety-seven steps above the ground.

'We must have been remarkably fit as children, as we climbed up and down those steps many times a day,' recalled Lady Maud Baillie, in 1972. 'We had to be down in the schoolroom at 7.15 for three quarters of an hour's work before breakfast at 8.00. We did over six hours of lessons a day but only three and a half on Saturdays, with a compulsory walk or ride morning or afternoon.' Each activity meant a change of clothing, and the lacing up, or unlacing, of high laced boots. All clothing was under the supervision of the nanny, and was therefore kept at the very top of the house.

There were French and German governesses, she explained, with a rule that no English was spoken during meals. The two ladies, 'goaded by aggressive children', often disagreed and 'frequent Franco-Prussian wars took place'. During the Christmas holidays the Devonshires' children were expected to take part in a play. 'This was no voluntary or spontaneous effort which we enjoyed, quite the reverse. It entailed hours of work, both in learning our parts and rehearsing.' In the winter of 1908 they staged the trial scene from the *Merchant of Venice* in the long gallery.

Unlike many of their generation and station the children lunched in the dining-room with the adults after reaching the age of five and the older ones ate both breakfast and tea at the refectory table in the great hall.

There was no electricity, no central heating and they washed in a few inches of tepid water in hip or flat round baths; the children's bedrooms were lit by candles, or a very small lamp, and Lady Maud found the darkness of the rooms terrifying. This spartan and demanding upbringing under the approbation of a loving and affectionate father, was to produce five women remarkable for their stamina and resilience, known collectively in the future by the present Duke and his brothers and sisters as 'The Aunts', eccentric, lively women who were generous to their nephews and nieces.

Chatsworth and Hardwick were only two of the five houses inherited by the Duke, each of which he was to occupy conscientiously for a time every year, until the war, but Chatsworth was much the most impressive with its painted hall, its superb pictures and furniture, palatial rooms, lavishly decorated chapel and incredible air of faded opulence, and the Christmases spent there were occasions to be remembered always by those who went. From 1909 until 1916 the Devonshires lived at Chatsworth in November, December and January and then moved on to the Irish estate, Lismore Castle, where they stayed until early May. Their London house in Piccadilly claimed them for the first three months of summer, with a quick return to Chatsworth for the Bakewell Agricultural Show, before a train journey to Bolton Abbey for the grouse shooting in August, an event followed in the autumn by partridge shooting at Hardwick Hall, the last being most loved by the Duchess, who was to spend her widowhood there, working on the tapestries. Chiswick House, another inheritance, they sold to meet death duties, but in addition there was Compton Place at Eastbourne, where the Duke had a few racehorses, and which was now mainly for recuperation after illnesses. 'As a family,' Lady Blanche was later to recall, 'we seemed always to be packing and unpacking as we moved from one house to the next. We thought it all quite normal, but it must have been an extraordinary feat of organisation for the servants as each of us children had our ponies and they would always travel with us. There were our nannies, nursery maids and grooms, and for the elder children there were the French and German governesses. For us it was all great fun and it wasn't as unsettling as it might have been as we always had our parents and the same servants with us.'

The daughter of the water bailiff at Bolton Abbey remembers her father trying to teach Dorothy and her sisters to fish. 'They were hopeless. They all looked alike, dressed in white with long hair tumbling down their backs. We couldn't tell one from the other, they were just the girls to us.' They did not themselves feel important in any way. 'We seemed a close-knit, rather ordinary family, and we were emphatically not brought up to regard ourselves in any way superior to anybody else,' commented Dorothy's sister Anne in 1980. 'Certainly we were aware that we were the daughters of a duke; what we were not aware of was that this was in any way exceptional. One result of this was that most of us ended up married to fairly ordinary people, instead of automatically going for the very rich or the very grand.'

But of course everyone else knew that they were exceptional, and, although the Duke and Duchess did not entertain widely apart from patrician relations and close friends, Royalty certainly came at least once a year. King Edward stayed for the shooting at Bolton Abbey in 1908 and the Prince of Wales the following year accompanied by his wife Mary, who was to appoint the Duchess Mistress of the Robes when he became King in 1911. There was also an annual dinner party of great distinction given at Devonshire House before the Derby, to which members of the royal family were invited.

The girls' failure to appreciate their high standing in society was partly due to the fact that they never went to school and partly due to moving too often to acquire close friends.

The Duke's uncritical love for them was countered by their mother's impatience and acerbity. Described by a brother-in-law as 'an unpleasant woman, accustomed to authority', she pointed at her daughters' faults with relentless regularity.

The child of brilliant but strait-laced parents, who found nude statues an affront, Evelyn Fitzmaurice, daughter of the fifth Marquess of Lansdowne, was incapable of showing affection, preferring places and works of art to people. Unable to meet emotional demands, 'She was,' says the present Duke of Devonshire, 'a fine-looking rather than beautiful woman.' Sargent's portrait of her, in Chatsworth, catches an air of restlessness in a face which suggests vitality, refinement and nervous tension, a face which bears little resemblance to Dorothy's as we know it from photographs and memories. Why, relations wondered, was this duchess so critical of her offspring? A courageous, dominating woman, she was, perhaps, envious of her daughters as they moved into girlhood, glowing with the youth she was beginning to lose; or possibly she was following an innate pattern set by her own mother which she was unable to break or understand. Significantly her sons did not entirely escape the lash of her tongue, although they fared better than her daughters, so that one daughter-in-law was to exclaim later with chagrin, 'If only she would count ten before she speaks!'

But, during all the moves, there was one stalwart figure — counterbalancing the nannies and governesses who came and went, the disturbing elements of the relations who took to drink — the redoubtable Elsie Saunders, the Duchess's secretary; a level-headed, sensible woman whose tact and good nature were an antidote to a mother's capricious tongue. Miss Saunders's room was a refuge, its occupant an example of goodness on which the girls could model themselves if they wished. She was a friend who did her best to protect them from the more vicious criticism, 'the putting down' as the present Duke described it.

In character the Duke was his wife's opposite, a large easy-going person until his stroke in 1925. Heavily moustached, a little florid, fond of racing, shooting and drinking; a countryman who liked to be present when his animals calved or foaled. Indeed, caring little for clothes, he often looked more like a farmer than a duke, yet his public service was varied and far-ranging, filling ten lines in *Burke's Peerage and Baronetage*, and he was deeply disappointed that he had to resign his seat in the House of Commons after inheriting his title.

So, Dorothy's adolescence was passed in frequent predictable moves in the British Isles in the most privileged circumstances, a fair taste of a life at the top which would stand her in good stead in the future.

Then came the cataclysm of the First World War, changing her course of life. Edward joined his regiment. The Duke became civil lord of the admiralty, while many male servants left to bear arms.

When Christmas arrived in 1914 the Duke wrote with appalling calm considering the carnage to come: 'In many ways a sad day but a great comfort to see the children happy and bright' — a sentiment which in the future was to bring consolation to Dorothy as a mother. In 1916 the Duke was appointed Governor-General of Canada. And this move involved his daughters in responsibilities which gave Dorothy the courage and experience to face great political events later on.

The Duke and Duchess sailed for Halifax that autumn with hosts of servants and loads of furniture, arriving eventually at Ottawa on November 13th. For the Duchess it was something of a home-coming, for her father had held the same post for five years from 1883 before becoming Viceroy of India, and she already knew and loved Government House, also known as Rideau Hall, and was well accustomed to the looser, easier customs of Canadian society.

But almost at once the Duke started typically to miss his children and was soon making arrangements for them to sail on the *Olympia* only to torment himself thereafter about the dangers they were facing on the high seas from enemy forces. They arrived on December 8th 'All very well,' he wrote in his diary, 'and do not even seem tired. It is really an enormous relief to have got them here safely over, especially as one or two raiders are supposed to be over the coast of Ireland.'

The Devonshires' daughters, an immediate female attraction to the Duke's younger male staff, were given the oval room upstairs as their sitting-room, and bedrooms in the Minto wing, and were quickly plunged into a life of receptions, parties and travel; for their affectionate father, an inveterate explorer of the countryside, took them on many of his travels. Likened by one American guest to a 'sleepy eyed mastiff', and later to a bloodhound, he was especially popular among the farmers, who appreciated his keen knowledge of agriculture. Very soon the girls became expert skaters on the Rideau rink where Chatsworth footmen served hot soup and their mother was observed on one occasion in a yellow mink-cuffed and collared coat, skating with Mackenzie King dressed unsuitably in suit and bowler hat. There were, too, dances in the magnificent ballroom, maple sugaring expeditions to the Gatineau Hills where the Duke commissioned a Canadian architect to design him a summer retreat which they called New Lismore. In addition there were traditional visits to the Governor-General's residence in Quebec, with Dorothy always in demand to play golf but not to ride — she left that to her sisters, being in her own surprising words 'far too frightened!'

On November 9th 1918 Lady Maud married one of her father's ADCs, Captain Angus Alexander Mackintosh of the Royal Horse Guards, in Christ Church Cathedral with over one thousand guests, a pipe band and an arch of crossed swords. Ten months later she gave birth to a daughter, as the Western world suffered one of the most virulent influenza epidemics ever known. The Devonshires had Government House disinfected; they instituted morning prayers and arranged for their own cows to come from England so that they could be sure of uncontaminated milk, presumably with the possibility of tuberculosis another anxiety in the Duke's mind. But they could not protect their in-laws as well — Edward had married Lady Mary Gascoyne-Cecil in 1917 — and, just a month after Maud's baby arrived, Angus Mackintosh was taken seriously ill in Washington, and Dorothy witnessed for the first time the effects of a tragedy on a close relation. Maud was not yet strong enough to travel, so the Duchess went to see her son-in-law, but at six o'clock on October 13th the Duke learned it 'was all over'. His wife had arrived just in time for Angus to ask after Maud and the baby before expiring. An example as usual of exemplary good sense, the Duke waited until a doctor arrived before telling Maud. 'She was wonderfully good and brave. Though she cried a good deal, she was not hysterical and showed no sign of collapse.'

On October 16th he wrote, 'Afraid Maud did not have a good night. Poor child — it is pitiable to see her. Evie is very overwrought.'

But life of course went on and soon another marriage was to be planned. In early Spring 1919, the Duchess, Blanche and Dorothy returned to England for several weeks and on March 16th the Duke learned from his wife that his second daughter was engaged to Ivan Cobbold. 'Nothing can be too good for Blanche,' he wrote. 'I do hope she will be happy. Everyone who knows him says he is delightful. I did not know how to work off my feelings, so I walked up and down the sidewalk which is the only place where there is no ice, and also telephoned various people.' An illuminating entry because it suggests that Dorothy inherited from her father her excellent ability to turn instinctively to physical activity to counter the adrenalin which emotional stress produces, in direct contrast to her mother who would retreat to bed and minor illness when life was difficult.

On April 11th the Duke wrote 'Very wet and muggy. Macmillan arrived. Seems a nice boy.'

And there he was, a future prime minister, although no one at Government House suspected such a future for him; a sensitive, scholarly new ADC, sporting a monocle and a fashionable military moustache; another guards officer in need of a wife over whom the Devonshire girls could cast appraising eyes. And, although Anthony Sampson suggests in his biography that Macmillan's intellectual conversation sometimes bored the Duke, there is little hint of this in the diaries. On April 14th he recorded a game of golf with Harold. 'He plays quite well and is much better than I am. Very jolly on the course. Lovely evening. Macmillan is certainly a great acquisition.' While an idealist by temperament, more Whig than Tory, Macmillan, always conscious of the Lansdownes' and Devonshires' political and diplomatic services to the nation, was delighted to find himself in such august company. Although of humble stock, he looked back to the success of his paternal grandfather, Daniel Macmillan, founder of the publishing firm, with unalloyed pride. '. . . We were brought up on his struggles and achievements,' he once wrote and, in another context, 'I was determined to follow in his footsteps through my own will and effort.' As the youngest in a family of three he had spent much of his early youth trying to catch up with the others.

Macmillan's war, which he was to recall so vividly in later years, was tough, dangerous and bloody; although spared long months in the trenches, he had twice been seriously wounded, at the Battle of Loos and later on the Somme where he lay all day in no-man's-land with a broken pelvis, reading, he said later, Aeschylus between bouts of shelling and feigning death when German soldiers were around. He came to Government House after months in military hospitals, with a limp due to an unhealed leg wound, hoping to find health, but also with a commendable air of bravado which, from time to time seemed to contrast oddly with his more withdrawn image. He was, of course, a man of many parts, which made him all the more intriguing to the young women who had viewed his appointment with such interest. Almost at once he found himself unexpectedly happy and soon a central part of that happiness was the Duke's third and favourite daughter, who returned on May 18th and was marking time until marriage. On July 8th the Duke was recording that he had arrived at New Lismore to find Dorothy, Miss Saunders and Macmillan who were 'going to Braniwaki'. On July 26th he noted that 'Dorothy and Harold got up early to go to Mount Jacques to see the sunrise. Afraid it would not be clear.'

On Tuesday August 19th Harold and Dorothy played golf with him and on the 21st HRH the Prince of Wales arrived for his tour of Canada, seeming well although in 'rather a nervous state, but will settle down all right. He seems to make all the arrangements himself.' Although the Duke's comments were normally complimentary and optimistic, the Prince's tour was to be remembered for its traumas as well as its pleasures, for the heir to the throne had a habit of disappearing unexpectedly to play golf or dance even on Sundays. He was seen so often with Dorothy that inevitably romantic rumours started to circulate causing the Duke to complain that there seemed to be 'a set opinion that Dorothy is engaged to HRH. It is certainly very tiresome, but there is nothing to be done.'

Meanwhile Macmillan bathed, climbed, boated and danced with her and certainly few people looking for romance can have enjoyed so much encouragement from both the elements and events; even the sunsets often recorded in the Duke's diary were breathtakingly beautiful. Yet a computer would probably have suggested that Dorothy and Macmillan would not make a good match, for, in several ways, their tastes and attitudes to life differed widely. Macmillan's façades found no counterpart in Dorothy, who was always uncompromisingly herself. He was a deeply committed Christian, whose family revered *The Kingdom of Christ* by F.D. Maurice and fervently discussed religion and any other subject except food and money. As an Oxford undergraduate Macmillan had been caught between his Methodist mother's influence and the high Anglicanism and then Roman Catholicism of his close friend and mentor, the incomparable Ronald Knox; 'a great man with an extraordinary mind'. Dorothy, down to earth, and direct, was no soul searcher, the progeny of a family who were always doers rather than thinkers, comfortable Christians, astringent talkers irked by intellectual conversation, accepting, it seems, without much debate the ethics and practice of their faith. A regular churchgoer, she took religion more lightly, never suffering the spiritual dilemmas which led Macmillan so near to following Knox into the arms of Rome. Macmillan, in his own words, 'had come to books before people'; Dorothy, impatient with too much agonising, preferred, like her father, to find peace and wisdom from nature.

But in 1919 such differences hardly seemed to matter. The attraction of opposites was an accepted phenomenon. Captain Harold Macmillan, a Grenadier Guardsman and Old Etonian and therefore indisputably a gentleman whatever his breeding, was ready for love. Messages between the couple were carried by Anne, who was rewarded with tiny splinters of bone from Macmillan's unhealed wound or books from his family's firm.

Macmillan with his fine dramatic sense chose, during a tour of Alberta, one of the most beautiful places on earth in which to declare his love, Jasper Park in the Rockies; Jasper Park in the fall when the yellow leaves of the aspens were like gold among the darkness of the Lodgepole pines, where red squirrels and chipmunks ran blithely in deep forested valleys with lakes that shone like turquoises or emeralds or amethysts, or, on duller days, became muted as olives, on account of the glacial silt that everywhere gave colour to the water. A place where bears and elk, moose, sheep and mountain goats roamed at will and the silence was broken by the roar of tremendous falls.

Here, in his own laconic words, Macmillan learned that 'his affections were returned' and was naively surprised to find that everyone had anticipated the event. The Duke commented bluntly that 'Books is better than beer,' referring to Blanche's impending marriage into a brewing family, but was reluctant to give his consent before knowing more about the young ADC's means.

'Dorothy and Macmillan spent the whole day together and it is really rather difficult to have to maintain, but they are not engaged,' he wrote on December 27th. In the meantime Macmillan had obviously appealed to his parents for support and encouragement, for three days later the Duke was mentioning that Mrs Macmillan had written Evie 'a long screed', but it was 'doubtful what she was aiming at'.

By January 2nd 1920, however, the future seemed more felicitous. Macmillan had received a nice letter from his father stating that he would receive £3,000 a year but 'would be able to get more,' and on January 4th the Duke was writing that 'Harold and Dorothy want to have their engagement announced. A number of people seem to know of it, so it may be a good thing to get it out.' With Macmillan's term as ADC coming to an end plans were made for the couple to return to England with Blanche to plan the two weddings. On January 13th there was a tea party to say goodbye to Blanche and Dorothy; On January 15th a dinner party for Dorothy and Macmillan at the country club where 'Harold made an admirable speech'. And on January 19th the Duke was reporting 'a great atmosphere of unrest all through the house owing to impending departures in a temperature 34 below zero. We shall miss Dorothy very much,' he wrote, but not it appears Blanche who perhaps had been less happy because of the long separation from Ivan Cobbold. On January 20th the couple left with Blanche, Dorothy rather low at the precise moment of leaving, 'but soon cheered up' wrote the Duke. 'Evie settled not to come.'

Back in London the engaged pair, now delectable food for the gossip columns, started to make arrangements for a wedding nine days before Blanche's, which was to plunge Macmillan into a world of pomp and publicity to which he was only just becoming accustomed; a calculated step, cynics might incorrectly suggest, in the right direction for a future politician. In fact he had fallen in love with the daughter of a man he both admired and liked, a sensible choice in some respects, as he must have seen endearing likenesses to the Duke, but as I have said earlier a match with possible drawbacks.

For weeks before the wedding presents arrived, many of them listed in *The Times*. 'All certainly very nice and in good taste,' wrote the Duke whose understanding of his daughters was based on his instinctive affection for them rather than insight into their characters. Certainly the money spent on gifts and clothes would have kept many poor families for over a year. The value of the jewellery alone was more than enough to buy a racehorse. Among this plethora, presented to Dorothy, were four diamond brooches, from King George V and Queen Mary, Queen Alexandra, the Duke and Duchess of Devonshire and Lady Astor. Macmillan's parents gave her a diamond cross while he bought her a diamond ring, in addition to a gold and composite necklace. The Ormsby-Gores gave a diamond box and Prince Paul of Serbia an onyx trinket box with a gold rim. There was plenty of furniture for them both, too, including a Sheraton table and an historic chest from the Duchess of

Wellington, and there were antique candlesticks, fantastic old spoons of quaint design, clocks, a tortoiseshell inkstand, an ivory case, and gold candelabra from the Duchess of Rutland. There were books from Sir Otto and Lady Beit, a silver urn from Lord Frederick Hamilton and a statue of Winged Victory from Lady Lyttelton and, most touchingly, because of the time given to its execution, a portrait of Dorothy by the artist who painted it, Philip de László, whose picture of her father hangs at Chatsworth. A glance at the long list of presents, in which donors' names read like pages from *Debrett*, suggests that few of the givers understood the character and taste of the bride, for there must seldom have been a young woman of her station so adverse to dressing up, so totally uninterested in adorning herself with jewellery. Lady Bordern's workbox was perhaps nearer the mark, although Dorothy was no seamstress, or the umbrellas sent by humbler friends. Whatever the thoughts behind the giving, rivalry or pride played a part for everyone eventually knew what everyone else had given and the result was so overwhelming that the splendidness of many of the presents must have been devalued by the abundance of the riches bestowed upon the young couple. It was to be Dorothy's last happy compliance with the extravagance and competition of high society.

So on April 21st 1920 before two o'clock, the crowds gathered outside St Margaret's, Westminster to gape at the arrival of royalty and members of Britain's most illustrious families for the wedding of the grandson of a Scottish crofter to the daughter of a duke. According to *The Times*'s report they saw, among others, Queen Alexandra resplendent in purple with a cloak of shimmering brocade, Prince Albert, the future King, the Duke of Connaught, Princess Victoria and her ladies-in-waiting, Princess Christian in funeral black velvet with sable furs, the Duchess of Wellington in black too, but with a plumed hat, and Lady Knaresborough in a 'radium silk' foulard dress and picture hat. The Dowager Duchess of Buckingham and Chandos wore an ermine cloak over a gown of regal velvet. Lady Frances Balfour was graceful in black Chantilly lace and the Honourable Stuart Montagu wore, according to *The Times*, a cavalier wrap cloak of 'nigger charmeuse'.

Macmillan's guests were naturally less newsworthy, his mother's clothes were unreported; but for a mere commoner he had done well, with Lord Morley and Lord Bryce on the bridegroom's side and also Thomas Hardy, rosy-faced from the country. Mr Arthur Penn, a family friend, was best man, and Alastair Wedderburn, a barrister from Macmillan's Oxford days, one of the ushers.

Lady Dorothy wore a gown of rich tanagra, its Florentine bodice garlanded by orange blossoms, her full train also held by a wreath of orange blossom entwined with sprigs of myrtle, symbols of fertility. There were orange trees in the chancel and white lilies at the altar, but Dorothy, who adored flowers, carried only a simple vellum prayer book. Her bridesmaids in sky-blue dresses with silver brocade at their waists included her sister Anne and cousins Diana and Sybil Cavendish.

Devonshire House in Piccadilly was up for sale, so the reception was held in Lansdowne House, the London seat of Dorothy's maternal grandparents. For the socialites, the name-droppers and the sensation hunters it was a day to be remembered and exploited over the tea cups and dinner tables, but for most of the thousand guests it was none of these things; their own daughters, brothers or sisters would have merited as much or more. For Harold Macmillan it was an initiation as well as a marriage ceremony, his acceptance into the world of the aristocracy in a country where class was still of prime importance. It was to take him almost a lifetime to discover that like Dorothy he was really happier among the less exalted, that creative people were often more fun, that the top dogs, though normally neither complacent nor arrogant, were frequently boring, the Cecils being a notable exception.

For the host it was a happy day. 'Dorothy's wedding really went off very well indeed — a great number of people . . .' he wrote. 'Mother got there in a bathchair and quite enjoyed herself. Everyone nice and kind. Dorothy looked very well and was quite at ease. The small children, pages and bridesmaids behaved admirably. A big crowd at Lansdowne House. I spent most of my time with the Queen who was charming.'

For the Duchess, who watched expenses so carefully that she was known to summon a footman to steam off a halfpenny unmarked stamp for future use, it must have seemed an enormous but, maybe, necessary extravagance.

The honeymoon was spent in England and Italy, the first part at Bolton Abbey in the castellated shooting lodge, once gatehouse to the priory whose ruins still stand. The couple were waited on and watched over by Devonshire servants curious, no doubt, to see how the shy young commoner measured up to expectations. There were horsehair mattresses on the beds, candles and oil lamps for lighting, and from the front windows views of spring pasture leading the eye across the river upwards to the brown moors on which Macmillan was so often to shoot. For a man who in old age still claims to suffer two days of misery and stomach pains before making a major speech, those first weeks cannot have been without moments of anxiety, but, although there are couples nowadays who will admit to discord or embarrassment on their honeymoon, Macmillan allows no inkling of uneasiness to break through the armour which protects his private life.

'The post-war boom was at its height,' he says, 'we were young; we were happy; everything smiled upon us.' They bought a house on the borders between Pimlico and Belgravia, 14 Chester Square, where their first baby, Maurice Victor, was born just over nine months after the wedding. 'Delightful to get the news,' wrote the Duke, 'seems strange to think of Dorothy as a mother. She's only a baby herself.'

Soon Nanny West, a rock on whom Dorothy would lean for forty years, was employed and a strain of enmity between Mother and Grandmother became obvious, the result of two dominating women struggling to influence the same two males; two women with a flair for organisation, strong wills and an unusual degree of self-confidence who would eventually, because they were also basically good-natured, learn to live together without rancour when necessary. Macmillan now considers his mother to have been the most important influence in his life and it was perhaps no coincidence or trick of the brain's mechanism that caused him to say in 1944, 'Tell my mother I'm alive and well,' when he regained consciousness after bombing in Algiers; an automatic reaction which could suggest Dorothy had never quite succeeded in replacing Nellie Macmillan, who had then been dead six years. Certainly, as time went on, the wife recognised Macmillan's weaknesses, while the mother allowed her considerable ambitions to ride high on his strengths.

Nellie Macmillan, who was in all respects a remarkable woman, began life as Helen Belles, the daughter of an Indianapolis doctor. At twenty she left America for Paris after the death of her husband, a painter, whom she had married a year earlier. There, studying music and art, she met, sang duets with and married the diffident young Maurice, whom she persuaded to leave schoolmastering to enter the family publishing firm. A thrifty and astute housewife who kept her provisions under lock and key, she was nevertheless a dynamic woman with a thrusting intelligence.

It was partly through Nellie Macmillan's pressure that the text-book side of the family firm was started and entirely through her advice that *Gone with the Wind*, previously turned down by twenty-seven rival firms, was published under its imprint. It was also through her influence that Macmillan transferred from the King's Own Rifles to the more prestigious Grenadier Guards and was subsequently appointed ADC to the Duke. 'No one who has not experienced it can realise,' Macmillan has said, 'the determination of an American woman defending one of her children.' Indeed she once committed an almost unforgivable sin in the sensitive eyes of an English public schoolboy when she told the head master of Eton that his college's sheets were improperly ironed. This go-getting American saw before anyone else that Macmillan, for her the most malleable of her three sons, had the makings of a politician. Daniel, more academic, remained in the family firm; gentle Arthur, the most independent, became a barrister, while Harold was earmarked for the highest office. 'Publishing,' his mother once said, 'is like stockbroking, a trade.' And that trade she determined was only to be part of Macmillan's life.

The first positive step in his political career was his adoption in 1923 as prospective Conservative and Unionist candidate for Stockton-on-Tees, Durham, a constituency his party did not expect to win; a move that initiated Dorothy into a totally new way of life which was to fascinate her for the next twenty years.

'My wife,' Macmillan was to write in his memoirs, 'quickly acquired the art of canvassing, which after all is merely the art of being natural, simple and a little humble.' But this intrepid-looking girl in a felt hat with a turned-down brim, did more than that; she ventured down streets where respectable women would not go; she banged on doors in the shabbiest quarters and talked to nearly everybody in the same way whether they were rich or poor, dirty or clean, male or female. 'There was hardly a house in Stockton or Thornaby where my wife's face was not familiar,' Macmillan was to say in years to come. And certainly at twenty-three she was something of a heroine. 'It is no exaggeration,' Lord Boothby has declared, 'to say that they adored her.' For Dorothy that first campaign was an eye-opener that changed her whole attitude to society. In Chester Square she had been protected from the effects of the slump; now the suffering and poverty, despair, courage and the friendship of those much lower down the social scale than herself filled her with admiration and affection for the working classes.

This campaign brought Dorothy's most useful qualities to the fore; her infectious enthusiasm inspired the other Conservative workers and drew people towards her; she dressed rather drably, but zest and vitality lit up her face, and her absolute simplicity of manner, breezy humour and intense interest in the way the under-privileged lived won her friends.

'The poorer they were the nicer they were,' Macmillan was to remark in 1983, a fact which must have hit the over-protected young couple right between the eyes. And Dorothy loved all the hurly-burly too, the pushing and shoving of street politics which Mary Wilson was later to loathe; the improvised school meetings when caretakers always seemed to provide chairs only suitable for infants, the visits to factories, the tea parties for the women workers when she was hostess, the kind Mr Kirk, a supporter who put the Mac-millans up for years at election times. Campaigning lapped up her phenomenal energy which was so abundant that even in middle age she would run rather than walk; campaigning threw her also into a world she had not known existed, warm and real, vibrant with suffering and hope, bubbling with north country hospitality, friendly handshakes and banter, endless cups of tea; and a doorstep welcome which sometimes may have been especially kindly because she was a duke's daughter, who unwittingly flattered the poor by her total lack of side and genuine concern for their troubles. She could look at their problems with new insight, because by now marriage and the birth of two children, Maurice in 1921 and Ann Caroline in 1923, had widened her knowledge of the complexity of life and human relationships to a degree she cannot have envisaged in those youth-ful, innocent days in Canada when romance seemed a simple matter. Love had not, it seems, come up to her expectations and conjugal life had left a crucial part of her nature hungry for more. But character-istically what shortcomings there were did not in any way dilute the support she gave her husband. In politics he could count on her loyalty, and although the Macmillans lost that first election by seventy-three votes, they won the next in 1924 with a comfortable majority of 3,214, a success they celebrated by hiring a special train, a familiar experience, of course, for Dorothy, to take three hundred of their supporters for a day out and a meal at the Pavilion Restaurant at Bolton Abbey. Peggy Read, the head forester's daughter whose grandparents ran the restaurant, looks back nostalgically to those days. 'The Cavendishes were our friends,' she told me. 'I know it sounds feudal, but that is how it was. I remember Lady Dorothy telling my mother that Harold Macmillan tried out his speeches on her, saying that if she could understand them everybody else in the land would. She was so cheerful, so natural.'

So in 1925 an optimistic Nellie Macmillan, with her usual foresight, gave orders for a small pseudo-Georgian mansion to be built at Chelwood Gate, near Haywards Heath, adjacent to Ashdown Forest, where she and her husband already owned Birch Grove estate with its many acres, farmhouse and cottages. She stipulated with a confidence infinitely more American than British that the size, proportions and style of this new residence were to be in keeping with the needs of a prime minister.

Such a belief in life's bounty was countered somewhat by an event which was to affect all the Devonshires and especially the Duchess for the next thirteen years. The Duke, broken-hearted that Stanley Baldwin had not offered him a place in the 1921 cabinet, took his family to Lismore for the spring holidays and suffered a severe stroke on Easter Sunday, after eating three dishes of potato cakes. 'Collapsed in a foolish and uncomfortable way after breakfast. Sort of fainting fit,' he wrote bravely afterwards. 'Got two nurses and a doctor and went to bed.'

All his adult life the Duke had worked and played hard. He had seen that his children were capable in the occupations usually followed by the upper classes. The girls could ride, skate, swim, handle boats, dance, manage servants and plan dinner parties. His diary shows that he frequently visited Blanche and Dorothy in London after their marriages, and he had passed on to his third daughter his gusty enthusiasm for life.

Now he was a changed man, but still determined to enjoy himself when he could.

On August 15th, with courageous obstinacy inherited by Dorothy he wrote: 'Found I could shoot all right so have silenced the critics.'

But the experience had changed him. This kindly, loving person was transformed into a monstrous man who swore abominably and struck with a stick at people who crossed his path. The Duke's illness tempered for Dorothy the usual pleasures of those great annual Christmas house parties at Chatsworth, still organised by her mother, when all the servants worked overtime. On these occasions the Devonshire children and grandchildren arrived with valets, ladies' maids and nurses to be housed according to rank; Edward, the heir, was allotted the finest bedrooms for his family and Dorothy, as third daughter, the fourth best. But despite the rigid patterns of the past which after Stockton must surely have struck a false note, there was still the joy of a homecoming, the pleasures of five sisters meeting again, laden with presents, ready to gloat over the latest babies, to watch the little ones playing together, to discuss households, children and husbands and to revisit old haunts recalling the myths that abound in every large family.

For the women it was renewal, for the husbands, overwhelmed with so much domestic chatter, it was an occasion to be left as soon as politely possible, but normally not until the family photographs had been taken, with the Duke holding his latest grandchild in his arms. Strangely, children and animals were spared his anger, and that innate love for the little and the helpless remained. In 1926 Harold and Dorothy presented him with another grandchild, Catherine.

The Duchess of Devonshire's life was now curtailed, while her third daughter's expanded as she built up a relationship with the man who was to fill an emotional gap in her life.

Macmillan, his social awareness considerably increased by the ordinary soldiers he had met in the war and the people of Stockton, now became a left-wing Conservative belonging to a group ironically known as the YMCA and among these forward-looking idealists was Dorothy's friend, the hedonistic Scotsman, Robert Boothby, with whom she fell in love. Divorce was a disgrace which in those days would have caused suffering to all three, destroying the men's political careers. Dorothy remained married but gave part of her heart to Boothby. He has described the relationship in a recent letter as 'a romantic friendship in the true Victorian tradition' and, in an interview quoted in the *Daily Mail* on 10th May 1978, as an association not sexual, 'but an emotional one that cuts much deeper'. He would have married Dorothy had she been free. As it was, to Macmillan's distress it became known in the political world that Dorothy was a woman with two men in her life; the one, in his own words, insecure, but with a deep-rooted religious belief from which he drew strength to bear his tribulations; the other a gambler with great vision but little wisdom, who chose his friends carelessly and was, on the whole, sexually adventurous, an ambitious, ebullient politician, charming, tolerant and self-indulgent; a colourful, lovable man attractive to both men and women.

Macmillan and Boothby treated each other with astonishing civility. Indeed Boothby was awarded a life peerage after a heart attack while Macmillan was prime minister. Together they gave Dorothy as much as any woman can sensibly expect from life, appealing to the different facets of her character, the serious side which prompted her devoted work for charity and her appreciation of the ludicrous which made her see through so much that was pompous and false. She strove with her husband for social justice, peace and his own political success, and with Boothby she found other degrees of happiness, sharing his love of racing, attracted by that childlike streak in his nature which appealed to motherly women and his anti-hero attitude which matched the debunking strain in her own character. Both men accepted her bossiness in small matters, appreciated her honesty and integrity, and loved her for her cheerful humour. She refused to take either seriously. 'Harold is about to play a part,' she would joke before he made a speech. 'But the question is which one — that is quite unpredictable.' And of an inebriated Boothby, laughing, 'you must meet him again when he's sober, and see how charming he is.' 'Men,' she told an audience of schoolgirls, 'are notoriously comfort-loving, selfish creatures and they all like good-looking girls.'

And so, while recognising their faults, she cared for them both in different ways which cannot have been easy as she tried to balance each one's claims on her time with her own physical and emotional needs. But she never, it seems, tried to adapt her character to meet their desires. 'Her attitude,' the Duke of Devonshire has said, 'was that people could like her or lump her.'

Macmillan turned for advice to his sister-in-law, the delicate featured Lady Hartington, who, being a Cecil by birth, was more of an intellectual than the Devonshires and so more like himself, and through her counsel the marriage survived, and scandal was averted.

But now, as Dorothy knew, life was tough for Macmillan who, tormented again by old war wounds, lost Stockton; and the birth of a third daughter, Sarah, in 1930, did little to raise his spirits; he was down and when he was down he was very very down, and since she had contributed most certainly to his depression it was one of those rare occasions when Dorothy could do little to lighten the darkness. In 1931 Macmillan entered a German clinic for treatment for his wounds and a nervous disorder, while she, making amends where she could, diligently nursed his constituency. When the government fell she telegrammed to bring him back, still on crutches, to fight a noisy campaign which they won by over eleven thousand votes. She was again a heroine, so popular that for years after her death constituents wrote to Macmillan on its anniversary to commiserate.

Dorothy's character had now formed and she was to change little between 1931 and her husband's premiership. A warm-hearted hostess, who liked to remain in control of the proceedings, she possessed very strong likes and dislikes and did not relish the parties given by the hospitable society women of her day: Lady Colefax, Lady Cunard, Lady Londonderry and Mrs Greville. She made an exception for witty Lady Astor whose company she enjoyed possibly because she was an unconventional American, forthright like herself, and an enthusiastic golfer.

The delight Dorothy felt when her brother Charlie married Fred Astaire's sister Adèle, the actress, in the chapel at Chatsworth, was typical. Of all her brothers and sisters, Charlie was her favourite, a weak, lovable, drunken man, who exuded great charm, but who never came up to scratch, a male who needed mothering. The Duke, who was to live another six years, was too ga-ga to understand fully that his youngest son who had caused him much anxiety over the years was marrying beneath him, but still wicked enough to break up his wife's parties with shouts of 'Gabble, gabble, gabble!'

Dorothy always found some compensation for the frustrations of a dual life in her children, although she feared from time to time that one or other of them might follow a Cavendish trend and take to drink. Catherine and Ann claim to have had an unusually happy childhood. Yet Dorothy could not have survived so well without the Macmillan riches, which paid for servants and a stable background. For who can tell how uneasy she might have been had she been deprived of the irreplaceable Nanny West, who smoothed her path for forty years, relieving her of many anxieties and alleviating the conflicting claims of husband and children which were to trouble Mary Wilson, and, to a lesser degree, Audrey Callaghan? In fact the daughters of dukes are rarely rich and Dorothy gained a good deal materially from her marriage; perhaps most of all in 1936 when life was especially difficult for her, and Macmillan inherited Birch Grove on the death of his father, so that, at last, the garden in which Dorothy had worked for years virtually became hers. True to the influence of Holker Hall she grew roses, shrubs, trees and bushes, and although she grew much else besides, roses remained her favourite flowers. With the stamina of a cart-horse, Dorothy dug (as her father had dug at Rideau Hall when things went wrong); dug and pruned and weeded: for Dorothy gardening was also an antidote to a temper shortened by age and the complexity of her life, to moments of anger which made her throw things, and on one occasion wrench a telephone fixture off the wall. The mid-thirties were especially trying for her, because in 1935 Boothby had tried to 'straighten out' his life by marrying Dorothy's cousin, Diana Cavendish. The disastrous union was dissolved in 1937. 'You can't have a successful marriage when you love someone else,' was Boothby's alleged comment in 1978.

Macmillan's temper was carefully controlled. When he was hurt or angry he would retire, usually to his study, and rejoin his family only when he could be entirely civilised. Indeed he always treated his wife with notable courtesy.

Over the years Birch Grove's garden gave Dorothy incalculable pleasure. In summer she would have her bed brought out so that she could sleep there under the stars and waken to birdsong and the dew-scented grass. In winter, undeterred by rough weather, she would sometimes work into the night, hot water bottles strapped to her legs, to keep out the cold and damp, her miner's torchlight breaking the darkness. Indoors, she would often occupy herself reading countless newspapers, or with jigsaw puzzles which, she told one journalist, became something of an addiction.

At the same time she continued to work for the National Society for the Prevention of Cruelty to Children and the East Sussex Nursing Association, while Macmillan wrote his book *The Middle Way*, and Britain edged slowly towards war.

When it came, Maurice joined up and the Macmillans, who usually responded generously to a humanitarian cause, offered Birch Grove as a children's home and the farmhouse as a temporary refuge for Czech refugees, just as the Duke had offered Hardwick for the use of Belgians in 1914, moving themselves into one of the cottages. Macmillan was no appeaser, and constantly attacked Chamberlain for complacency. He travelled with his usual courage to Finland with a group of volunteers to observe the Russian invasion at first hand. Dorothy took on the command of a section of the local Land Army as well as continuing her charitable work, being quick to accept responsibility if it meant practical organisation rather than intellectual effort.

Her first taste of life as a statesman's wife came in 1944 when, in Algiers as minister resident at allied headquarters in north-west Africa, Macmillan was 'immensely cheered by her arrival from London'. In Algiers she met General Eisenhower and General de Gaulle, with whom Macmillan had been working closely. She gaily entertained her husband's friends and associates in the villa he had been allotted. 'She enjoyed her time and certainly gave a great deal of pleasure to others with her simplicity and charm,' recorded the loyal husband. When he moved on to Italy she rowed Marshal Tito, very hot in his thick uniform, in a small boat on the Bay of Naples, while awaiting Churchill's arrival — an informal and enterprising middle-aged hostess in a floral dress. And Macmillan, changed by the war and a new job into a dashing, forceful diplomat, willing to gamble on his hunches, was a new man. It was fun to be with either or both of them; their vitality was a tonic in grey times. Macmillan indeed owed much to the war. 'If it hadn't been for Hitler,' he had remarked to Churchill earlier, 'you wouldn't have been prime minister and I wouldn't have become an under-secretary.'

For four months in Algiers and Italy the Macmillans worked together harmoniously and then for Dorothy it was back to England to the children's home at Birch Grove, the Land Army, her charitable work and the nursing of Stockton-on-Tees for the approaching election. It was a sad return, because 1944 was the year in which Charlie died, his life shortened by alcoholism, and her nephew William, heir to the dukedom and married to John Kennedy's sister, was killed in action in Belgium.

She saw that the majority of the British people were looking away from Conservatism to the new world of greater opportunity and equality which they thought post-war Socialism would bring and, despite all her efforts, Macmillan lost Stockton. In November 1945, however, he won Bromley in a by-election, after Randolph Churchill had generously withdrawn his own name as a candidate. In Bromley, a solidly middle-class constituency, Dorothy became well known not only as his wife, but also as his chauffeur, 'Always driving,' one constituent remembers, 'a very ordinary car'; a reliable driver, but dashing enough to be convicted for speeding in 1950. For the next nineteen years, although not adored at Bromley as she had been in Stockton, Dorothy was extremely popular among Conservative supporters. With her usual flair and wish to repay kindness and help, she arranged an annual visit to Birch Grove by coach, and a tour of the gardens and tea for all the constituency workers who cared to come, an event still remembered by many with pleasure and the familiar praise: 'She was so natural, so friendly. She treated everyone just the same.'

Once again she was almost certainly helped by her breeding, for working- and lower-middle-class Tories were undoubtedly flattered when a duke's daughter treated them as equals. For Macmillan the end of the war was something of an anti-climax; the Socialist victory brought disillusionment: he had experienced power, enjoyed negotiating on matters that changed the course of history, and was now a warrior without arms. 'It was a personal pessimism,' writes Anthony Sampson, 'by no means shared by all his party and it seems worth enquiring whether it might have a cause beyond his evident private unhappiness at that time.' Certainly he seemed to feel that he was finished, too old, on the scrap heap, a sensation which was to return from time to time for the rest of his life, to be turned into a family joke and dismissed by Dorothy with fond breezy humour. But underneath this there was a wider, less personal sense of despair that Britain was losing the opportunity to take on the leadership of Europe, the consequences of which would be felt for decades to come. And, in addition, there was Dorothy's unabated devotion to another man, the continuation of that deep and loving friendship which Lord Boothby has said first developed between 1925 and 1930. And yet it may be that Dorothy's visits to Boothby's house in Eaton Square, her need for the warmer more mercurial and exciting man, was the spur that eventually drove Macmillan on towards the

premiership, a contented husband not always being the best politician. In short, without Dorothy's friendship with Boothby, it is
possible that Macmillan might have turned back to family life and
publishing and left the long gruelling climb to the top. But he had
too a vision of a new England; his aim, surely shared by Dorothy,
was to abolish the proletariat and make them all bourgeois. He
wanted the workers to own their own cars, and their own houses,
without depriving the rich of their wealth.

But after all his despair, his efforts in Africa and Italy were not
forgotten, and in 1949 he was appointed to the Consultative
Assembly of the Council of Europe along with Churchill, Boothby,
Maurice Edelman, Hugh Dalton, David Eccles and others; and after
the first year, when he took his daughter Catherine, Macmillan was
accompanied to the annual conferences at Strasbourg by Dorothy
who enjoyed the company there of both her men, as well as excellent
meals which contrasted strangely with the rationed fare in victorious
Britain. Such events kept her up with world politics and, in particular, the people who struggled at the top; it was the people, rather
than their politics, that caught her imagination and kept her interest
alive, although she made no close friends among them, giving often
but rarely taking. And the fact that Macmillan took her to these
conferences demonstrates how great was her grip on those who loved
her. By now time and her lack of vanity had stripped her of the
charms of youth and she looked rather a battleaxe. Yet two men
were to need her and lean on her for another seventeen years; she
held the deepest affections of them both until death and was the only
woman to whom Macmillan ever became romantically attached. Her
power to enchant seems to have lain partly in her directness; she
spoke her mind and played no games, never consciously using her
sex as a weapon or bait. At a superficial level at least, men knew
where they were with her, and yet she had all the warmth of the most
female of women for those she loved, and she knew how to pander to
male weaknesses. In addition she was blessed with the aristocrat's
supreme advantage of not caring what the outside world thought of
her behaviour; tittle-tattle was to be ignored; a certain innate
arrogance has always given the nobility a freedom not enjoyed by the
bourgeois. Boothby had picked up along the way a similar disregard
for accepted middle-class Protestant codes of conduct. 'Distrust the
man who puts salvation before happiness,' he advised in a rectorial

address at St Andrew's University. Macmillan, the ardent Christian, turned to God to alleviate his suffering and tried to do what he felt was right, and that included forgiveness.

In 1950 Dorothy's brother Edward died while cutting wood, his favourite pastime.

'Poor dear Eddie,' Chips Channon commented in his diary, 'was a frustrated man, hated being a duke and was really a bit bored by all his possessions and palaces. But he was gay at heart and loved life, ladies, and above all, port. He was kind, old-fashioned, shrewd, loyal and intelligent, though not quite intelligent enough to rise high politically.'

Meanwhile, the Macmillan children had all except for Sarah found themselves spouses. Maurice had married into the aristocracy when he wedded the Honourable Katharine Margaret Alice Ormsby-Gore in 1942, a girl never liked by Dorothy; and Ann had married Julian Faber in 1944. Catherine, a striking beauty, married Julian Amery in 1950.

In 1951 with the Tories back in power Macmillan was offered the ministry of housing by Churchill, a disappointment to a man who aspired to statesmanship, but very much in keeping with his aim to raise the proletariat, a desire soon echoed throughout the country by the slogan prophesying a 'property-owning democracy'. But before accepting the post Macmillan characteristically consulted Dorothy, who had driven him over to Chartwell and was walking in the gardens with Mrs Churchill. Her advice, he knew, was generally sound. 'She was in no doubt that I ought to accept.'

She was right, for Macmillan enjoyed housing more than any other cabinet post, mostly because it produced tangible results. A brilliant organiser, he met all his targets, helping to rebuild Britain's housing and promoting happiness among the less fortunate, causes very close to the heart of a wife shocked by the Stockton slums. But Dorothy actually found more personal fulfilment when, after a spell as minister of defence, Macmillan became foreign secretary in Anthony Eden's government, and moved to the official residence in Carlton Gardens. Perhaps prime ministers' consorts are best prepared if their spouses have first been foreign secretary, an advantage enjoyed by Lady Home and Audrey Callaghan, but not, significantly, by Mary Wilson or Denis Thatcher. Certainly Dorothy slipped into her new role with enthusiastic ease. Now Macmillan was to travel very widely taking her with him when he could. The Geneva Summit in 1955 was to remain a landmark in her memory.

Macmillan's change of appointment from foreign secretary to chancellor of the exchequer came as a shock to a wife who was just getting into her stride as a statesman's spouse. Dorothy, Macmillan wrote, 'had thrown herself with great vigour into the world of the foreign office and the duties which fell upon her.' Indeed Dorothy advised him to resist the change, typing the letter Macmillan drafted in Paris in reply to Eden's request. She knew that he had been happy with foreign affairs 'instinctively', Macmillan wrote, '— for she had an inborn and inherited shrewdness about public affairs — she felt the change was a mistake. On looking back upon it I feel sure she was right.' Sir Gladwin Jebb, British ambassador to France, almost certainly echoed her views when he wrote of Macmillan's popularity: 'It was not only the head officials who appreciated your brilliant qualities; but it was also the little people right down to the typists and messengers, who thought you were the kindest and most considerate secretary of state they had ever known.'

Dorothy had no interest in figures or economics, but she went dutifully to the House, with a daughter, after dining with the Queen the preceding evening, to hear Macmillan present his budget. Only his introduction of premium bonds, launched with the help of the Dagenham Girl Pipers in Trafalgar Square, aroused her special interest, appealing to her sense of fun and the gambling instinct which she shared with Boothby.

Yet that reluctant move to Number 11 in December 1955 was, although the Macmillans did not realise it, a step in the right direction, with the Suez crisis and Eden's downfall only months away. Macmillan, who had earlier thought the foreign office a suitable summit for his career, had, he has said since, no eye on the leadership. But others considered the choice to be clearly between him and R.A. Butler, a man always disliked by Dorothy partly perhaps because she saw him as her husband's rival and partly because he was too donnishly intellectual and not decisive enough to win her admiration. Yet Macmillan's eventual selection as prime minister in January 1957 took her by surprise, as though her thoughts had been elsewhere during all the drama and manoeuvring.

'Harold,' she exclaimed in her clear humorous voice, when seeing him in morning dress on the day of his appointment. 'Why on earth are you wearing those ridiculous clothes?'

And that evening he dined not with his wife but with Edward Heath on oysters and champagne at the Turf Club.

Now suddenly Dorothy was forced to think about her own wardrobe. The Devonshires' attitude to dress had always been strangely contradictory, in that their footmen were turned out impeccably, powdering their hair until 1938, while the dukes cared little for their own wear, often owning only a couple of suits. Dorothy followed the paternal rather than maternal side of her family in this as in so many ways. 'I suppose I shall have to get another gown,' she allegedly told William Hickey of the *Daily Express*. 'My best one is my Coronation dress. It's silver and is rather nicely made . . .' A Bromley constituent remembers visiting Number 10 when a Macmillan daughter was running into trouble trying to make her mother buy a new dress, and the Duke of Devonshire recalls an occasion when he invited Dorothy to a formal dinner and she asked whether she should wear her best or second best dress. She refused to spoil herself. Although Dorothy dressed casually and was fond of walking and golf, she never wore trousers, favouring tweed suits, twin sets and pearls, sensible shoes, close-fitting off-the-face hats, with a preference for red, and floral-patterned summer dresses, none of which flattered her figure. As prime minister's wife, she like to wear black in the evening, her ample chest setting off her jewels, chin up, blue eyes in a strong face, a nose now fit for an emperor, fine capable hands often still ingrained with dirt from the garden. She was inclined to be late for appointments, often changing her shoes in the car or running up the steps of Number 10 still in her gardening clothes with only minutes to spare in which to drag on a smarter dress. Macmillan, meticulously punctual, saw to it that her invitations were advanced fifteen minutes to ensure that she did not hold things up.

Prime ministers' consorts were less newsworthy in 1957 than now; Dorothy was unoppressed by publicity and played herself down with easy charm. 'I feel a little lost,' she admitted when facing reporters for the first time, but of her new situation she said, 'It's an achievement; it's fun and exciting and interesting . . . I see my husband more than I used to, but I don't know what to do between engagements. Now, at home in Sussex I could be tidying up or gardening or something.'

Then with her usual brisk decisiveness she turned her attention to the furnishing of the flat at 10 Downing Street ordering that the walls should be papered in white Regency stripe, the floors carpeted in Celadon green and the window seats covered in turquoise ribbed cotton. And, surely with a rush of blood to the head, she bought yards and yards of floral material to curtain the place throughout — red and green garlands of flowers on a white background. The drawing-room sofa she had done up in rose and the chairs in beige.

She made a bedsitter for herself on the top floor under the roof, saying she would go to Chequers when her servants needed a rest, 'but it's like living in an hotel. It isn't home.' She also told reporters that she couldn't make a speech. 'I should lose my place if I tried to read it. The only joke I ever made in my life — when I said I had married a publisher and look what I got — went over the world. I shall never be able to think of another one.'

Dorothy neither avoided nor exploited the press. 'There is nothing to say about me,' she remarked on one occasion, 'except that I do not like London.'

But very soon after moving into Number 10 she started to give tea parties for MPs and their wives and later other Conservative supporters. 'She never asked me,' Boothby writes, 'because she thought and said I would hate it. But I was told by many guests that she always contrived to create an atmosphere of total informality, which made everyone happy.' She also filled the house with flowers, all arranged expertly by herself, sometimes staying up until two o'clock in the morning to achieve the exact effect she wanted.

Catherine Amery and Maurice Macmillan were eventually to have four surviving children each, Ann Faber five, and Sarah, who had married Andrew Heath in 1955, adopted two babies. The Trooping the Colour was an annual excuse to give a party for them and their friends, for her one of the nicest parties of all. Indeed Number 10 was often bursting with children and grandchildren for she 'made sure', in Harold Evans's words, 'that it was cheerful. It could hardly have been otherwise,' he adds, 'with Lady Dorothy's bustling presence, her robust down-to-earth comments on the passing scene and, above all, her deep interest in people in whatever role she encountered them.'

She made friends with the Garden Girls, those chic personable young members of the typing and general secretarial staff: as always she admired beauty in others while neglecting her own potential. Her grandchildren were inclined to leave toys in the main hall, so the most distinguished figures might find Dinky cars underfoot, but who cared about that? Not the Macmillans, for whom children were the expression of life itself. She did however take the precaution of pinning up a notice saying 'No roller skating on cabinet days' — she had as a child roller skated in the sculpture hall at Chatsworth — and, looking critically at the garden, she instructed that scrubby bushes should be replaced by colourful bedding plants. She also hired a first-class cook, although Macmillan, who had put photographs of his mother and of his grandfather's Arran croft in places of honour in his study, cared little about food and when pressed would normally plump for cold meat.

'I'm only social up to a point,' she told a *Star* reporter after a year in Number 10. 'I prefer the non-social life . . . I am just like many of the thousands of other housewives in Britain who have to work jolly hard to keep their husbands going.' This was not true of course and an affront to those struggling for female equality, for Dorothy on her own admittance was totally undomesticated and could not boil an egg, although, unlike thousands of other housewives, she knew how to run a large household and gave orders that soup in a flask should always await Macmillan after a late sitting. But although Macmillan had a certain faded style, his clothes did her little credit; his drooping cardigans were sometimes grubby; he wore paper collars as her grandfather had because she said they were cheap, despite a Sudbury firm's offer to supply him with, and launder for a year, a dozen linen ones without cost; for she had inherited her mother's thrifty streak and she would ask a porter for change for a shilling so that she would not over-tip him, and could keep a few pence for other things. On the other hand, Dorothy complained that Macmillan would not use anything new she bought him, and preferred clothes and objects to which he was accustomed. There was perhaps a certain grandeur in the way that this prime minister and his wife flaunted convention by dressing shabbily. On one occasion Macmillan played cricket at East Grinstead in brown shoes and pin-striped trousers, creating his own unflappable image of untidy elegance with just a touch of bravado.

'Calm deliberation disentangles every knot,' he wrote, quoting from *The Gondoliers* on a notice he pinned to the door leading from the cabinet room to the private office. For him matters such as the colour of shoes were trivial; the wider sweep of history, the international scene occupied his talents and time.

In 1960, when Dorothy's mother died in her ninetieth year, the foundations of Number 10 were found to be crumbling and the Macmillans moved into Admiralty House on the opposite corner of Horse Guards Parade, where they remained for three years, returning to a prime minister's official residence that was smarter, safer and more convenient.

Dorothy was fifty-eight when she went with Macmillan and her ladies' maid, the redoubtable Edith Baker, to India, Pakistan, Ceylon, New Zealand and Australia and sixty when she undertook the more arduous 'wind of change' trip to Nigeria, Ghana, Rhodesia, the high commission territories and South Africa; but she was always indomitable, despite her age, even with a badly gashed leg which needed stitching in Broken Hill Hospital: the wound dripped blood at Kariba on the red carpet of the plane against whose steps she had stumbled, and she entered the plane as an injured woman, 'swearing hard (with apologies)', determined not to delay the flight. 'She brightened our lives,' Harold Evans wrote of that tour, remembering too how he had rested his head against the cushion which covered the same leg, now poulticed, at Pretoria; how as 'cheerful and zestful as ever' she worried about the fieriness of his sun tan while ignoring most of the doctor's advice to herself and 'positively refusing to submit to any pain or discomfort'. A poor sailor, she suffered from stomach upsets on board ship, but when recovering enjoyed the boat drill and gossip, and returned home with funny rather than dire stories: a favourite was about John Wyndham's predicament when he realised that at Government House, Zomba, he had retired to sleep in one bed and awakened in another without any idea how the change took place. She joked frequently about Macmillan, seeing him always as a husband rather than a VIP, and she related how on a trip to Canada he had been found wandering outside his bedroom in Rideau Hall wearing a shirt but no trousers and had asked plaintively, 'Where is the office? I want a young lady.'

But in press interviews it did not occur to Dorothy to mention her husband as one of her interests — gardening and her work for charities were top of her list — and much of the help she gave him was totally unselfconscious. 'She serves to remind me of the realities of life. These are so often concealed in White Papers and departmental briefs. You learn quite a lot from having four children and eleven grandchildren,' Macmillan said, selling himself to a conference of Conservative Women at Church House. 'If I show signs of becoming remote from those everyday problems that perplex women in their homes, then my wife brings me back to fundamentals.'

With a good wife an immeasurable help to a politician, the Macmillans' apparently sound marital background reassured the British people. And whatever the drawbacks Macmillan was always proud of Dorothy's background which opened doors to a world of country house parties, shooting and sport which he loved, reflecting a conflict within his character summed up by R.A. Butler as 'the dual character of the Macmillan experience, namely the soft heart for and the strong determination to help the underdog and the social habit to associate happily with the overdog'. The high standard of hospitality offered by the Devonshires at Chatsworth and Rideau Hall had provided Dorothy with examples which made her critical of others. And, unlike the wives of following prime ministers, she did not hesitate to complain of shortcomings when among friendly diplomats. Harold Nicolson described in his *Diaries* an American embassy dinner when Dorothy talked about a visit to Rambouillet. Madame de Gaulle, she said, was a poor *maîtresse de maison*. 'There were about forty men servants with silver chains, superb food, but no soap in their (the Macmillans') bedrooms, no waste paper baskets, no writing materials.' It was so cold that she had to go to bed in a 'woolly'. When Dorothy asked Madame de Gaulle if there was anything special she would like to do on her state visit to London she aroused Dorothy's scorn by only being able to think of visiting Gorringes and Mrs Leo Amery, who was bedridden. Talking to the General's wife was, gardener Dorothy said, 'like digging at clay with a trowel', a criticism more like her mother's sharp comments than her father's occasional complaints. 'The Baden-Powells arrived. They are rather tiresome,' was about as far as the Duke would go in admitting to any irritation caused by guests.

But although Dorothy made little of them, her time as prime minister's wife had definite advantages and sometimes she even admitted to having enjoyed parties more than she expected. Yet, probably, apart from her family, Macmillan's greatest contribution to her happiness was not connected with his stature; it was Birch

Grove and especially the garden which provided a source of income for her charities and of pleasure for those who she felt deserved her thanks.

Dorothy's life cannot in the end be separated from Birch Grove that was ironically the claim on her time which often made her duties seem less welcome, while being also a home they both loved, so helping to keep the marriage together. It is doubtful that in later years she would ever have left Birch Grove for good; too much of her had been given to it and too much was an expression of herself. And the Macmillans always preferred it to Chequers for entertaining.

The de Gaulles stayed there, Madame once again earning Dorothy's criticism. 'She's a very difficult woman to entertain. She has a thing about people. She won't go to the hunt nor the cripples' craft school nor even the pavilion at Brighton.' In the end they settled for a drive to Beachy Head via Alfriston. John Kennedy came too, to be greatly admired by grandson Alexander handing round the cakes, who studied the president with 'rapt attention' for in the country also the children were given every opportunity to share the great moments of political life. But most important for her were the Open Days, so that, even while Kennedy was at Birch Grove, she was worrying about the siting of the posters to advertise the next one. For fifteen years until Dorothy's death the gardens were open to the public twice yearly in aid of charity. And she was always there. On wet days in an old mackintosh, wellingtons and headscarf — supervising arrangements, nailing notices on posts, cancelling orders given by local police about parking in the grounds when she thought them ill-advised. And whenever possible Macmillan supported her, staying up with her one night until two o'clock autographing photographs to be sold the next day. In later years they opened part of the house too. And the more people came the happier Dorothy was, two thousand visitors in two hours were no exception and, although she could not cook and did not prepare the teas, she would turn her hand to almost anything else, remarking on one occasion on the cussedness of the Chatsworth footmen who would never help wash up even in an emergency because they felt it was beneath their dignity.

Although the Government Hospitality Fund staff might help when important visitors came, there were only the cook, housemaid and ageing nanny as permanent servants at Birch Grove and lesser guests would be asked to bring in logs and take on other minor chores, while sometimes the grandchildren waited at table, all bossed gently in exactly the same tone of voice. 'One of the nice things about getting old,' Dorothy once said, looking as usual on the positive side, 'is that you seem to be more and more at home with the young and they with you.'

But others found her less easy, suggesting that although many considered Dorothy to be an exceptionally conscientious wife for a prime minister the view was not shared by those who supported R.A. Butler. 'That awful woman!' one such person remarked, while others high up in the women's side of the Conservative Party complained of her bossiness. Impatient of inefficiency, when crossed she would sometimes curtly demand a quick remedy, her mother's authoritarian anger for a moment rising above that wonderful warmth and friendliness which came from her father. She could put shy people at ease and she could be, as we know, a delightful travelling companion. Boothby, who never saw her lose her temper, nostalgically recalls a trip to Portugal with her, while Macmillan said in 1963, 'What I really like to do is go off with Dorothy in the car alone to Scotland. Where the hedges end is real freedom.'

Occasionally, during Macmillan's premiership, Dorothy could seem a little muddled. One now distinguished journalist recalls going, when twenty-nine, to a party at Number 10 when, despite his age, she insisted that he had been a friend of Stanley Baldwin. Ignoring the journalist's polite denials of any such relationship, Dorothy continued to question him closely about Baldwin while she showed him round the house.

Macmillan's love for the aristocracy and a rather outdated confidence in breeding, especially in the Devonshire shrewdness, perhaps made him overrate her wisdom and, surprisingly, Dorothy, like her father, trusted her own judgement, rarely hesitating to give a decisive view about people and tactics. On the eve of Macmillan's famous cabinet purge, she urged him to send out at once the letters requesting resignation. 'Women,' he said, 'have an instinct about such matters.' But was her instinct always right? Did she for example advise him after rowing Tito on the Bay of Naples before the Yugoslavian Chetniks, prisoners of war, were sent back to their own country and execution? Much later, of course, she saw Macmillan through the traumas of the Test Ban Treaty, 'the wind of change', the collapse of Britain's effort to enter the Common Market, the Vassall débâcle and the Profumo affair, and whatever her feelings for Boothby, Macmillan felt confident of her protection always; a fact very evident when the dying Gaitskell was surrounded by pressmen and Macmillan, characteristically foreseeing his own death, said, 'A man should be allowed to die in peace, and Dorothy will keep them away.'

When his illness came Dorothy was stalwart, unruffled by deep anxiety but concerned, taking his resignation with equanimity and maybe with relief, for she knew a spent force when she saw one and inevitably his retirement would give her more time at Birch Grove. But, unlike Mary Wilson, she had not yearned for the end of a personal ordeal, because with her sense of balance, she had always kept the sacrifices she made on Macmillan's behalf within limits she could cheerfully endure.

After his recovery Macmillan took on the chairmanship of the family firm of publishers, pleased to return to an occupation he loved, particularly since it brought him to London twice a week. Sixteen months after his resignation as prime minister domesticity palled and Macmillan confessed that it was nice at Birch Grove being looked after by Dorothy, but he got a little fed up of 'being surrounded by women'. (Three had taken up residence in one of the cottages to help with the research for his memoirs.) He badly needed male company, his London clubs, Oxford, and a chance to exercise his considerable skill as a raconteur. And so we are left with the feeling that he was basically a man's man, whereas Boothby was a charmer who enjoyed the company of women. Perhaps this is one aspect that put a strain on the marriage. And perhaps, paradoxically given his weaknesses and his strengths, there was no woman who would have made a better wife for him than the unpossessive Dorothy who in the end asked for no more than he could give.

Their time together was now limited. She occupied herself as usual with family, gardening, golf and her charities rather than with personal friends; she was always in demand to raise money for good causes. In 1964 she was awarded the GBE for her charitable and political work and was afterwards known by most of her grandchildren as Dame Dot. In 1965 there was a special opening at Birch Grove, with a brass band playing, and her beloved gardens looking as beautiful as ever. On May 20th the following year Dorothy organised a fête at which £400 was raised in aid of Sussex's historic churches, displaying her usual energy and enthusiasm, protective towards Macmillan's health but never towards her own. No one now suspected that her life was ebbing towards its end, but the next day at Birch Grove she complained of feeling unwell when preparing to go out. Moments later she collapsed, struggling for breath, a collar of pain gripping her chest. There was no time to summon help, to supply oxygen, before she was carried away by a massive heart attack.

The shock to her family and those who knew her was all the more severe because it was unexpected. News of her death was given to the Queen at Newbury Races. Others heard it on the BBC one o'clock news. She died intestate, leaving £62,441 of which £5,000 eventually went to her husband, along with her belongings, and the rest on trust to her children. Despite the suddenness of her death funeral arrangements were speedily made, and her obituary announcement in *The Times* the next day carried details of the funeral with the times of appropriate trains to and from Victoria. Although the service on May 25th at St Giles Horstead Keynes, where the Bishop of Chichester gave the address and the Bishop of Lewes read the lesson, was attended by many distinguished people, the mainstream of the British aristocracy waited for the memorial service at St Margaret's Westminster on June 24th. Here, on a sadder and infinitely more sombre note, was a replay in some respects of the wedding forty-six years earlier. The names of those present read once again like pages from Debrett, with the addition of the prime minister, five ambassadors and Field-marshal Alexander, whom Dorothy had known first in Africa.

Lord Home had already spoken of her 'simple and homely goodness'. Quintin Hogg said she was one of the most gracious ladies ever to occupy Number 10 that he had ever known, 'a charming hostess and a tireless worker'.

Lord Boothby, who married Wanda Sanna in 1967, wrote to me in April 1983, 'Lady Dorothy was a close friend of mine for forty years . . . I shall miss her for the rest of my life.'

Nearly twenty years later the present Duchess of Devonshire echoes others in her praise: 'She was the most vital and charming person and one of the few people I have met in my life, who was *exactly* the same, no matter who she was talking to, king or dustman.'

Macmillan in his memoirs wrote: 'For my part I could not have sustained the excitements and the frequent disappointments of the early years, or the heavy burden of the later, without her wise and loyal support.'

LADY HOME

Lady Home was born on November 6th 1909 at Shrewsbury
School, where her father was head master. She was one of six
children, the second of four daughters of Cyril Argentine Alington and
Margaret Hester Lyttelton: fair, blue-eyed and quick-tempered.

When she was seven her father became head master of Eton,
succeeding his brother-in-law, Edward Lyttelton, where he stayed
until 1933. For the girls Eton was an unconventional place in which
to grow up; boys almost everywhere; Father an Olympian figure
whose word was law; strange school rituals; legends that were, like
religion, part of life. Their nursery looked out across the provost's
garden and their schoolroom on to College Field and the famous wall
where over the centuries Eton boys have played their unique game.
The head master's house is on the north-east corner of the cloisters, a
place of great charm with a spacious drawing-room, curving staircase and, in the Alingtons' time, a fine panelled dining-room. There
were five main bedrooms, three small ones looking out across the
cloisters and five turret rooms each with views over the head
master's garden. There were attics for the lower servants. One door
opened on to the gallery where the Alington children played, racing
between the picture-lined walls. At the bottom of the fellows'
garden, which lay on the far side of the house, was a pleasant
meadow sometimes grazed by the horses Elizabeth rode with her
father to watch the future leaders of the nation playing games. In this
garden grew a great cedar and an old mulberry tree, who converse in
one of Cyril Alington's famous fables. Thinker, writer, classicist and
theologian, Cyril Alington carried his cares lightly. He was the ruler
in Elizabeth's world as the Duke of Devonshire had been in Lady
Dorothy's. The fact that neither father became arrogant was due in
part to a certain natural humbleness and also to the fact that each had

a wife with a sharp eye for weakness, although Hester Alington was infinitely kinder and more understanding than the Duchess of Devonshire. Nevertheless the children of these marriages had plenty of opportunity to observe that rulers may have feet of clay and, perhaps because of this early experience, as prime minister's wife, Elizabeth, like Lady Dorothy, would never stand in awe of the world's leaders.

Cyril Alington was second son of the Reverend Henry Giles Alington (invariably known as Giles), a Lincolnshire clergyman, who was a school inspector, living in Tunbridge Wells, during his children's youth. Cyril Alington was to recall later how he used to ride round the schools with his father, holding the horses while his father carried out an inspection. Despite the fear with which many of the teachers regarded Giles Alington, Cyril decided early that he too wanted to be a schoolmaster. A double first in classics at Trinity College, Oxford, under the tutorship of the incomparable Charles Cannan, fine aquiline features, a lively nature and reasonable success in the cricket field, gave Alington a running start. When he became head master of Shrewsbury he was younger than any of the regular teaching staff. At home, life revolved round him; his needs always came first; he liked macaroni cheese, so macaroni cheese was there, day after day; everything was arranged so that he could perform the tasks that lay before him, teach, preach (he was ordained in 1900), write his books, poetry, hymns, fables, detective stories and lectures with the least possible disturbance. He could be infuriating, but never dull, intolerant of other people's short-comings but not of the people themselves. He was a loving and affectionate father who chronicled his children's lives in a scrapbook kept by their mother. When he wrote to them, it was always in verse rather than prose. He was the sort of man whose spectacles were for ever parted from their case.

Elizabeth remembers herself as a naughty child, whose smallness inspired the names 'Tiny Wee' and 'Miss Wee', in the days before wee became synonymous with pee. 'I was really beastly,' she says now with customary candour, going on to describe how her beloved Nanny, Ada Shirlaw, had cuffed her on the platform at Reading Station, only to be accused by a fellow traveller of cruelty to that 'darling little girl'. Mortified, Nanny, who had been carrying Elizabeth's sister Lavinia at the time, wrote to Mrs Alington, 'I am sorry to say that Miss Wee is beyond my control.' Elizabeth was then three. Matters were smoothed over, but a legend was established, which suggests that the Alington's upbringing must have been remarkably gentle if such a small act of violence could loom so large in their lives.

What caused Elizabeth's frequent naughtiness? She doesn't know. Was it partly because her eldest sister, Kathleen, a dark-haired beauty, was so talented as a musician, and her younger one, Lavinia, academically brilliant — sibling jealousy? 'No, no, nothing like that, just childish devilment,' replies Elizabeth, not one to make psychological judgements. Her early life was very secure, very safe. 'Mummy,' she says, 'was a saint,' and Nanny 'a lovely person.' Then where did she come in? What was her talent? 'She was an organiser,' a family friend says, 'the one who brought the black hats for her sisters to wear at Nanny's funeral thirty years later, and provisions including a brace of home-bred pheasants because she knew that without Nanny domestic life in the Alington household would come to a halt, so great in those days was the upper classes' reliance on the good practical sense of the lower orders. Elizabeth alone in the family was not absent-minded, the sister who took the trouble to watch what the servants did, thereby learning how to run a household. She saw herself as an efficient organiser, someone who could anticipate trouble and stop it happening. Her brother-in-law, the dramatist William Douglas-Home, highlights this watchfulness when he writes in his biography of his brother's absent-mindedness:

> . . . 'Peking, Alec, Peking,' his devoted wife, Elizabeth would constantly repeat to him while walking behind him down the steps of an aeroplane when he was foreign secretary. 'Peking, Peking, Peking,' in order to prevent him saying to his hosts, as he stood before the microphone, 'I'm happy to be in Montreal (or Rome or Washington or Moscow).'

Elizabeth's mother, Margaret Hester Alington, was of noble birth, related by marriage to the Cavendishes and fifteenth child of the disastrously fertile, but far from rich, fourth Baron Lyttelton. Hester Alington's own parents were in many ways remarkable. Her mother's first husband went mad on his honeymoon, but she refused to put him in an asylum, and lived with him until his death six years later. Then, after a decent interval, she fell in love with and married Lord Lyttelton, whose first wife had died uncomplainingly and almost certainly of excessive childbearing. Lyttelton gave his new wife, Sybella, three baby girls in four years, the last being Hester, and committed suicide in 1876 by throwing himself over the banisters.

Hester Alington, however, brought up in her mother's strong religious beliefs, seems to have been exceptionally stable. Always welcoming, talkative and good-natured, with a fine sense of the ludicrous, she became an unforgettable figure at Eton and later in Durham. Round-faced, blue-eyed, unfashionably dressed and inclined to plumpness, she had a surprisingly deep voice, and was famous for her wit, and often strange vocabulary which at times left her listeners speechless. In youth her red hair was so bright that some people used to stop her in the street to say, 'You look on fire.'

In several respects a feminist in outlook, she protested violently, but unavailingly, when her husband proclaimed a school holiday, first at Shrewsbury and then at Eton, at the birth of his sons without having similar celebrations for his daughters. A radical, Hester Alington entertained some of the leading Socialists of the day when they came to talk to members of Eton's Political Society, not caring for a moment that her husband was a Tory. Yet it is doubtful that she really believed in equality, except before God, for she accepted that everyone had a station in life and that servants should wait on her, freely admitting that she had never been into a shop to buy provisions and would not know how to choose a leg of lamb. It has been alleged, perhaps unfairly, that when her own mother blew her nose she threw her handkerchief down for a servant to pick up and take to the laundry. But, while never suggesting that workers were anything but a race apart, except if they won a scholarship to one of the great educational institutions, Hester Alington would work tirelessly to improve the lot of the poor and underprivileged. She cared deeply about suffering, wanted to alleviate it, but would not willingly have countenanced a drop in her own standard of living to improve theirs. For, within the circles in which the Alingtons moved, they were financially ill-favoured. Pomp and circumstance, Cyril reflected wryly, had their disadvantages; a fixed income, however large on paper, did not 'respond with any elasticity to large increases both in taxation and the expenses of maintaining a decent standard of hospitality'.

Hospitality was, it seems, the Alingtons' greatest extravagance.

They considered the services of a butler, nanny, cook and other servants to be essential. Although their entertaining was neither so lush nor so luxurious as that provided at Chatsworth in Lady Dorothy's youth, it was much more frequently bestowed, more informal and warmer-hearted. It was also so well appreciated that the sheer number and variety of visitors could be bewildering — Lytteltons, Clives, Talbots, Cavendishes, aunts, uncles, cousins, and countless friends from all over the globe, in addition to those whom the head master of Eton might be expected to entertain. Among the last, unexpectedly and unforgettably, came Mahatma Gandhi with two female European sympathisers, two detectives, and a secretary. Of course the Alingtons were accustomed to foreigners, there were always a few among the Eton boys, but Gandhi was different and Nanny was irritated when requested to boil in her nursery the twig with which he cleaned his teeth, for the upper servants naturally had minds of their own and were often more prejudiced and conventional than their employers. She gave way, but Mrs Alington the feminist was firm when asked whether Elizabeth Slade, the principal sympathiser, might sleep on the mat outside Gandhi's door or in the adjoining dressing room. 'No, my dear,' she said, 'not while I'm president of the Mothers' Union.'

So Elizabeth learned early to meet important and renowned people. She saw that her parents treated the stream of visitors merely as an enjoyable if sometimes expensive fact of life, that colour and creed made no difference to the way in which they were received, that tact, diplomacy, friendliness and occasionally firmness were the order of the day. She learned to put on a good face at breakfast whoever might be there, although some guests, like her future husband, who were at eighteen more interested in cricket than girls, paid her scant attention. Later many of these Eton boys who came so apprehensively to eat with their head master would fill key positions in the great professions, lead armies, command ships, operate on kings, and so much more. And these boys, when men at the top of their particular tree, would be glad that they could *place* Elizabeth not only as the wife of Lord Dunglass, Sir Alec Douglas-Home or Lord Home, but as the girl they saw at Eton. They would remember her as the daughter of the head master, who it was said, had produced one of the finest generations of scholars Eton had even known; the preacher, the inveterate talker, the man who probably recommended them for their first job. For the old school network has continued to be a powerful force in England where connections are often important at every level in society. Eton gave the Alingtons a unique advantage, nurtured and developed by their own outstanding abilities, an advantage which was to impinge on almost every aspect of Elizabeth's life.

But in all this success, this status among top people, there was a counterbalance that forbade the children swollen heads. The influence that probably contributed most to Elizabeth's lack of side and the disarming diffidence, which masks an iron will, was Hester Alington's Christianity supported no doubt by Nanny. In Mrs Alington's view no laurels were won, no achievements made but for the grace of God. Religion coloured everything she did. She would talk of God as naturally as others would speak of friends or relations. Not even the horrors of the Great War, nor death closer to home nor deep personal disasters, shook her convictions. Her faith was absolute and everlasting. And with this her husband, respected theologian and revered preacher that he was, agreed. However much Cyril Alington might decry his own self-centredness, his unbounded optimism, his refusal to heed the darker warnings of the Gospel and his small misdemeanours, he was simply not as innately good as his wife. He loved life, loved his own successes and expected special treatment as a special person; the one most glaring example of this being his rather spoilt attitude to food; when he was invited out to dinner his hostesses would be told beforehand what Dr Alington liked to eat and if he were served a different menu he might leave the food on his plate. So now if you ask Lady Home about her father she is more reticent than when speaking of her mother; too loyal to criticise she leaves you with the thought that, in spite of all his rueful efforts, sainthood would not have come his way. In fact it was fortunate for his children that he possessed some shortcomings, because to live with two parents you believe to be paragons of virtue is surely no preparation for life, especially in politics where so often nothing is quite what it seems. In short, the gap between what Cyril Alington preached and what at times he practised, narrow though it was, was a mild antidote to his wife's Godliness. It kept his children's feet on the ground.

Yet because his childlike failings were so small and obvious, and his enthusiasms so contagious, because he cared so deeply about causes and, on the whole, people, because he was never pompous or censorious, he was a most lovable man. And most important he adored his family, whom he often took abroad during Easter holidays where Elizabeth painted in watercolours, and at other times to his wife's houses first at Ross-on-Wye and later to Ramsbury near Marlborough where Elizabeth rode in Savernake Forest. He rented school houses for them too at Westonbirt and Canford where they swam in the new pool, so that they might escape the sometimes inbred atmosphere of Eton.

With so much going on Elizabeth grew up accustomed to change. There was little time for boredom, few silences and much humour. Elizabeth, Lavinia and the youngest daughter, Joan, thrived in this cerebral hot-house, but Kathleen who was different in looks and temperament, developed anorexia nervosa, turning inwards away from food. Little was understood about the condition in those days. 'We did all the wrong things,' Elizabeth recalls. 'Doctors tried to *make* her eat.'

'But she was by no means,' Elizabeth is quick to say, 'a melancholy child.' As the first in the family she had been especially cherished through babyhood. Her parents' scrapbook with their records of her weight, height, first words and growing intelligence bear witness to their love for her. Indeed, for a short time, she must have been a centre in the head master's house at Shrewsbury, an enchanting child who grew into a dark-haired beauty, different in style and temperament from the others. 'She could play absolutely everything by ear,' Elizabeth told me, 'from the greatest classics to the current musicals, so she was always in demand for sing-songs and had a host of friends.' Her intermittent bouts of refusing to eat nonplussed them all and turned into a major tragedy when, weakened by undernourishment, she died of meningitis in the thirties, the first cause for deep grief in Elizabeth's life, which must have emphasised most painfully the fragility of the human frame. It was an event from which her parents never entirely recovered.

But, while Kathleen's musical career could not reach the heights expected, Lavinia blossomed and went on to Oxford. The elder girls were taught by a governess who lived in, liked but not loved as Nanny was. Elizabeth, intelligent rather than intellectual, failed to learn foreign languages, a fact she characteristically blames on herself rather than on the governess. Cyril Alington, ahead of his time, cared more about his daughters' education than most fathers of his generation, and Joan, who went for a time to a small girls' school in Eton and then to Durham High School, followed Lavinia to Oxford. But he did not push them as they grew older. His sons were shaped by Eton; his daughters were brought up to be conscientious, well-informed young women who would make good hostesses and wives in a man's world. In his day, charm, prettiness, innocence and intuitive intelligence were of paramount importance. Blue-stockings, usually pictured as confirmed spinsters unable to arouse male desire, were often considered warped women trying to compete with men. So strong was this view in some academic circles that Alington's near contemporary at Oxford, Sir Arthur Quiller-Couch, refused his daughter Foy any education so that she was forced in the end to teach herself to read and write. Of course, Mrs Alington would never have accepted such deprivation for her children and it is interesting that Lavinia, the research doctor, became the academic, putting work before appearance, not caring at all if her elbows showed through the sleeves of coat or cardigan.

It was not long before Elizabeth, with her usual practical approach to life, obtained a camera and became the recorder of family events. From this small beginning grew the ninety-three volumes, splendidly bound in dark green or red, at The Hirsel, which she describes as her life's work. 'Scrapbooks,' she tells you with a faint air of self-disparagement. 'I started them shortly before I was married.' And here in the first ones we see scenes from her early life; the drawing-room at Eton, with Chinese wallpaper and carpets, with flowers everywhere and antimacassars on the chairs, comfortable rather than smart and a little too 'busy' in today's jargon to please modern eyes. There are snapshots of Italy, views and churches. Elizabeth, a slightly lumpy adolescent in jodphurs, riding a bay gelding called Felstead at Canford. But mostly we see in these pages other members of her family because, of course, she was usually the photographer: Nanny, with a little bonnet with strings, Mother, looking a little dumpy but open-faced, Father leonine with a mane of white hair and classical profile — how could so handsome a man with such a distinguished career expect to remain unspoilt? — and brothers, sisters and countless other relations. But a succession of silver poodles — one named after his master Argentine, another MU after the Mothers' Union — steal the show, cherished, sure of themselves in arms, on rocks, in doorways or cars. These are nearly all happy snapshots, depicting aspects of an enviably full and happy childhood. Everyone knows no childhood is entirely happy; where then were the drawbacks? Why did Elizabeth become an organiser? Her father was an inveterate talker; her mother's play on words was unique and unfettered. Elizabeth appears reserved in comparison, perhaps keeping in check words that would have bounded from her parents' tongues like ping-pong balls. Did she become the quiet and efficient organiser in the background because when she was a child there was never any room in the foreground? Was she a little overshadowed by her brilliant father and mother? Old-fashioned in her loyalty, she would not admit it if she were. More pertinent perhaps was Lady Astor's comment when Hester Alington broke a leg. Turning to one of the Alington daughters the outspoken American said with humorous but cruel candour, 'None of you white trash are a patch on her.' Thus she voiced an opinion which Elizabeth still holds today; that good, kind and delightful though they may be it is doubtful that any of the Alington girls could be described as a saint.

Be that as it may, Elizabeth's organising ability was channelled into use when she went in 1927 to St James's Secretarial College, Grosvenor Square, where early reports comment on her natural speed but inaccuracy in transcription and later ones speak of her conscientiousness. 'Elizabeth has trained excellently in every way,' is the final assessment. The job which followed might have been tailor-made for the future wife of a foreign secretary. For three months Elizabeth was the right hand of Mrs Henry Stimson, wife of the American secretary of state and chief delegate to the Conference on Naval Disarmament. It was a post where a knowledge of social shibboleths and the correct way in which to address the British nobility were almost as important as shorthand and typing. Her office was at the Ritz, where Mrs Stimson was staying, and Elizabeth was so well paid that when the job ended she had earned enough to buy herself a secondhand Morris Oxford. More important for the future, she had learned much about diplomatic entertaining, and the social side of international conferences. She had shown herself to be a capable organiser well aware of social niceties.

In 1930 Elizabeth met again the young Lord Dunglass whom she had first seen at her father's breakfast table, not directly but through his younger brother William. William, who was putting on a play at

Eton which he had written, needed help in dressing the cast. Could Elizabeth lend a hand? And could she also arrange an invitation for his sister, Rachel, to stay at the head master's house so that she could see the performance? Elizabeth readily agreed to both propositions, became close friends with Rachel and was invited back to The Hirsel.

For a time the emphasis was on the girls' friendship. They met frequently, allowing the relationship between Alec Dunglass and Elizabeth to ripen slowly and respectably into love. A mutual interest in *The Times* crossword was one strand which brought the couple together, for Elizabeth was formidably well informed and always more competent than she would allow people to see. One of their joint efforts published on October 13th 1933 (the vital clue: 'the first swallow' — the answer: 'early morning tea') won them a prize of five pounds, an auspicious start to that close co-operation which was to be a hallmark of their married life.

Once again Eton gave Elizabeth an inestimable advantage, for the Homes' three eldest sons, all Etonians, seem to have venerated her father, at least in retrospect (inevitably there were boys in the Homes' Houses at Eton who mimicked their head master's voice and gestures). Alec, a president of Pop, was to remember forty years on that Alington's effect on 'boys of my generation was profound . . . He had a fine presence, classical features and a good voice.' 'And what,' he asked in his autobiography, 'did Eton give me? An introduction to life in a large and varied company, a sniff of the value of independence; tolerance; self-discipline accepted as infinitely superior to orders; responsibility shouldered lightly; to feel but not wear one's feelings on one's sleeve; a perception of the fun of living; a recognition that power and authority must be exercised with restraint. All that — while the peace and beauty and the tradition soothed the soul.'

And now in 1933 a little bit of Eton came to The Hirsel in the form of Elizabeth, who had absorbed the same values, and as a young woman bore a striking resemblance to her father, now very apparent again as old age advances. Like Alec she respected the establishment and had been brought up to obey parents, nanny and butler. Like him she had been knocked down to size every so often by brothers or sisters, to whom both had remained attached. At a time of great unemployment neither had cause to seek urgently for work. Alec, after Oxford and following a cricket tour of South America, had been allowed a two-year sabbatical in which to shoot, fish and read, and decide on a career. In 1931 he became a Unionist Member of Parliament for South Lanark. After working at the Ritz, Elizabeth took positions with charities where she was not severely tied down by her duties. Such freedom from pressures and, for Alec, outlets for aggression on grouse moor, cricket pitch and in rivers, must have diluted any unlikely seeds of youthful rebellion. Both remained products of a privileged world however much they might later take on washing up and other menial tasks, but they were infinitely kinder and more considerate than many of their counterparts, and if there had been a revolution they were surely the sort of people whose servants would have striven to save them from execution.

Photographs of this period in Elizabeth's scrapbooks show Alec, often in plus fours, with a sandy moustache hedging his wide mouth, ears prominent below tweed caps, and Elizabeth, at The Hirsel, tall in well-cut tweed suits, her hair gently waved in the fashion of the time, not beautiful but with a fine skin and good bone structure, a Sloane Ranger of the thirties, but always frowning a little as though the sun is in her eyes. Hers was a face that belonged to the *Tatler* or *Queen* of the day, to the Ritz or Savoy rather than to the Café Royal or the continental restaurants of Soho.

But it would be wrong to suppose that life at The Hirsel was very similar to that at Chatsworth or that the servants were as regimented. Lady Home, Alec's mother, saw that the living was good but frugal for everyone. There were no second helpings at meals, because all the food disappeared the first time round. She gave Alec, his brother Henry and sister Bridget their earliest education with religious teaching every Sunday. 'God was to be loved and feared. He would approve us if we were good and punish us if we were naughty.' And Alec, like Elizabeth, cared deeply for his parents, believing now that his father 'was the nearest thing to sainthood. He could think ill of no one.' In fact the Earl of Home could be endearingly eccentric. He would dress sometimes very shabbily and, other times, rising early, would waken the servants by singing hymns loudly in the passages. The butler Collingwood, immortalised in William Douglas-Home's *The Chiltern Hundreds*, would tip the Home children when they ran short of pocket money. The head gardener at the Homes' other seat, Douglas Castle — demolished in 1938 — would give them large bunches of grapes from the greenhouse with a caution not to let the elders see.

The Home children were then all healthily hungry, energetic and high spirited and Elizabeth, accustomed to large families, fitted in. After a time Alec began to see her when they were both in London, not often at first, but now and then. He took her to the races, to the theatre and out to dinner, growing to know her gradually. Even a computer would probably have recommended the match. Elizabeth's pedigree was right, as well as her character and looks, for the Lytteltons were famous for cricket and politics, so embracing two of Alec's most enduring interests. Perhaps his courtship of Elizabeth, careful and well-mannered by today's standards, sums up their later successes. No abnormal sensibility in either was to test their growing love with the devastating ups and downs of some relationships. The man who had taken more than two years after university to decide upon a career took three years to fall in love with his sister's friend (perhaps the safest choice a man can make). In the summer of 1936 he took Elizabeth to the Oaks, where they backed the winner and won the tote double, and afterwards, jubilant at their success, they walked in the gardens at Dropmore in Buckinghamshire. Here the azaleas and rhododendrons, shrubs dear to their hearts, were gloriously in bloom. The scene was set; the moment right; love was confessed. When they left the gardens they were engaged to be married.

The wedding was on October 3rd 1936. The sun shone all day. The newspapers made great play of the fact that the pages and bridesmaids were to be dressed in green, and that there would be thirteen of them, including the youngest baronet in England, Sir John Riddell, aged two and three-quarters. Flaunting superstition again, Elizabeth Alington and Lord Dunglass met on the morning of the wedding, touchingly to take communion together before their marriage. This was held in Durham, where Dr Alington was now dean, in the great Norman cathedral which stands above the city, looking down in all its majestic splendour to the river. Outside the crowds waiting to see the bride were so thick that three women fainted.

Elizabeth wore a stiff gold brocade dress of stately medieval style, with a veil of gold tulle, and carried a bouquet of gold-tipped lilies. Her father and the Archbishop of York officiated. Her younger brother Patrick gave her away, retrieving her handkerchief, according to one newspaper, the three times she dropped it walking up the aisle.

Dr Alington had written a hymn specially for the occasion to a tune suggested by the Earl of Home. The last verse called on the Holy Ghost to

Be present in our hearts today
All powerful to bless and give
To these, thy children, grace that they
May love and, through their loving, live.

He was somewhat irritated afterwards when he heard guests telling the Earl of Home that he had 'done rather well with that hymn'. Others were well tried favourites. *Praise my Soul the King of Heaven* and *Holy, Holy, Holy*, and the psalm, entirely suitable for someone with Alec's love of nature, *I Will Lift Mine Eyes unto the Hills*.

The customary wedding photograph, taken outside the cathedral, does not flatter. Moustached, looking a little sickly, Alec smiles bravely at nothing, while Elizabeth's distinguished face seems oddly out of proportion, as though someone had put it in a clamp to press her mouth and nose up towards her eyes, while leaving her brow high and her chin determined and pointed.

They left after a reception in the deanery for a motoring honeymoon through the Rhine and Switzerland into the Italy Elizabeth already knew so well. It was Alec's first trip to the continent, a prelude for all the travel to follow. They returned to Springhill which the Earl had presented to them as his wedding gift, so sparing them the housing problems which beset the Wilsons in the early years of their marriage. Alec was devoted to Springhill which is five miles from Coldstream, where he had spent the first years of his life, a modest place in comparison with The Hirsel, but with a grace and charm not frequently found in Scottish houses. Shaded by lofty trees, sheltered by well clipped hedges its lawns looked across the River Tweed to the Cheviots, into Northumberland and Roxburghshire, views embracing some of the most beautiful country in the world.

Elizabeth, like her mother, accepted the house with the job, taking over The Hirsel and Castlemains, originally the Factor's house for Douglas Castle, with her usual calm efficiency when the old Earl died. The photographs in her scrapbook were now mainly family groups, with Alec's brothers: Henry, William, Edward and George, and his sisters Bridget and Rachel, in crumpled tweeds with guns or dogs and Elizabeth herself, still frowning as she smiled, as though looking into the sun; photographs which suggest a relaxed, happy but tough family life. These are men and boys who would walk ten miles a day with a gun without turning a hair, who needed no central heating to weather the raw climate nor bothered about wet feet nor cared too much about how they looked.

Elizabeth grew very fond of them all, especially the playwright William whom she still describes as 'glorious'. And her husband she found to be 'the least shy person I have ever known'. And in keeping with that engaging self-confidence was a complete lack of showmanship, the air of an amateur in the days when gentlemen were not supposed to be professionals and careerists were considered both vulgar and suspect. If Alec reached the top it would again be through the grace of God, not because he had pushed harder than other people. It was a good beginning for a marriage, yet the happy Elizabeth was just nostalgic enough to plant cowslips to bring a little bit of England to The Hirsel's drive, an act, she says, gently deplored by the Earl because they are alien to the Borders.

Spanning three centuries, built in warm grey stone, The Hirsel which has meant so much to her cannot be categorised; its tower and elevations recall fortified Border castles while the rest is undeniably domestic, mostly a mixture of Regency and Queen Anne, graceful yet a little severe, but softened by the climbers on its walls, trees and that general air of peace and happiness which is so much part of the estate.

Inside you find a curving staircase, parquet flooring, fine carpets, passages papered in soothing green, portraits by Lely, Ramsay, Romney. There are great bowls of flowers arranged by Alec in beautiful profusion, elegant furniture, comfortable chairs and sofas. Without opulence, it yet has the kind of trappings, the works of art and antiques you would expect to find in a British country house which has been owned by one family for centuries. Unlike Chatsworth, The Hirsel has the air of a home; the servants have gone, but dogs and children have run down its passages, clustered about its fires, lain stretched out reading on the floor. The garden is well cherished and remarkable for the age of several of its trees, (most notably for the rare tulip tree planted in 1742), in summer full of colour, birds and butterflies. And, beyond the drive curving away to lead visitors to the house, the public come to walk over the grounds to see especially the lake and Dundock with its rhododendrons and azaleas, the woods and the river Leet, to picnic with their families. For the Homes allow everyone to share their estate without cost so long as the country code is kept, with the extra stipulation that dogs must be on a lead, a rule which has caused Alec, unrecognised, to be reprimanded more than once by visitors for allowing his labrador to run loose.

In Coldstream the Homes' popularity is evident; any mention of their name invites praise. Pausing there before my first visit, I talked to an old man who kindly came out of a terrace cottage to bring water for my dog. I told him I was nervous.

'You don't need to be,' he replied at once. 'No one needs to be. *She* won't let you be. They're too nice. They'll make you feel at home.' The old Earl, the man said, used sometimes to roam the hills dressed like a tramp. They were a lovely family, very natural. And then there was Caroline, Caroline and her horses.

He was right, of course. I was a stranger, the only guest, coming self-invited with my biographer's begging bowl and the Homes did their best to make me feel welcome, and worried afterwards because they had not invited in my dog, not knowing until I was leaving that she was outside in the car. She must have been cold, Alec said, down there all by herself, revealing that weakness for dogs which has allowed the housekeeper's crossbred terrier to ingratiate herself into the drawing-room where she sits pressed against Alec's legs hogging the fire.

In 1936, Elizabeth's parents in Durham provided a useful stopping place on the drive down to London, where Alec, already a Member of Parliament, had a house near the Macmillans at 32 Chester Square, an appropriate setting for Elizabeth, who even now seems to belong to Belgravia and Knightsbridge rather than Chelsea or Hampstead. She was, a Nottingham reporter suggested, 'a welcome addition to the ranks of young political hostesses in London'. She also went to many of the parties so disliked by Lady Dorothy Macmillan. Elizabeth wanted a large family and hoped to provide the desired heir to the Earldom. She produced three daughters in under four years; the first, Lavinia Caroline in 1937. At that time Alec, who, as Neville Chamberlain's parliamentary private secretary, seemed set for a promising political career, was in the thick of things. It was he who delivered to Sir John Simon in the House on September 28th 1938 Hitler's crucial invitation to the Munich meeting and it was he who stood in the entrance hall at the Führerhaus in the Königsplatz, waiting for the subsequent talks to finish, wearing one of William's landlord's shirts because he had been summoned so unexpectedly that he had no clean one to hand. Elizabeth stayed with her baby, intensely caring about, but not yet deeply involved in her husband's political life.

Though housebound, she saw how loyally Alec supported Chamberlain against attacks from Churchill, Duff Cooper and others, unwisely declaring in East Kilbride in November 1938 that war between England and Germany was more remote than it had been for years, so finding himself on the other side of the fence to Macmillan. His own prep school days, she knew, had been clouded by his father's departure to fight in the First World War, but having served in the OTC at Eton he was nevertheless in 1938 already a territorial officer in the Lanarkshire Yeomanry.

On that awful Sunday when war was declared, with Elizabeth out of London, Alec turned, as he always does in moments of anguish, to nature, walking off his tension looking for Chalk Blues on the Downs. She realised his judgement had been wrong, but all through that long cold winter, when she bore a second daughter, Meriel, and everything was strangely quiet on the western front, he continued to support Chamberlain, staying at his post as PPS rather than joining his regiment. When May came and Chamberlain tumbled, Alec planned to enlist. Pale and drawn, determined to take up arms, he cleared out his drawer at Number 10 and went home to Springhill, where Elizabeth was expecting their third child. He was thirty-seven, underweight and sleeping badly, but Elizabeth, who later was to become so watchful of his health, was not unduly alarmed and neither husband nor wife anticipated for one moment that they were about to meet a watershed in their lives. It was only after Alec had twice been turned down by an army medical board that it was decided to seek specialist advice. The result was a bombshell which was to shatter Elizabeth's faith in Alec's constitution for ever. A tubercular spinal cavity threatened to cripple or even kill him; nothing but a dangerous operation offered any hope of recovery and even then the chances of his walking again were no better than fifty-fifty. In the 'forties a diagnosis of TB was close to a death warrant. Alec, who now admitted to having felt washed out and tired for years, had never complained, merely grown whiter and thinner, perhaps not wanting to face a killer. But now typically he decided without hesitation to risk the operation; the only choice for a man of his leanings and temperament; in Western Europe greater dangers were taxing the courage of thousands, putting his own position into perspective.

Elizabeth, pregnant, stayed in Edinburgh, where he was in hospital for about a month. He emerged eventually, a sad face above a shell of plaster from shoulder to thigh, the cavity repaired with bone from his shin without injury to the spinal cord, but with a two-year sentence of almost complete immobility. Changed spiritually as well as physically by the operation, he felt he had looked over the edge, and 'glimpsed the infinite'. Now each afternoon Elizabeth read to him; at mealtimes she fed him, and she wrote all his letters, for everything about her upbringing had prepared her to meet such a challenge bravely and sensibly. Although there were moments of despair ('I often felt I would be better dead,' Alec wrote of the first months), both were fortunate in their unswerving religious faith supported by the combined prayers of the Homes and the Alingtons, who surely had direct lines to the Almighty if such lines there be. And now there was another Godly relation to swell the ranks, who would eventually take Holy Orders, for in 1940 Joan Alington had married John Comyn Vaughan Wilkes, a classicist who had taught at Eton for seven years before becoming warden of Radley College in 1937. Joan, a typical Alington, was to give Wilkes four sons and a daughter before adopting two coloured children. The Homes' third child, Diana, was born in December that year.

Meanwhile Elizabeth had Alec's bed brought down to a room on the ground floor from which he could see his beloved Tweed and the Cheviots. The next summer, a revolving summer-house was constructed for his use, which, with his arms free of plaster, he could manoeuvre to change his panorama. When he began to read biographies of all the nineteenth-century prime ministers and books on Eastern European affairs and communism, and, in addition, to enjoy short bouts of embroidery — he completed eight dining-room chair covers in petit point — Elizabeth knew that he had turned a corner. And yet with the German bombers 'droning up the Tweed to Glasgow' he was still riled by his helplessness, particularly as his brothers Henry, William, Edward and George, and Patrick Alington, had all enlisted.

The best Alec could do was to work towards a return to the House of Commons and an equitable and lasting peace. Knowledge gained from reading was supplemented by visits from the courageous Count Paul Stavzenski, one time private secretary to the Polish foreign minister, Colonel Beck, now stationed at Douglas Castle: a man who undoubtedly strengthened Alec's own distrust of the Soviet Union and the communist policies in general.

Those two years with Alec helpless were of the kind that make or break a marriage; for the Homes they simply cemented what was already there, strengthening their belief, confirming love and reinforcing the pleasures, as they returned, of normal companionship. When Alec came out of plaster he weighed fifteen stone, compared to his usual eleven, and his knees were locked. Horrendous months followed, with the final crippling adhesion broken only as he slipped on a rock 'when with a crack like a pistol and a sweating stab of pain the last adhesion went.'

Now there was physical love again, the chance of more children and a political life stretching ahead as Alec returned to parliament. There was also grief. In 1943 Elizabeth and Alec were each to lose a brother. George died flying in Canada and Patrick at Salerno. But Nature carried out one of her balancing acts; Elizabeth's fourth baby, born in November the same year, was a boy: David, the heir, whom Alec would teach to fish and shoot; another future Lord Dunglass for Eton, another hostage to fortune.

On his return to politics, Alec briefly held the post of joint under secretary at the foreign office before losing his seat in the 1945 Labour landslide, the year that Lavinia Alington married Old Etonian and distinguished classicist, Roger Mynors. So for five years after the war Elizabeth had the pleasure of her husband's company at home at least in the evenings, during a crucial time in their son's development, while Alec looked after the estate and sat on committees concerned with Scottish affairs becoming president of the Conservative Party in Scotland. She also accepted with good humour the hours Alec spent away from her with gun or rod, understanding his addiction to fishing and shooting, adapting herself to meet the needs of a sportsman as well as a politician.

Alec returned to parliament in the 1950 general election, only to give up his seat the next year when he inherited the Earldom on his father's death, a deep blow that knocked him sideways for he had greatly loved the man, who, he wrote in his memoirs, 'could not think ill of anyone'. When Alec's brother Edward had been a prisoner of the Japanese working on the notorious railway someone had said to his father, 'Never mind, one day we'll have our revenge,' and the Earl had asked, 'What would be the point of that?' a reply which had profoundly impressed his eldest son.

The death of this kindly and remarkable man brought Alec not only grief, but financial complications, massive death duties and business problems and that year, struggling to sort everything out, he was fined for driving through traffic lights at red.

But now with Alec automatically a member of the House of Lords, the new Earl and Countess of Home were spared the ardours of electioneering and very soon James Stuart of Findhorn, under whom Alec had served on a Scottish committee, provided the crucial leg-up which was to set Alec on his way to the foreign office. Stuart, who was married to Lady Dorothy Macmillan's sister Lady Rachel, had just been appointed secretary of state for Scotland and when asked whom he would like as his minister, suggested Alec. 'All right, Home sweet Home it shall be,' said Churchill.

So once again Elizabeth was saved from a political wife's usual conflict of loyalties. Alec was more often in Scotland than London and most of their formal engagements were in Edinburgh, memorably the banquet given for the exotic Queen of Tonga at the Castle. By 1955 when Eden appointed Alec secretary of state for commonwealth relations, Caroline, Meriel and Diana, who had been educated by governesses 'so that they could enjoy home life', were teenagers and David was safely at Eton. Sadly, Cyril Alington died while living with the Mynors, in whose Herefordshire house he had set up a little chapel with an altar for communion and prayer. Three years earlier, still berating himself at eighty, he had said, 'I was a schoolmaster and as the great Lord Halifax once said, "the occupation of teaching doth often cause a man to forget he is a blockhead." As I look back I marvel more and more at all that I have failed to learn.' The year after his death, Elizabeth's brother Giles Alington, dean and senior tutor at University College, died.

Meanwhile, at a time when many wives of her generation were struggling with the menopause and a sense of redundancy, Elizabeth was to turn nomad. Alec, wishing to become better acquainted with the Commonwealth, planned a 35,000 mile tour of Australia, New Zealand, India, Pakistan and Ceylon, and Elizabeth went to the prime minister himself to ask that she might accompany him. 'I said,' she will tell you, 'that I could not be parted from him for so long.' And once Eden agreed the pattern was set. In 1956 it was Canada and Newfoundland. In 1957, Rhodesia and the Federation, a whirlwind tour with one hundred engagements for Alec and many tours of hospitals and schools for Elizabeth. The Mayor of Bulawayo complained that twenty-three hours in his town was too short in comparison with six or seven days in Salisbury, and so on and on into a world of strange faces, old and new civilisations. She insists doggedly that she never worried. 'We're not the worrying kind. I never worry. My husband is even more an unworrier than I am. I mean, after he's done his best he just stops worrying.'

But her eye was ever-watchful, her feeling always that she must anticipate and avoid pitfalls, which is surely anxiety's sister. She must be there just in case. And if you ask to meet her today she will say, 'It depends whether my husband needs me'.

But Elizabeth is no servant, no lesser being. The Homes' marriage remains the fusing of two wills working towards the same end; it is never a subordination of one to the other. She is the organiser. He is the man up front. She will push him on small matters, get him to the right place at the right time, put names to faces he has forgotten, remind him, as we know, where he is when he is about to make a speech, but those who say (and the comment is more common than the Homes may realise) that Elizabeth is a formidable woman and that Alec would not have reached the top without her, miss one vital point. His absent-minded good-natured air, his casual hand in pocket saunter, hide a profound pertinacity and on the rare occasions when their wills clashed on an important matter outside the family, he won. It may be that without Elizabeth he would not have survived his illness so well, or taken on so many arduous duties. Hers has been the voice at the elbow saying, 'Go on, you can do it.' But of the two he was actually the more formidable, because he was the one who would go, if he felt it necessary, into any fray and face the music. Like Callaghan he needed no cronies; he amended his own speeches often without consultation; obstinately he salvaged hours for personal leisure out of crisis in which to think alone as well as to enjoy himself. He did not necessarily consult Elizabeth on the graver issues of state, but was and is happy to have a loving and devoted wife who enjoys acting as his private secretary. She told a reporter in 1964, 'I don't make speeches. I'm a hopeless speaker and Alec is not in favour of me making speeches.'

Before the commonwealth office led on to the foreign office, Elizabeth's mother died, sadly bereaved of three out of six children, crippled by arthritis but game and religiously faithful to the last. Hester Alington, who had been awarded the CBE in 1949 for her charitable work, has remained a central influence in her second daughter's life, an example against whom Elizabeth can measure her own performance and, in her father's fashion, find herself wanting.

After Suez (when Alec supported Eden but felt British action should have been swifter and more far-reaching) Alec was appointed foreign secretary and the Homes moved into 1 Carlton Gardens from the last of various London flats they had occupied since leaving Chester Square at the outbreak of war. Here in the elegant Nash house with its graceful staircase, its gold embossed ceilings, fine fireplaces and glittering candelabra, the Home children established themselves in a small room overlooking the gardens of Marlborough House, well out of the way of the frequent distinguished guests. It was, Elizabeth says, 'a glorious time'.

A little over twenty miles away was Dorneywood, a twenty-bedroomed house deep in the woods of Buckinghamshire near Burnham Beeches, which had been given to the nation by Lord Courtauld Thomson for the use of ministers entertaining overseas visitors. Standing in two hundred acres, built in Tudor style but with Georgian-type windows, it was a delightful country place for a family accustomed to spaciousness; simple in design but of special interest to art lovers because of the Rex Whistler decorations in the inner hall. During Alec's years first at the commonwealth office, then at the foreign office, Dorneywood was the scene of many splendid parties supervised by Elizabeth but paid for by the Government Hospitality Fund, an arrangement happily embraced by the convivial Homes, who still entertain with undiminished enthusiasm at The Hirsel and Castlemains, with a steady flow of guests from all over the world.

Elizabeth Home and Lady Dorothy were now to see more of each other, since Macmillan favoured summit meetings and travelled more widely than any previous prime minister, frequently accompanied at least for part of the time by his foreign secretary. And when they could the wives went too. Elizabeth was already connected to the Devonshires by marriage, Hester Alington's half sister Lucy Lyttelton having married Lord Frederick Cavendish, and the two women liked each other. Both had married Old Etonians, Oxford graduates, sportsmen and politicians; both were educated at home, reared by parents and nannies who were practising members of the Church of England, and in certain directions careful with money. Both had been brought up to loathe pretentiousness and swank and to develop their own courage and stoicism. Certain codes of behaviour were intrinsic for Lady Dorothy and Elizabeth Home: displays of deep emotion were kept for the privacy of the home; gossiping was left to the servants; vanity, sloth, greed, mindless extravagance, whining, screaming, shrieking were all out. Duty, endurance and good temper in the face of adversity were to be admired. In short, they both possessed that now ridiculed and perhaps underrated British quality known as 'the stiff upper lip'. For their husbands such characteristics and beliefs were invaluable. These wives had been trained by example from the beginning to marry eminent men and the training showed. With outstretched hand, smiling face and words of welcome or appreciation on their lips they travelled the world, conscious that they were ambassadors for their country. Perhaps they embodied what the world expected British women to be: not chic, not beautiful, but always friendly, eminently sensible, accommodating and good-mannered. Of the two, Elizabeth was more closely set in the conventional role of diplomat's wife, better dressed, more relaxed with intellectuals and totally committed. But Dorothy with her breezy good humour could be more disarming, creating a special rapport with her husband's colleagues.

Although the appointment of a member of the Upper House had been greeted with fury by some Conservative members and by the Opposition, both Alec and Elizabeth felt he gained from being in the Lords, being spared vociferous attacks in the Commons and finding more time to think in the quieter House. Alec's job, Macmillan had said, was a killer; 'It killed Bevin in three years [*sic*] and nearly killed Sir Anthony Eden.' But over the years he had become a great conserver of his own energy, knowing when to switch off.

'Of course my husband has no qualms about the job,' Elizabeth told newspaper reporters, adding staunchly, without a sense of prophecy, 'As far as I'm concerned he's able enough for any post in the government, even prime minister.'

He made eleven trips abroad in the first six months, with the girl who had remembered black hats for Nanny's funeral, ensuring with meticulous care that he had the right clothes in the right places. As foreign secretary's wife Elizabeth's first trip abroad included a state visit to Nepal by the Queen and Duke of Edinburgh. A game hunt on elephants, described by the *Church Times* as 'organised butchery', was undoubtedly arranged with the sporting inclinations of the Earl of Home and Prince Philip in mind. Scores of tents were pitched, some superbly equipped for royal and distinguished guests; 327 elephants provided and countless servants and hunters employed. For Elizabeth, trying to adjust herself to the swaying gait of her huge mount, the whole event took on a nightmarish quality when it decided to run away. Mistaking her calls to slow down for enthusiasm the mahout encouraged the elephant to overtake the entire train including the Queen, while Elizabeth frantically hung on. Alec hardly fared better for when asked to shoot a lone tiger who had been driven out of the bush (Prince Philip having declined to do so on account of an injured wrist), he missed three times and it was killed by someone else. Later he and the Queen's secretary, Michael Adeane, combined to shoot a rhinoceros. 'A decadent occasion,' exploded the *Church Times*, to which the Queen should not have been invited, not seeing that Alec's position had been impossible, for as a diplomat he had to put his hosts' feelings first and to plead a disability as the Prince had would have been an irretrievable snub to the people who had set up the whole event at such enormous expense.

Mercifully for the Homes, the next state visit, at the end of April 1961 was more conventional and less demanding — Naples and Rome with a royal gala performance of *Falstaff* — and in May there was a trip to Lisbon and Madrid. Others followed with disconcerting frequency.

Sometimes, Alec told a meeting at Ayr on April 20th 1961, he felt like a soldier who had answered a recruiting poster to join the army 'and see the world'. Occasionally he wondered whether Macmillan was judicious in arranging so many summit meetings. But Elizabeth's statements were always appreciative and occasionally almost schoolgirlish in their jollity. 'It sounds enormous fun,' she said, when the idea of meeting Khrushchev at a Russian seaside resort was mooted. 'I shall certainly pack a swimsuit for myself. My husband is not very keen on swimming actually, but I think we can put a hand on a costume for him somewhere.' There was no suggestion, of course, that a new suit might be bought for the occasion, for most of the British aristocracy hesitate to spend money on clothes. 'Fine feathers,' their nannies have told them in childhood, 'do not make fine birds.' In the end there was no bathing with Khrushchev either before or after the Test Ban Treaty was signed, and the Homes flew on to join the Macmillans in Sweden where at Harpsund — the Swedish equivalent of Chequers — Macmillan sang *My Bonnie Lies over the Ocean* and *Little Brown Jug*, while Alec beat time. Another day they lunched with the King and Queen at Sofiero, and went to the opera at Drottningholm Palace Theatre.

The Home children brought friends home to Carlton Gardens. 'I never know when I go to bed how many are sleeping in the house,' Elizabeth cheerfully told a *Woman's Journal* reporter. 'Of course it does mean that lights are left blazing in every room and cupboard in the place and that's one thing Alec does get furious about.' A telephone pinger bought in an attempt to control the duration of calls was left unused. Such problems were peripheral, however. 'I love it all,' she claimed in April 1963. 'I love eating foreign food, Japanese food was marvellous. I can eat anything. I only wish we could stay longer in all the different places.' On one Canadian trip, she said, they slept in twenty beds in twenty-eight days.

But Alec's health remained a deep concern, and Elizabeth the conscientious housekeeper cooked assiduously when necessary, to keep him healthy, always providing porridge for breakfast, leaning towards casseroles — oxtail a favourite — and nursery food, rice pudding and stewed fruit which counterbalanced the richness of official dinners. He was careful too, balancing every glass of wine with one of water. And yet despite her efforts there were times when she felt desperate because he looked drained, particularly on television, always his *bête noire*.

'I know why you think my husband looks so poorly,' she told a newspaper reporter in spring 1963. 'I was watching him on TV and I got an awful shock. He looked simply appalling, all hollows and bones. I was terrified and rushed upstairs to have a look at him in the bedroom where he was changing. It was a recorded interview, you see, at some airport. I just stared at him and said, "Are you all right? You looked terrible downstairs." Then I could see he was all right.'

So a thin strain of anxiety persisted while she continued to combine with liveliness and good temper the roles of foreign secretary's wife and mother of children who had moved into adulthood, coping with jobs and young love and the heady invigorating life of the early sixties, handicapped at first perhaps by that very protected childhood. A trip with Alec to Karachi and Teheran was missed because she was preparing for Diana's wedding to James Archibald Wolfe Murray, a distillery executive. When asked what she would wear, she replied, laughing, 'The dress I bought for the royal wedding. Not very enterprising am I?' And she continued to work intermittently on the scrapbooks, her contribution to posterity, including in them the nasty cartoons and caricatures of Alec and most of the bad as well as the good press.

Then came Macmillan's illness, the leadership crisis, all the talk behind closed doors, the semi-secret manoeuvring, which was to make Alec feel later that he had come in 'sub rosa', despite the fact that his lack of guile in the matter and his hesitation over accepting the leadership were widely remarked.

His eventual selection, welcomed by Elizabeth, presented, as she knew, formidable problems. No seeker after fame or adulation, Alec enjoyed a leisurely life. At the same time he liked to be where the action was, and his highly developed sense of duty was never in doubt. When it became clear that he might be offered the job his feelings were mixed. 'If you get into a terrible jam,' he replied diffidently, 'what I will consent to do — and nothing else — is to go and see my doctor and see if I'd be fit.'

He was, he wrote in his biography, 'filled with deep doubts about becoming a commoner once again. It entailed renouncing a peerage which had been held for many hundreds of years; it meant taking on a new constituency and fighting a by-election in order to be able to sit in the House of Commons; and it meant assuming the most testing and responsible of all the political offices in Britain, with all the physical strains which go with the occupancy of Number 10 Downing Street.'

He recalled that overstrain had brought on TB in 1939, that his eyes were troubling him and he jibbed at the thought of 'such a convulsion' in his life. He was, in short, without the ambition which usually drives those who become prime ministers.

Like Macmillan he would have been satisfied with the foreign office as the peak of his career. But, in Alec's words, 'the escape route was closed' when the doctor pronounced him medically fit for the job.

He then discussed every aspect of the appointment with his wife and children. Few prime ministers can have taken on the premiership so reluctantly and so carefully, nor have felt so doubtful of winning support in their own party, while all the time Elizabeth was determined that he should accept.

'In the end,' he writes in his biography, 'I concluded that if — and only if — convincing evidence was brought to me that a substantial majority in both Houses wished me to take on the job I would do so.'

When this stipulation was met there was no time to tell Elizabeth, who heard on the radio that her husband had left for the Palace and, knowing that he had had no opportunity to change his clothes, exclaimed, 'Heavens, in that suit!'

Elizabeth was plumper now than in the fifties, and although English very Scottish-looking with that high brow and dignified air, a woman more confident about her role than Mary Wilson was to be and more excited than Lady Dorothy had been on Macmillan's appointment.

Accustomed to royalty, Elizabeth had little cause for nervousness; she had met the Queen of Romania while at Eton and had first visited Buckingham Palace to be presented in 1928, wearing the obligatory court dress with 'feathers and a train'. There had been frequent royal encounters while Alec was foreign secretary. Unhampered by serious anxieties, she was soon to become the most skilful of prime ministers' wives since the war at promoting a husband's image both as an attractive human being and a leader.

'Anyone who underestimates him,' she announced proudly, 'does so at their peril. He doesn't look nearly so tough as he really is — he can really lash out. I don't flinch at the thought of Mr Wilson cutting him up.' And, softening the image later, 'He never gets very wound up about criticism or any toodleoo. He's just frightfully good-tempered. The only time he ever gets annoyed is in traffic jams.' Then, perhaps remembering to remind people that the Homes knew what ordinary life was, 'We have a cook for the first time ever in London.' 'Toodleoo' was a throwback to childhood, one of those invented words which had given her mother's conversation an idiosyncratic flavour in strange contrast to Alington's classical precision.

Elizabeth was diplomatically polite about her predecessor's taste, her Christian beliefs allowing her the occasional white lie for kindness' sake. 'It's all delightful. I shall make no changes at all,' she said of the Downing Street décor, though in fact she soon decided she could not bear Dorothy Macmillan's identical chintz curtains in *every* room.

Like her predecessor, Elizabeth possessed the self-confidence that allows self-depreciation. 'There's nothing distinguished about me, I am very ordinary,' she told a newspaper reporter to ward off further personal questions, using a well tried defence mechanism as well as expressing a mood that overtakes the more positive side of her nature from time to time.

Despite these occasional moments of self-disparagement, everyone who knows Elizabeth is well aware of the dynamism behind the calm front, the suppressed emotion, which in her youth once caused her to faint when thwarted while others less well-mannered might have exploded into abuse. This is the flame behind the guard which helps to keep her going despite the afflictions of approaching old age, the rheumatism which attacks knee or shoulder. It is a force well recognised by her children who so good-naturedly, 'out of love favour and affection', assisted their father in renouncing his title. In 1963 the young Homes were grown-up and mildly unconventional in the lively way of many of their generation. After Sir Alec Douglas-Home had won the by-election at Kinross and West Perthshire, to be truly prime minister, his three youngest children arrived at 10 Downing Street 'carrying clothes over their arms, coat hangers, guitars, Beatles records and piles of books.' The doorman, no doubt expecting more obviously upper-class young people, barred their way requesting their names. 'Dunglass,' said the boy, hanging on to his gun case. 'Douglas-Home,' the girls claimed. Only after checking with the staff upstairs that these cheerful, casual young people were really the Homes' progeny did the doorman let them in.

Diana's first baby, Fiona, was to become a familiar presence in her pram in the garden at Number 10, watched over by the secretarial staff. Meriel, who was later to regret her lack of conventional schooling, was working in Bumpus, the bookshop, David was still at Oxford. Caroline, who disliked London, was soon to study estate management in preparation for managing The Hirsel, but in 1963 she was an Extra Woman of the Bedchamber to HM Queen Elizabeth the Queen Mother. The Home children appeared to take a certain amount of mild harassment from newspaper men in their stride. Meriel in black stockings and shiny black mackintosh, which contrasted delightfully with her long blonde hair, reacted with aplomb when questioned by reporters who pursued her into Bumpus where she was trying to sell biographies and travel books. 'For the last few days,' Alec joked, referring to the loss of titles, 'the girls have been calling themselves "near misses".'

So despite the seriousness of the moment the whole family retained their light-heartedness. Elizabeth continued to keep a joke book for Alec, in which she wrote down anything that would come in useful for speeches. And back at The Hirsel they would sometimes return to their old pastime of playing Scrabble or Racing Demon, sitting on the floor, with Elizabeth umpire, a position entirely in keeping with the family's view of her efficiency. Yet despite her proven ability as an organiser, when offered the services of a secretary at Number 10, she agreed only unwillingly, saying that she was 'not nearly competent enough' to use such help, and was more accustomed to taking than dictating letters.

Much of her mail as prime minister's wife came, she said, from friendly lunatics. They wrote to say that Alec was wonderful, but she should fatten him up. 'Does he have to wear glasses?' asked one correspondent, longing to improve his image. 'Feed him cheese then; it's good for eyes; strengthen him by giving him warm milk and honey every two hours.' Other sad people wrote needing help or money. There were persuasive invitations to attend public functions which she usually refused, preferring to back up Alec rather than go on her own. More than any other pair discussed in this book, the Homes were invited out together, with Alec normally finishing his work early enough to be with his wife in the evening. He did not wish to discuss problems with his colleagues far into the night, nor would he relish dining in a London club, as was often Macmillan's custom. Home life was immensely important to him; he felt that leisure kept a man sane; wisely he would delegate when necessary and leave the person concerned to get on with the job.

When you ask Elizabeth about life in the flat at Number 10 she will laugh and say, 'We were hardly ever there!' When they were there, being accustomed to space, they would take their after-dinner coffee in one of the state rooms. In the mornings Alec would wake at about six-thirty and work until breakfast — porridge — around a quarter to nine. There was no anger, no shouting, the atmosphere was calm and civilised. Elizabeth, with her ability to see small problems arising, always fretted more than her husband if things seemed to be going wrong. The way of life at Number 10 came naturally to her because her parents had always lived at their place of work, constantly on view and available to callers, the top people at Eton as she was now a top person in Westminster. Now like her mother she kept open house for friends, and since she was accustomed to servants, there were few adjustments to make. One of her chief regrets was and remains that her parents were not alive to share the Homes' success and pleasures. 'They would have enjoyed it all immensely,' she says, and one can picture the Alingtons, the one so distinguished, the other assured enough to allow herself eccentricities, lively as crickets at receptions, deeply involved in every crisis. Elizabeth, faithful to her class and generation in having a great respect for connections, felt she could best help her husband by 'getting to know people and helping them to know each other'. She already knew many heads of state, and was totally accustomed to state occasions. Her equanimity and presence of mind when arrangements went awry were perfectly exemplified at President Kennedy's funeral, when she quickly offered her seat to the Duke of Edinburgh, whose place appeared to have been overlooked.

Undoubtedly she enjoyed herself at Number 10 and would gladly have stayed longer. Although clothes continued to be a bore, for she had, she said 'no flair for fashion', she still played safe, becoming noted for her pearls and discreet good taste, following the upper-class dictum that it is better for the hostess to be underdressed than overdressed. Very occasionally she splashed out just enough for the more conservative-minded to wonder whether she was wearing one of her daughters' frocks, whereas she had merely given way to a natural but frequently suppressed exuberance.

With the children needing her less, Alec became the centre point of her life, his career was her career and to some extent she lived and continues to live through him. Always conscious of his image, she was sometimes nettled by *Private Eye*'s caricatures of him as the mad Scottish laird, Lord Baillie Vass, while he took them as good fun. Cartoonists, she said, always made his upper lip stick out. 'It doesn't. It's concave rather than convex.' Deeply involved in his politics, she rarely missed an important speech, and went regularly to the House.

There were worries, of course. The economic situation was bad and did not begin to improve for several months. There were particular difficulties for the new countries in the commonwealth. Coming in as prime minister at the tail-end of a government presented special problems, particularly for a man accustomed to the quieter House of Lords. Officials at Central Office, with another general election approaching, were determined that Alec should become well known to the electorate. He had to be seen and, with this in mind, he made sixty-four full dress speeches and one hundred and fifty 'whistle stop chats' in the first five months of his premiership, still supported whenever possible by the enthusiastic Elizabeth. In addition, his ignorance of economics meant that he had to rely heavily on the chancellor, Reginald Maudling. Ironically his appearance on television remained unattractive, despite his fair open face, which won friends and supporters in the field. Unlike Macmillan he had no acting ability. In his autobiography he describes a conversation he had with a make-up girl before a prime ministerial performance in 1963.

'Can you not make me look better than I do?' he asked.

'No,' said the girl.

'Why not?'

'Because you have a head like a skull,' she replied.

'Does not everyone have a head like a skull?'

'No,' she said.

To improve his image, and against Elizabeth's advice, he took to wearing half moon spectacles (known as Homes) which she later claimed lost him the election. Certainly they made him seem years older.

Another anxiety on her mind was the reckless way he turned his pages when making speeches so that occasionally two were flicked over at once, which could cause more than a little confusion. Kenneth Young has described how he rewrote the speeches his aides produced for him, 'writing in his own hand with a 3/9d Biro pen on thick white sheets of Basildon Bond', a process described by his staff as 'basildoning'.

But tired and worried though she might occasionally be, Elizabeth always appeared confident. In January 1964 she was saying, 'With Alec all things are possible . . . I cannot imagine him ever trying to put on an act. We always try to be absolutely ourselves.' And on another occasion 'He's very kind and extremely good-tempered. He has excellent judgement . . .' and so on, always friendly, always polite, with no chink in her armour, no absurdity for the cartoonists to caricature. And yet there is frequently, even now, a suspicion of shyness in her, picked up by the antennae of any sensitive interviewer, which accounts sometimes for sudden spontaneous bursts of conversation rather than steady dialogue.

At Number 10 Elizabeth continued Lady Dorothy's practice of giving tea parties for MP's wives and constituency workers, only now it was Alec who arranged the flowers if he had time. They invited a Scottish joiner, Tom Hodge, with his wife and three-year-old son to celebrate the Trooping the Colour with them. This family had been allotted the 10,000th house to be built in the new East Kilbride town, which the Homes visited at the celebrations held to commemorate its completion.

'Now that I have seen your house,' Alec had told Tom Hodge, 'you must come and see mine.' And he was as good as his word, although rumour had it that the joiner was a Labour supporter.

Inevitably, the country-loving Homes spent weekends when possible at Chequers, which they loved with the one reservation that it needed an additional smallish room for entertaining, a shortcoming remedied by Edward Heath. Alec tells a story of commonwealth leaders, who are traditionally entertained at Chequers, leaving one by one after dinner for London, to the Homes' consternation because they had been invited for the night. It later transpired that the less sophisticated had been afraid to sleep in the four-poster beds, a discovery which might have given many a hostess a broken night. But Gandhi with his toothbrush twig and the strange Miss Slade outside his door had prepared Elizabeth for anything. Her own manners might be impeccable but she was not bourgeois; she could take strange behaviour in her stride so long as it was not barbaric or rude.

In June 1964 Meriel married Adrian Darby, an Oxford economics don. Dropping political life for a few days, Elizabeth was in her element making the arrangements. Characteristically she drew a master plan which she pinned to a board at The Hirsel, so that each member of the family should know his or her duties both before and immediately after the wedding, with Alec's main chore, apart from the usual responsibilities of the bride's father, the arranging of the flowers in the church. She also detailed on the plan the exact arrival and departure times for the guests and to whom slices of wedding cake should be sent.

It was this reliability which won Elizabeth the high regard among Alec's aides, civil servants and diplomats which survives today. Whatever her private torments, she was rarely fractious or difficult and could be counted on to be in the right place at the right moment.

But she feels now that their time at the top was too short; they were thrown into a general election before Alec had had time to put new policies across, to improve his television image or more fully understand economics. He is, she knows, a man who does not like to be rushed, and although he insisted upon a daily walk in St James's Park while in London, to the anxiety of his security guards, and escaped to Scotland whenever reasonably possible, she believed that he needed more thinking time in which to amend his speeches, to cut out a few cold statistics and bring in a little human warmth, to appeal to the best rather than the purely materialistic side of human nature.

The general election was rough for the Homes with noisy barracking from Labour supporters, which proved a trying experience for a couple normally protected from such shows of violence by their upbringing, natures and status.

'At open air meetings they used to pack the area immediately below the platform,' Alec remembers. 'Two or three hundred young hooligans would collect under the microphone and proceed for the necessary time to bawl their heads off.'

No orator, he could not hear himself speak and had not realised until then that he needed the sounds of his words to reassure himself that he was presenting a coherent argument. The strain showed both in his face and in his response to the uproar and, with the television cameras projecting his image into millions of British homes, the result was disastrous. A meeting in Birmingham Rag Market was the nadir of his campaign. Labour supporters had been carefully planted in the audience of 10,000 to cause the maximum disruption. They kept up a steady chanting which drowned every word Alec spoke. It was a far cry from the quiet good-mannered response of the people of Coldstream to their past Earl and friend, from the ordered rivalry of the cricket field on which Alec had excelled, the decorum of diplomatic negotiations and the sometimes noisy but basically good-natured debates in the House of Lords. He had coped with the spontaneous outbursts from Lanarkshire miners in the past, and occasional sabotage, but organised hooliganism was another matter.

When I mentioned to Lady Home at the end of 1983 a leading politician's remark that there were advantages in having a male rather than a female secretary because when annoyed you could 'bawl him out' without fear of feminine tears or hurt feelings, she exclaimed in genuine surprise, 'How extraordinary! I cannot imagine Alec ever bawling anyone out.' And there were, of course, Labour constituency workers well aware of this basic gentleness, who planned their opposition accordingly.

Humiliated at Birmingham, Alec was delighted when he managed to divert a kick at his own leg so that it landed on another heckler's kneecap, and the two louts set about each other.

Yet the dismissal of these stupid, ill-mannered men as louts in Alec's book, *Where the Wind Blows*, is perhaps symptomatic of the reluctance of two people brought up in loving, well-endowed households to look deeper into the cause of such behaviour. It is easy to despise louts if you have never been underprivileged or forced to live in over-crowded conditions with uncaring parents in the seedier outskirts of industrial towns. The lout who kicked Alec was 'ugly' too; one of nature's less glamorous specimens who came to ruin the speech of someone more blessed, more brilliant, richer and happier than himself. But Alec, statesman rather than psychologist, resists such ideas as false. He says firmly that the men who shouted him down were ordinary thugs — partly 'rent-a-crowd' — and that he had been accustomed to them as such for many years in his first constituency, which included some very noisy mining communities. This comment, of course, begs further questions and suggests that Alec does not see himself as a figure to be envied; a man who, partly because of the tremendous advantages he has enjoyed, can inspire hatred as well as admiration among those who do not know him personally. Attaching labels, a practice also adopted by the louts, can sometimes be a convenient way of dismissing and dehumanising a complex problem worthy of deeper thought.

As a young woman, Elizabeth had, as we know, worked among the poor in Durham when the deprived accepted patronage and were grateful to wear the cast-off or outgrown clothes of their better-off brethren. She understands and responds to every call of help if it is within her capability to do so; her many kindnesses are renowned. If there is a failing it may be that she does not see all the shades of grey between good and bad, hate and love. Perhaps because of over-crowding, lack of opportunities and awful parents, rude urban youth have problems right outside the Homes' experience. Maybe if the 'lout' who kicked at Alec had grown up a wanted, presentable child surrounded by love, kindly servants and caring parents, he might have been a Conservative and a cricketer too or a dedicated, well-mannered Socialist. These are impossible questions to answer, but perhaps the Homes would have been even better politicians had they tried. Be that as it may, Elizabeth electioneered with rare alacrity and loyalty, while never pretending to be anything but upper-class, in contrast with Wedgwood Benn and his well publicised penchant for fish and chips. Her patrician face and style of dress, her very walk suggested breeding; her smile, her voice, her elegant hands confirmed it. She was and is a 'lady' in the old-fashioned sense of the word and those poorer people who appreciate a 'real lady' love her for it. In addition, she is that special variety of person known in the thirties as 'a sport'.

Looking in her scrapbooks you will find an undated piece by George Gale about the 1964 campaign.

> If I wore a cap, I would be doffing it to Lady Douglas-Home. For the past few weeks she has endured with the utmost aplomb the slings and arrows of outrageous opposition, innumerable uncomfortable seats on lorries, carts, flower-decked platforms and in the backs of cars, aircraft and helicopters . . . Throughout she has preserved a kind of stoic calm and craggy dignity, and determination never to let the side down.

Introducing Alec at a meeting Norman St John-Stevas turned to him to remark, 'I have no wife at the moment, but if I can do half as well as you have done, sir, I shall be well pleased.'

Three months earlier, speaking to women Conservatives, Elizabeth had said, 'If we are sufficiently convinced that we are going to win — and we are — we shall start an epidemic of optimism that will sweep all over the country.'

As everyone knows, this hope was not realised, although Elizabeth will say now, 'I think we did jolly well, because we very nearly won.' And remembering how low was the government's standing when Alec took over, you know that she is right. It was a very close fight. Only after many tense hours of waiting, did the last vital results come through on October 16th. The Labour overall majority was four; their seats 317 against the Conservatives' 304 with the Liberals winning nine. Vain attempts were made to advance Alec's audience with the Queen, who was out walking the dogs. While he went upstairs to change into morning dress with tails and top hat, the rest of his family started to pack. They had no English home, so arrangements were made for them to spend the weekend at Chequers.

It was a sad but not unexpected moment. 'I enjoyed being PM,' Alec said afterwards. 'I think the responsibility is something one can carry and therefore I am disappointed that I am not continuing being PM. I have no regrets. In politics you take the rough with the smooth.'

The Wilsons arrived to a great cheer from an assembled crowd as their predecessors were about to leave, so the Homes slipped down into the basement and made their way out through the garden. Both were wearing tweeds. They got into a Daimler with, a reporter noted, five cases, two hats, three coats, one worn leather briefcase and one unrolled umbrella, and were driven away. The premiership was over but not the politics. During the next nine months Alec was to be leader of the Opposition, a post which gradually weakened his self-confidence, as men pressed behind the scenes for a younger leader and his rating in opinion polls decreased. He was, Kenneth Young writes in his biography, wounded at suggestions that he had got the premiership by 'the back door'. By April 1965 he was characteristically beginning to question whether he was a help or a hindrance to his Party in its struggle to win the hearts and minds of the electorate. Quick to feel self-diminished he could fight for a cause but not for himself, and murmurings of discontent in the background only fed this mounting depression. Elizabeth remained stalwart, certain of his ability. As supporters gathered round Edward Heath, she urged Alec to fight and, with many back-benchers and old friends still with him, he declared his intention, during the weekend July 10th–11th, to remain. By the 21st he had changed his mind. Despite his wife's exhortations and advice he had decided to go, a decision reached alone. Kenneth Young sums up: 'Sir Alec would oblige, indeed, at no matter what cost to himself, even to the shedding of ancient peerages and sweating under tele-vision lights; he would fight the Opposition because that was like fighting in a cricket team to score more runs than the other team. But to remain top dog only by snarling and biting dogs beneath him — no!'

So he kept his dignity, and his popularity among the Conservative general public. Edward Heath as the new leader was happy to appoint him shadow foreign secretary. After the 1970 election he was again foreign and commonwealth secretary. In 1974 he received a life peerage and returned to the Lords. 'These days,' a Labour member recently promoted to the same House, told me, 'Lord Home's more respected than he's ever been. He was widely con-sulted and listened to at the time of the Falklands War.'

Now Elizabeth is housekeeper, cook and secretary in their small flat in Victoria. She types his letters, articles and books, and drives him back and forth to the House of Lords. They are still invited out so often that they welcome a quiet evening at home. When he has attended a special luncheon she will say, 'Only biscuits and cheese for Alec tonight.' And she is, of course, available to others only if Alec does not need her. Clothes no longer bother her; an old dark blue mackintosh, scuffed black shoes, ordinary skirt and blouse are fairly standard wear in London. In her seventies she is slim enough to look well in a quilted floral jacket and buttoned denim skirt, so that the image is modern, although her face wears the cares of years of devoted service and passionate endeavour.

In Scotland she drives an Austin Princess with dash and self-assurance. She organises the house parties which are still an important and enjoyable feature of the Homes' lives, supported by The Hirsel's caretaker and housekeeper, the sensible and kindly

Anthea Montgomery. Friends from all over the world know they will be welcome in this house which remains grand without being intimidating. And at Christmas it fills with son and daughters, sisters and brothers, grandchildren, great-nephews and nieces, for the woman who feels a family of four to have been too small still loves the young, and spends much time finding her grandchildren the right presents. They call her Grandmummy, and descriptions of their activities often enliven her conversation. Her scrapbooks are a legacy to them. Speaking of Alec, grandson Matthew Darby says, 'He doesn't disapprove of the younger generation. I think he accepts it. If any of us got into trouble, my grandmother would be very upset, but he would be very forgiving.' And Elizabeth has probably been upset more times than she cares now to remember, partly because as a perfectionist her standards of behaviour have perhaps been too high. 'I am conscious of the supreme good fortune too that I found the perfect partner in life who was able to combine the hurly-burly of political life with that of bringing up four lively and happy children,' writes Lord Home.

But the story is not yet over. There are more books to be written, more scrapbooks to be filled, more speeches to be made and journeys taken across the world to see friends. It is no rarity for Alec to travel by sleeper on a Friday after an official dinner to spend a day's shooting at Castlemains, before entertaining guests in the evening, then, after some formality in Edinburgh or elsewhere, to return to London and his duties at the House of Lords by sleeper on Sunday night. No mean feat at eighty. He suffers from deafness, she from aches and pains in the joints and muscles and from asthma. He has become stringy with age; she has fined down, so that there is not an ounce of spare flesh on the lean, lined, distinguished face. They appear to have no enemies; even those who see their failings recognise two totally civilised people, a little crafty perhaps, but never devious; a husband and wife who have risen to the top after a running start without ever putting on an act and who have retired to a lower level in the political world with their integrity intact. Regrets there must be, but one suspects no remorse, because starting on the right foot, they have been able to live their lives without meanness or envy. Inevitably, given their upbringing and standards, they wish they could have done better, but there seems to be still time to do more, so long as Alec can speak and write with Elizabeth beside him.

MARY WILSON

'I saw this young lady playing tennis,' Harold Wilson said, 'and I thought: life isn't all about *Dr Faustus* and *Hamlet* and *Cymbeline*.'

He was looking over a fence in Bebbington at a slim eighteen-year-old, golden-haired, blue-eyed typist who worked at Lever Brothers on the Wirral; a girl who dreamed of becoming a poet and knew the Bible by heart, whose head was full of quotations and contradictions. Mary Baldwin's face was not distinguished like Lady Home's, but possessed a flower-like prettiness which was immediately attractive. She was at an age to fall in love romantically first rather than physically, the only daughter of highly respectable parents of working-class origin who had themselves waited many years for marriage.

The fair schoolboy, two months her junior, barely hesitated, immediately overcoming a youthful shyness to join the tennis club, so beginning a relationship which was to take them both on a long, hard, emotionally turbulent path into the quieter waters of old age.

This couple, who were once popular subjects for satire and ridicule, praise and assessment, and adulation, can sometimes now be seen wandering hand in hand in Vincent Square which is close to their Westminster flat; unlikely Darby and Joan figures, a man and woman who refused to merge into that close joint existence, that sharing of interests, which is for some people the essence of marriage.

You will never hear from Mary Wilson, who sees herself as a feminist, the qualification, 'It depends on whether my husband needs me.' In her own words a loner, she grew up in East Anglia where a certain stubbornness is endemic, where people are wary of strangers, and known for their individuality; where you are judged for yourself rather than your associations.

Her father was an able, hard-working Congregational minister, as serious as the books he read, dark-complexioned with grey eyes and black hair, and everlasting faith. He hated bigotry, enjoyed poetry, especially the work of Wordsworth which he quoted liberally from the pulpit, and stuck by principles. To Mary a figure of undoubted authority as well as love, this Lancashire lad had started work in a cotton mill at the age of twelve to help support his young brothers and sisters. No scholar's life could have been further from that of Dr Alington and the ninth Duke of Devonshire than his. Starving himself to buy theological books, studying at night, he learned Hebrew and Latin and became a lay preacher while still in his twenties, continuing mill work by day.

Ordination came in 1912 when he was thirty-one, after studying on a grant at Paton College, Nottingham, followed by a pastorate at Brosely and marriage to Sarah Bently, the loom worker he had loved since a boy; a usually merry but quick-tempered girl, fair-skinned with the blue eyes — more azure than violet — which Mary inherited, and light-brown coiled hair, a woman who was content to be a minister's wife.

Their son, Clifford, was born in 1914 at Padiham in Lancashire after Daniel Baldwin's appointment as minister to the Congregational chapel at Diss. Gladys Mary, who was called by her first name until 1963, was born in 22 Frenze Road, Diss on January 12th 1916. The First World War ensured that life was uneasy, so sad sometimes that a sense of tragedy must have intruded even on a young baby's life. Yet Diss was a favourable place from which to discover the wonders of the natural world, which have always attracted Mary Wilson. Near the chapel is the Mere, a silver oasis surrounded by trees and grass with birds and wildfowl, and Frenze Road runs out into the countryside. 'My first memories,' Mary says now, 'are of my father rowing a boat on the Mere and an uncle wearing khaki puttees coming back from the war at the wheel of a huge lorry.'

It was at Fulbourn where the Baldwins moved when she was six, that Mary found herself. Here, home was a pale Burwell brick manse at the corner of a tree-shaded road where she became aware of her father's mission and importance and the seeds of nostalgia were

sown, which the mellowness and frustration of middle age would
bring to life in verse.

> Oh what a longing, and a burning deep desire,
> Here in my father's house, to be a child again;
> To see the lamplight and the winter fire
> Or smell the garden after summer rain!

The schoolboy looking over the fence at the girl with the sparkling
face had no inkling how strong would be the call of that past,
memories which would sometimes be more potent than the reality of
the present. Fulbourn, says Mary, turned her into an egalitarian.
She went to the village school, gleaned corn for her mother's hens
along with poorer children, yet as a minister's daughter was invited
to parties at the houses of the nonconformist middle class. There
were many other contradictions in her life. The manse was spacious,
solid and Victorian, with four bedrooms, but only an outside earth
closet as a lavatory. There was no electricity; water came from a
pump in a stone sink, and money was scarce, because the minister
relied on the generosity of his parishioners for his income, and, by
and large, although some were generous, congregationalists were
not rich. Yet the Baldwin children were destined for private education, and, therefore, different from many of their schoolmates.
Clifford was brilliant enough to win a scholarship to Cambridge
County School, becoming another subject for nostalgia, as he moved
out of Mary's life.

> My brother mounts his clean new bicycle to ride
> The long white Cambridge road that winds up
>   Windmill Hill.
> I watch him disappear with shaky pride.
>
> And then a silence wraps the garden, 'til
> My long dead friend comes calling at the gate —
> The village school bell clangs — we shall be late!

The long dead friend died as a grown-up, but another, Joyce
Payne, perished of peritonitis at the age of eight, a blow to Mary of
the kind that brings a sombre threat into the merriest child's life.
Joyce was buried by the path that led to the chapel door, her small

grave, passed regularly by Mary, a constant reminder of the fragility of life.

Mary had started writing poetry when six years old with Dorothea Drury, the deacon's daughter, inspired, she says, 'by the splendid imagery of the Bible', and the hymns which she heard sung every Sunday in the simple white chapel. There in a sense her father was king, and she was a princess, the little fair girl usually chosen to present bouquets to important visitors, the reciter of poems at the chapel's social evenings. She soon made her mark at school too, twice winning the coveted prize for the best Empire Day essay.

There were other less happy times, of course, long enforced silences after grace at meals, discipline for a girl whose humour bubbled up, the awful warnings of the Old Testament, the restrictions of a puritan's household.

'Time to a man,' her father quoted with absolute conviction, 'is more than cash, so waste it not in talking trash. But in few words say all you require and then without delay retire.' This message stuck in the child's retentive mind, clipping the wings of spontaneity, reinforcing a latent shyness which was to grow as puberty approached, so that even now Mary remains keenly aware that her presence might not be welcome, that wasting people's time is offensive. The inhibition is so entrenched that when, as prime minister's wife she visited her old home in Diss with Sir John Betjeman, she would not ring the doorbell in case she might be a nuisance, despite her longing to see inside the house.

'It would not be polite,' she said, still too uncertain of her own worth even as premier's wife to suppose that the occupants might have been thrilled to meet her.

A year after Joyce Payne's death, Daniel Baldwin left Fulbourn in November 1926 to become minister of Hucknall Congregational church, exchanging a country village for a small mining town in Nottinghamshire, which Mary later described as 'permanently enveloped in a thin pall of smoke'. For Mary, who is always happiest with long established friends and rural landscape, the move was little less than catastrophic; her sense of security, essential to a person of her character and sensibilities, disappeared overnight. The familiar villagers who knew her by name were replaced by black-faced miners with gleaming teeth, the friendly shopkeepers by strangers, the flat summer-gold fields by murky streets. The teachers and children at the school — larger than Fulbourn's — spoke with alien accents. In addition, her father was deeply absorbed in managing a larger parish and congregation, her mother was busy settling into the new house, and Clifford went away to boarding school. Alone in sorrow, baffled and bewildered, Mary withdrew, took to her bed, stopped eating.

'I grew paler and paler,' she says, 'thinner and thinner and nobody, not even the doctors, knew what was wrong.'

'A classic cry for help,' a more enlightened parent might say today, the speechless appeal of a child who feels deserted and out of her depth, a symptom of heartbreak and shock. But perhaps because in the 'twenties such traumas were little understood and psychiatric treatment unavailable to most people, it was a year before Mary emerged, pale, asthmatic, but ready again for life, with reams of paper covered in verses which had been her outlet and her therapy. 'Naturally,' she says now, 'the illness coloured my whole life.' Then she adds, ironically, 'It was only when I gave up the struggle to live that I began to get better.' The influence of mind over body and vice versa remains so complex that the exact cause of the anorexia-like illness can only now be guessed at, but the breakdown does seem to suggest that Mary was, unlike Lady Dorothy Macmillan and Lady Home, deeply susceptible to change, a disturbing handicap for a woman who was to move twenty-three times in forty years.

Meanwhile young Harold Wilson, an enthusiastic traveller, had already visited Australia, where his uncle was a Member of Parliament and, later, president of the Senate. While Mary put her feelings and fantasies into verse Harold was concerning himself with political elections, undeterred by moves, a boy more interested in argument and thought than landscape and surroundings.

James Harold Wilson was born on March 11th 1916, in Huddersfield, the son of an industrial chemist, Herbert Wilson, whom he describes as a Liberal Radical, and of Ethel Seddon, a teacher. The first time he can remember thinking systematically about politics was on election day, when he was seven, and in hospital with appendicitis. Already a socialist he told his visiting parents not to stay too long in case they were too late to vote for the candidate he favoured — Philip Snowden.

At home politics were often discussed, especially at meals. Herbert Wilson had been sub-agent for Winston Churchill in the

1908 election campaign and Harold's great uncle, James Herbert Thewlis, a successful umbrella manufacturer, was Churchill's constituency chairman the same year, and one-time Lord Mayor of Manchester. The Wilson family, all Nonconformist, saw the world was unfair and wanted it changed, but in an orderly way through the ballot box. Proud and respectable, they kept Herbert Wilson's period of unemployment between the wars a secret, for outward appearances were extremely important to them. They were, Harold says, Nonconformist by religion, but radical by temperament. 'In my boyhood it was chapel and the scout movement. The fourth scout law was a lasting influence: "A scout is a friend to all and a brother to every other scout." ' When Harold was twelve he won a competition in the *Yorkshire Post* writing on why Baden-Powell was his hero in less than one hundred words, and his loyalty to the 'kitchen cabinet', on which he relied as prime minister, subscribed to the same ethos.

Harold's attitude to women was influenced by his mother, a remarkably witty woman whom he deeply loved, and his sister, both teachers with a gift for exposition. 'Mother,' he says, 'was a very calm, saintly person.' But undoubtedly Ethel Wilson drove her son, so that at times he may have felt that her love was conditional on his success in life. 'He had,' Andrew Roth wrote in his biography (which was later banned) 'to be not only the kindest and most polite little boy, but also the best dressed, the most clever and the most successful ever.' His parents were strict about homework, too, and much later he was to recognise a puritan strain in himself. 'I have always been driven by a feeling that there is something to be done and I really ought to be doing it.' A far cry from the relaxed upbringing of Lord Home, but closer to that of Harold Macmillan, who, of course, was similarly motivated by the ambitions of a mother he loved. In addition, Harold's sister, Marjorie, seven years his senior, a future headmistress, would certainly have urged her small brother to learn his tables and grammar. Yet to him this sister was also a rival, competing for his parents' affections; a fact well illustrated by his reaction when Marjorie triumphantly announced that she had won a scholarship to Huddersfield High School for Girls. 'I want a ship, too,' he cried. When the meaning of his sister's achievement had been explained he decided to try for a scholarship himself, dropping his previous rather macabre intention to be a carpenter and undertaker, a choice perhaps calculated to draw shocked attention to himself.

Academically talented with an extraordinary memory for facts and figures, Harold moved from Milnsbridge Council School to Royds Hall School from which, having survived typhoid, he won his scholarship to Wirral Grammar. His strength lay in mathematics while his future wife was interested in English and history.

After that dismal year at Hucknall, Mary's existence had been transformed with the award of a bursary to Milton Mount College, a sister school to the Caterham Congregational Boys' School where Clifford was making his way as a scientist. It was a move which lifted her out of the working-class milieu. After years in unmodernised manses supported by neighbours she suddenly found herself in surroundings of remarkable splendour.

Founded in 1870 at Gravesend on the same lines as the Hoylake Female Seminary in north America, Milton Mount had moved temporarily to Cirencester during the war before finally taking over Worth Park, a stately Victorian mansion built for the Montefiores and lavishly redecorated for a visit from the Prince of Wales which never materialised. Truda Uffen, another Congregational minister's daughter, has left a colourful description of this extraordinary house, published in the centenary issue of *The Miltonian*. 'It was,' she writes, 'far larger and more magnificent than any palace. The entrance is full of wonder. Up some huge steps and through a glass door with ionic marble pillars . . .' She dwells on the polished wood floors, the beautifully patterned windows, the electric lights in every room. Here for the poor daughters of impoverished ministers was a fairy tale world of luxury and glamour, surroundings they never forgot. No money had been spared by the Montefiores to make Worth Park's interior ornate and beautiful. The mahogany doors were magnificently proportioned; gilded and painted ceilings, great windows, mosaic floors, all provided a radiant splendour, into which Mary came carrying a small battered teddy bear and a few clothes.

Here, as one of the poorer children, she experienced no snobbery, no feeling of class divisions between daughters of Congregational ministers, most of whom received bursaries, and the richer daughters of lay Congregationalists whose parents supported the school by paying the full fees. All were equal in the sight of God, and knowing their Bibles the children were not 'greedy for filthy lucre'.

Neither were there any status symbols. Those who were top of the form were merely expected to help others lower down to catch up; talents were to be used for the betterment of others; self-regard was discouraged.

Mary Wilson remembers being called to the head mistress's room to receive a coat sent by the parish committee for a disadvantaged child. 'It was done very nicely,' she says. 'You did not feel as though you were receiving charity. And no one knew where the coat had come from.' And more importantly, no one asked. Personal questions were discouraged because private lives were to be respected.

Mary's hopelessness at games, apart from tennis, was highlighted at Milton Mount, where the odious habit of picking sides was used. Athletic girls, captains, whose achievements on the playing fields were ranked higher among their peers than academic success, would inviariably call out Mary's name last. Each time she would know that she was the least wanted, with the handicap of asthmatic breathlessness added to natural ineptitude, an ordeal which left a permanent scar.

At Milton Mount the headmistress, Mrs Henman, an elegant war widow, daughter of missionaries, graduate and mother, supervised Christian training following the original board of governors' desire for an institution which was to be 'very much the opposite of a merely fashionable boarding school', preparing pupils to be 'wives, mothers, teachers, and missionaries', to train them 'to love unselfish work and Christian usefulness'. Such high ethical and religious standards were to make it difficult for Mary Wilson to accept the deceptions, manoeuvring and broken promises which are inevitably part of political life.

Although domestic science was offered Mary did not learn to cook until later in life. For an aspiring poet, feelings and words, metre and rhyme were infinitely more relevant to life than food and housework. Mary went her own way, an intelligent rather than an academic individual who revelled in the loveliness of the long avenue, the camellia walk, the Dutch Lawn where once a year the Ben Greet company performed Shakespeare, the swans on the lake and the fountain. She was a keen gardener, though hampered occasionally by asthma. She read voraciously, unmoved by the library itself, a skilfully converted domed garden room of glass and marble, preferring the countryside, the changing skies, the undulating landscape, sitting with pencil and paper to write verse including *Eventide*, a poem published in the school magazine during her first year.

> The gentle breeze has dropped, and silence reigns

begins the third verse,

> Another glorious star is swiftly lit,
> The misty light softly and quickly wanes
> And leaves me breathless with the joy of it.

She responded intensely to natural beauty, which remains a therapeutic joy, a cure for low spirits so that she will say, 'I am feeling under the weather, so I am going to the Scilly Isles for a few days.' And there under a wider sky, the sea at her feet, she believes herself to be in touch with eternal values. And yet behind that passive nature-loving front there is also a sensuousness, of little use to a busy politician's wife on which she touches in *Mamzelle*, a poem which looks back at her schoolgirl crush on her French teacher.

> My mouth is dry as she goes by —
> One curving line from foot to thigh —
> And with unEnglish liberty
> Her bosom bounces, full and free;
> Pale skin, pink lips, a wide blue stare,
> Her page-boy fall of silky hair
> Swings on her shoulders like a bell;
> Oh how I love Mamzelle!

Romantic fantasies now replaced the puritanical influence of her father as she abandoned his hero, Oliver Cromwell, for Charles II, Bonnie Prince Charlie, Prince Rupert of the Rhine and Lord Byron. In *Mamzelle* she looks forward to other loves.

> Perhaps I shall forget her face,
> Her gentleness, her body's grace,
> Even her accents, deep and slow,
> May be forgotten. And I know,
> That I, throughout the coming years
> May love with joy, may love with tears;
> But shall I ever love so well
> As now I love Mamzelle?

The teacher left for another job. 'At the end of term I say farewell for ever to Mamzelle.' The secret frustrated longing of a sensitive adolescent died its natural death.

At sixteen Mary left Milton Mount. The brother she loved was now on a scholarship at Cambridge, an enviable position. But handicapped by that year in bed and unable to master Latin, Mary could never compete intellectually with Clifford. As Britain remained in the throes of a depression, Daniel Baldwin's meagre resources could hardly meet his son's needs. Jobs were few, but there was still work for girls who could type. So Mary, who would have made an admirable teacher, travelled home to Penrith, where her parents had moved in 1928, to start a shorthand and typing course. Her Carlisle college was hardly on the same social plane as St James's Secretarial College where Lady Home had trained, but the course was to lead on to a job with Lever Brothers, lodgings in the Wirral and that first meeting with Harold Wilson.

The year was 1934. Neither was ready for marriage or experienced with the other sex. Harold was cramming English for higher school certificate and Oxford, an engaging youth with pleasant blue-grey eyes. Although he lacked the supposed sharper elegance of the aristocrat, his features were well proportioned with a wide brow and an open expression, his was a workaday face, absolutely right for a man who has always claimed to be on the side of 'ordinary people', a little pouchy under the eyes but kind and lively. He laughed a good deal but his self-confidence needed the proof of frequent academic achievements to keep it on an even keel. His mother's people had traditionally worked for the Lancashire railway as clerks, engine drivers and fitters, and Harold at forty would not have looked out of place among them. In contrast Mary's character was infinitely more complex; her slight figure and very feminine attractiveness disguised that strong will, a waywardness coupled with a rebellious streak, which had surfaced briefly and superficially when she started a 'rebels' club' at her primary school. Her father's influence had brought inhibitions which may have contributed to her asthma, a disease which has been linked by some experts to suppression and a sense of loss. As a child Mary had been awed by the darker stories of the Old Testament; the wrath of God was a reality. Self-control, unselfishness, loyalty to the family and the Almighty were the hallmarks of goodness, and though she was later quick to identify and deplore examples of male chauvinism, she had deeply admired Daniel Baldwin, who stood for authority, and she had accepted her mother as a weaker vessel, the figure at the oven or the sink, whom she would never emulate.

'I decided to marry her the day we met,' says Harold.

'No, it was three days later,' retorts Mary, a stickler for accuracy.

On closer questioning she says, 'One didn't decide to get married at any particular time. It just became accepted that one would.'

So, without realising it, she establishes in one respect her class and background, for few aspects of life were so firmly entrenched before the last war as the differing forms of courtship in the different strata of society. Members of the upper classes invariably felt free to play the field until a formal engagement was announced, often only after a girl's parents had established that the suitor's prospects and finances were such that he could comfortably support her. Long engagements were discouraged as unrealistic or difficult to sustain. The respectable lower orders, on the other hand, walked out until their circumstances permitted marriage. They might be 'sweethearts' for years as Mary's parents were, whereas an upper- or middle-class man would not normally expect a girl to wait so long.

For a short time Mary and Harold both went to the local Congregational church with Harold walking his 'young lady' back to her lodgings afterwards, but from the beginning Oxford loomed enchantingly as the next step and when Harold went to Jesus College in the autumn of 1934 it was agreed that Mary should write to him twice a week and visit him at least once a term with his parents, who had already accepted her as his future bride. Sometimes they would take trains from opposite directions to snatch a few hours together at Leamington Spa Station as a staging post between Oxford and the Wirral. Now, with a steady girlfriend, the sexually well-controlled Harold was free to concentrate on work, feeling that his marital future was settled. So, as in childhood, he gave more time to his intellectual development than to his emotional, working sometimes eighteen hours a day.

In 1936 he won the Gladstone Memorial prize with an essay on *The State and the Railways 1823–63*, an achievement of special interest to his mother, and possibly inspired by her forbears. In October of the same year he was awarded the Webb Medley Junior Economic Scholarship, so relieving his father's often difficult financial position. Mary, already in love with Oxford — 'it symbolised so much for me', was there with the Wilson parents to see Harold receive his first class honours degree in politics, philosophy and economics, from which he went on to take up a senior research fellowship at New College, after his parents had dissuaded him from following a long but not deeply held ambition towards journalism. At twenty-one he was a don, at twenty-two he took a post with Sir William Beveridge at University College. Marriage, he thought, was at last a practical proposition. But Beveridge, who was against the union, pointed out that college rules forbade new fellows to wed until three years after election, an edict quickly bypassed when Harold discovered that it did not apply to juniors on research. The outbreak of war caused another delay, and then at last the date was fixed, and Mary, aware of her deficiencies, left the Wirral and went home to learn house management from her mother. In keeping with her don's wife dream, she decided the wedding should be held in Oxford at the Nonconformist chapel in Mansfield College. Since most of the guests were friends Mary and Harold had made at the university, she announced that the men were to wear academic dress.

Young as she was, she was already capable of standing outside herself, making assessments, and analysing her own character, which she frequently found unsatisfactory. More than Lady Dorothy or Lady Home she had a vision of herself as a person, as a wife and later as a not very efficient mother. She saw herself now as clearly middle class, an old Miltonian with literary interests. Clifford, a man after Mary's own heart, established himself as a lecturer in engineering as early as 1940, and everything about the Baldwin children's upbringing had persuaded them that a profession in the world of learning was to be desired. Almost certainly Mary's own idea of her future self as poet and a don's wife, entertaining undergraduates to tea and generally backing up Harold, was more reassuring than one of housewife, for the thought of cooking and shopping appalled her. Meanwhile she moved to Oxford in preparation for marriage and took a job with the Potato Marketing Board.

The venue and style of the wedding on January 1st 1940 was a sort of affirmation of her entry into the milieu in which she hoped to spend her life. Like Harold Macmillan she was joining a new stratum of society on the arm of her partner. Departure from the modest room she had rented above Northgate Café did not seem to fit into the new scene, so she borrowed a friend's flat, where she dressed in comfort. There was nothing grand or exotic or bohemian about her white wedding gown, her tulle veil or bouquet of carnations, for these represented the conventional side of her nature. Like Lady Home she was given away by her brother while her father helped with the proceedings. Pretty, fair and delicate she was every ordinary person's idea of a charming young English bride as she entered the chapel to the strains of *Gaudeamus Igitur* played and chosen by the Wilsons' friend, the distinguished organist John Webster, who had declared Mary's own choice of *Here Comes the Bride* to be too banal. No little bridesmaids from distinguished families followed this future prime minister's wife, only one contemporary, a schoolfriend from Milton Mount, Irene Price, who had promised to be Mary's brides-maid long before Harold had appeared on the scene. Dr Nathaniel Micklem officiated and Patrick Duncan, who was to die prematurely on the North West Frontier, was best man.

With the snow beating on the stained glass windows, fog coming down and the world turning white, Mary vowed to *cherish* rather than *obey* Harold, having decided beforehand that cherish was more affectionate and in keeping with her feminist views. No crowd waited outside as the fifty guests left for a buffet and fruit cup at the nearby Royal Park Hotel. Sir William and Lady Beveridge, unable to come, had given the couple Venetian glass bowls, but Harold's rich uncle disappointed them by presenting a still-life painting instead of the money they needed. Professor A.L. Goodhart made a witty speech likening Harold to a 'lively fox terrier'. Then, as the weather worsened and their driver feared for their safety, Harold and Mary left early in a whirl of snow and drifting fog in a book-laden car, taking with them the memory of a quiet but warm-hearted wartime wedding without the panache of champagne or the vulgarity of confetti. Perhaps this was a foretaste of the style Mary would try to adopt as prime minister's wife; pleasant, low key, intelligently joyous rather than exuberant, touched always with the respectability of those who believe in Nonconformist church ethics, despite her later rejection of some aspects of its puritan morality.

The honeymoon was spent at Minster Lovell in appalling weather with Harold and Mary nursing colds and reading a few of the books they had brought, some of which related directly to Harold's work.

These were the early days of war when everything seemed 'quiet on the western front', and yet the future lay before the young like uncharted seas, promising nothing, but murmuring of danger and death or a great swell which could sweep away all that had seemed permanent and safe.

After a week Sir William Beveridge cut the honeymoon in half when he summoned Harold back by telegram. Mary acquiesced, a sense of duty conflicting with disappointment and hurt, as she began to realise, perhaps for the first time, that war or no war Harold would usually put work first.

Inevitably, her idea of married life did not exactly match Harold's, for hers was based partly on that of her own parents and partly on marriages in the novels she read. Harold could not compare with Sarah Baldwin's man, who had shared the bringing-up of the children, helping them with their school work, teaching them manners and morality, a companion as well as husband and lover. Each of the Baldwin parents had played a specific role recognised by the children. Hence her increasing and sometimes self-deceptive nostalgia for the time when her ideas on marriage were first formed by parental example, recaptured in the last two verses of her poem *The Old Manse*:

> Within the study, where the sunlight never falls
> My father writes his sermon, hooded eyes downbent;
> His books of reference wait round the walls —
> He shapes each phrase, deploys each argument
> And turns from time to time, instinctively
> To the Great Bible open on his knee.
>
> I see my mother in the kitchen making bread
> Setting the pliant dough in shallow pans to rise;
> Her long brown hair is coiled round her head —
> How young her form, how shining blue her eyes!
> The door stands open on the morning sweet,
> And all the hens come clucking to her feet.

Drenched in nostalgia those days were to remain in Mary's mind as high peaks of happiness, the time before the illness, before a strain of irony entered her soul, before adolescence.

In wartime compromises naturally had to be made, expectations of happiness often put aside at least for the duration, and sexual deprivation frequently endured by the physically passionate who had vowed fidelity. The first dream to be put aside was the don's wife dream, books in the study, young men on the doorstep; erudition, scholarship, high-minded endeavour, Harold handsome in academic dress, spreading wisdom and truth. Romance, too, proved to be a dream. For many of Mary's generation romance meant more than many men could provide in wartime England; it meant a dedicated, passionate love which time and circumstances could not always allow, an emotional tie perhaps too deep for the average Englishman, a dream which perhaps no bridegroom could fulfil.

Life had to be prosaic for those on the home front. Very soon Harold moved to London to work as a civil servant, which resulted in the Wilsons living in a series of flats in Earls Court, Pimlico, Twickenham and Richmond. For a time Mary stayed at a friend's house in Oxford to avoid the worst of the London bombing; then she became an air raid warden in Richmond only to leave after the birth of their son Robin in December 1943, to stay for seven weeks with her parents at Duxford in Cambridgeshire, where her father now had a charge. By now Harold, the brilliant economist, was winning admiration and ensuring himself a promising future. In war-time the train ride to Duxford was long and slow, so sometimes he would bicycle over from London to see Mary, a journey of some fifty miles. She was back in London, however, in time for the flying bombs when, in her own words, she would 'stand over Robin's cot to protect him.'

Harold spoke now and then of going into politics when he was around thirty, but Mary underestimated the scale of his ambitions and kept her Oxford dream through the five long years of war . . . a little home, a nest in sight of the dreaming spires. 'My idea of heaven,' she said. 'The old buildings and very young people. There is everything anyone could want, music, theatre, congenial friends all in a beautiful setting and within a fourpenny bus ride.'

But none of this was in keeping with Harold's growing aspirations for, as he learned in the civil service as secretary of the Greene Commission's investigation into the miners' wages, real power lay in parliament; his commitment to nationalisation and the Labour Party deepened. While Mary coped with housekeeping despite 'the buzz bombs,' as they called them, and later the rockets, Harold's political horizon widened.

In 1944 he was adopted as Labour candidate for the constituency of Ormskirk near Liverpool, rather naively precipitating his resignation from the civil service, as the rules decreed. For a while Mary's dream of academia seemed about to leap back into life when University College, coming to the rescue, appointed Harold their praelector in economics and domestic bursar, which gave Mary the chance to move back to Oxford. She took up residence in rooms on Staircase 11, Back Quad, from which she could enjoy the fellows' garden, renew earlier friendships, especially that of John Webster, and take tea in the Cadena.

Because Mary, like everyone else, did not expect a Labour victory in 1945, Ormskirk, which had not been held by the Party since 1929, seemed to pose no threat to her happiness in Oxford. The meetings she attended with Harold only confirmed her dislike of politics. Noisy strife was totally alien to her upbringing and beliefs, and over the years she was never to develop any enthusiasm for campaigning. Seeing herself as a person of contemplation rather than action, she continued to play a background role as home-based wife, mother and poet. Besides, the Wilsons had little money to spare and train fares were expensive. Also, as a fond parent, Mary preferred to look after Robin who was blossoming as a personality.

So when Harold knew in the early hours of July 27th that he had won Ormskirk with a majority of 7,000 Mary was in Oxford, where she rejoiced for him rather than for herself. His appointment as a junior minister in Attlee's government in August further undermined the togetherness she had once expected from marriage, but for a while Oxford remained her home, because a shortage of economists gave Harold the opportunity to continue to teach on those Saturdays and Sundays which he could spare from politics.

Nine days after Harold's maiden speech in the House, Daniel Baldwin died following three weeks' illness, severing Mary's closest link with the past and cutting off the most profound influence of her youth. Few of her father's teachings had, however, prepared her to be a politician's wife. Power-seeking, self-publicising and deviousness he had abhorred; frivolity, vanity and worldly ambitions were to be avoided. Teetotal himself, he had persuaded Mary to sign the pledge when she was ten, and, although she was later to enjoy a sherry, she did not touch alcohol at all until she was twenty-six and deeply disliked drunkenness in others.

Harold's rise was now disconcertingly rapid for a wife who had hoped for a normal married life. At twenty-nine he became parliamentary secretary to the ministry of works and the next year was appointed leader of the British delegation to the United Nations' World Food and Agricultural Preparatory Commission's conference in Washington, so depriving Mary once again of his company. As he sailed away to America it must have seemed to his young wife that she and her husband would never set up a proper home together. She had not possessed the courage to ask the Attlees, who were friends, whether she might go too, and Harold, grabbing at every chance of advancement, perhaps did not consider deeply enough the feelings of the girl he left behind him. He was not very perceptive about female needs and emotions; his articulate, level-headed and undemonstrative parents had done little to prepare him for the temperament and desires of a hypersensitive wife confused by her own changing moods. From the beginning he did not appear to involve Mary in his political life, perhaps partly because he did not wish her to emulate Dora Gaitskell, whose influence was said to be so strong that some Members thought they must win her approval to gain access to Gaitskell's house and therefore, sometimes, his ear; a situation Harold would not welcome in his own climb to the top.

The Wilsons' marriage tottered, but it finally survived this new separation and after returning for Christmas, Harold took Mary back to Washington, while her mother cared for Robin. When she returned to Oxford, he started to look for a London house where they could live together permanently. His eventual choice could not have been more suitable for Mary, now again pregnant, whose need for quiet beauty was paramount. Number 10 Southway, to which they moved at the end of 1947 was unpretentious, cottage-like and pretty; a small house which caught the sun, part tile-hung, part gabled, pleasantly asymmetrical but beautifully proportioned.

Southway is in the heart of Hampstead Garden Suburb, leading away from its spacious centre which was designed by Lutyens, shady, fragrant in summer, and select. The square's two churches are notable for their simple magnificence and idiosyncratic design and the exceptional quality of their brickwork. To the architecturally ignorant the square can seem oddly foreign, perhaps because, unlike so much that is English, it has been formally planned, so that the paved walk under the regimented trees and general air of ordered charm seems to suggest a small French town, causing the uninformed to look instinctively for a café at the corner. But the terraced houses flanking the square and the air of quiet respectability are undeniably British. Southway itself, running downhill at the side of the school, is modest in comparison with the restrained grandeur of the square. Nowadays it seems exclusively middle class, but Number 10 Southway was built for artisans and its first owner arrived in 1907 with his bride in a horse-drawn cart, a fact which pleases Mary.

Hampstead Garden Suburb is devoid of ugliness, trim, cherished, untroubled by the dirty dustbin at the corner, the vagrant on the seat, the bands of disenchanted youth which can be found in other parts around the city. To some it may seem a mere enclave of unremitting good taste above the crematorium and the endless bustle of Golders Green. Here in March 1948 up on the hill where the winds blow and the birds sing and great trees cast shadows on the grass, Giles was born and named after Lady Home's elder brother, whom the Wilsons had liked and admired at Oxford. Here in Southway Mary found much of the peace and security essential to her happiness, sharing the anxieties and joys of bringing up children with congenial neighbours, several of whom became close and lasting friends. She worshipped at the Free Church in the square. There were, of course, problems, her mother's old age and her own asthma being two, but she found to her surprise that she could cope reasonably well with her children and housekeeping, leaving a list at the local shop so that her groceries could be delivered and walking down to Golders Green for fresh vegetables, for Hampstead Garden Suburb was at that time without buses, trains, pubs or shops. Mary never learned to drive because, she says, at this stage in life Harold always took their only car to central London. She never learned to row a boat either, or to organise holidays abroad for herself and her children when Harold was unavailable. But in Hampstead the Wilsons were a family at home at last. They enjoyed their boys and employed a Swiss au pair. As time went on Mary was anxious to emphasise that they were a very ordinary family, portraying Harold as just another father. 'He drives the children to school every morning; we have the usual rush to get breakfast for everyone in time.' In fact there were many occasions before he became leader of the Labour Party when Harold took Mary breakfast in bed. The ordinariness was a false picture, for the Wilson boys eventually went to University College School, which is not open to children of average intelligence, and were brought up in the best traditions of the British middle classes, with extra emphasis on service to others rather than personal material gain. So Mary passed on the ethos of Milton Mount, milked of its puritanism, with greater understanding and even sympathy for those who erred from the path of duty.

In 1953 the Wilsons moved next door to Number 12 which had been built in 1909 and was more spacious than Number 10, another sunny house, asymmetrical, part tile-hung, sash-windowed, exuding Edwardian charm and looking through pink hawthorns and larger trees to the primary school and tennis courts. Here the boys had bicycles, a harmonium, stick insects and a Siamese cat called Nemo. Frayed nerves were soothed in spring and summer by the busy hum of bees, butterflies in the buddleia. From the top of the hill you could see the woods of Hampstead Heath and, all around, gardens and children. It wasn't Oxford, Harold wasn't a don, but there were compensations and Mary was learning to compromise; yet her poem *Winter Parting* suggests that there was a strain in her nature left unsatisfied, a corner of her heart without occupation. She says it is wrong to assume that all her work is autobiographical, but fantasy can sometimes be as potent as reality, the hunger of the imagination as fervent as that of the actual. She made her poem personal, challenging her readers to believe that the woman at the end of the love affair was herself.

> 'Mary,' you said, and 'Mary!' once again,
> You grasped my cold, cold hands within your own
> Too tightly, but I did not feel the pain,
> I could not think or speak — my heart was stone.

Be that as it may, her family in the end brought her more pleasure than she had once thought possible. And, for a time, she had the 'little nest' she had craved, a refuge from politics: no intrigues, no political bargaining or theorising, no dinner parties where useful contacts could be cemented, took place within its walls. The boys were protected from all rat-races except the educational one, and, like other Westminster widows, Mary found her own friends. Although attached to Harold, she was neither political nor saintly enough to bear with constant equanimity the demands the House made on him and his ever-increasing obsession with politics. Despite those mornings when she wasn't well and Harold waited on her, she was in her own words 'a lark', rather than 'an owl' like the rest of her family. But life changed dramatically when the Wilsons went on holiday, when Mary could persuade Harold to push back politics and be simply husband and father, and he lay, brown and relaxed, on Cornish beaches.

In 1956 Harold took a step which was to affect his career and Mary's life in several ways. He employed Marcia Williams, a dedicated and highly-charged young woman, as his secretary. Unlike Clement Attlee, Harold was not a political loner; his natural conviviality demanded the devoted interest of someone wholeheartedly with him, not as a rival but as a right hand on his travels to the top. Marcia was ready to enter into the trials and triumphs of his career with total and sometimes emotional enthusiasm. Intelligent, single-minded and occasionally tempestuous, she was impatient of others' inefficiency and, as time went on, ready to advise, cajole and drive as well as serve her employer. Tall and blonde with a long, very expressive face, striking blue eyes alive and limpid in turn and prominent teeth, Marcia is a woman of great charm as well as quick temper, much more attractive than photographs of her suggest. She cannot be ignored; arouses keen emotions of admiration and affection or strong dislike; she is never lukewarm, always positive and swift to act when aroused. In a small way, she probably replaced the influence of Harold's mother, becoming the encouraging figure at his shoulder, as well as the woman who warned him if he was going too far, and spotted dirty marks on his clothes or shabby shoes. When Harold flew back from America in 1963 to join the Labour leadership battle after Gaitskell's death, it was Marcia who drove the family car, with Giles and Mary, to meet him at the airport, and later it would be Marcia who found the Wilsons a house to rent when they were temporarily homeless.

Meanwhile Mary's happiness was immeasurably increased when Harold bought a plot of land in the Scilly Isles in 1958 on which they built a grey bungalow of reconstituted stone, with three bedrooms, looking three hundred yards across flat fields to the sea.

They named it Lowenva at Harold's sister's suggestion, which means in ancient Cornish 'the House of Happiness'. Its building, and the purchase of 12 Southway, was made possible by Harold's job as consultant to Montague L. Meyer, the timber importers, followed by a similar post with Marchon Products. Lowenva was completed in 1959, the year Mr Baldwin died, and became Mary's most cherished possession, especially because the mortgage was paid off by the royalties from her first book of poetry. It has provided that sense of independence which she feels every woman needs. She is merrier, lighter-hearted and more relaxed in the Scilly Isles than anywhere else, and with the town of St Mary's close by shopping is easy.

So the early 'sixties were another peak of happiness for her, although they were the beginning of the end of tranquillity. Harold became leader of the Labour Party in 1963 and Mary could no longer remain outside politics. A modern image was necessary so she dropped Gladys for Mary at the same time as one of the secretaries agreed that her name Elsie should be upgraded to Eileen. Now Mary had to be seen: mother and wife, an ordinary person, a housewife, as she at first portrayed herself, very different from the two aristocrats who had preceded her at Number 10. The message she wrote on the back of one of Harold's election addresses tells us the simple values uppermost in her mind, values which in politics can be the hardest to keep. 'I am confident you will return my husband to parliament again. He is a good man. He is conscientious and sincere; and as you all know, and as many have had material proof, he is deeply concerned for the welfare of the people of Huyton.'

As leader Harold Wilson fought and won three elections, the first in 1964, the second in 1966 and the third in 1974. He lost the 1970 election to Edward Heath and resigned his premiership on April 5th 1976. Mary was therefore prime minister's wife for almost eight years, a task she neither relished nor enjoyed except occasionally. Sometimes she was caught up in the excitement: 'You can feel the terrific tension in the building during a crisis. Everybody walks that bit faster. You hear the voices outside, feel the electricity, it is nerve-racking, but somehow it carries you along with its own momentum,' she told journalist Donald Zec in June 1970. At other times, as we shall see, she was an outsider. She did not enjoy elections or electioneering, but when her sons were no longer dependent on her she began to be seen more often in the political arena. She did not like formal entertaining or public functions, but her sense of duty, of occasion and history, ensured that she was at her husband's side when the importance of the event demanded her presence.

Her confidence in Harold could not in any way match that of Elizabeth Home's in Alec's basic gifts of leadership and diplomacy. In several respects Mary considered women to be superior to men.

'My wife would have voted for Shirley Williams or Barbara Castle rather than me,' Harold jokingly told reporters with more than an ounce of truth after the 1964 election.

For Harold that win was a personal as well as a Party triumph. When he took his father, wife, sons and secretary to the swearing in at the Palace he was driven by his chauffeur and friend, Bill Housden, whom he had known since his days at the Board of Trade in 1951, a man he had requested to be his driver within hours of the Labour victory.

But euphoria, heightened by the cheering crowds outside Downing Street on the Wilsons' return, was short-lived. Monumental problems waited to be solved: an £800 million trade deficit, a seemingly unsympathetic civil service, a governor of the Bank of England who appeared to abhor Socialist philosophy, and the approaching Defence Conference at Chequers, not to mention the Rhodesian question and a whispering campaign against Marcia Williams.

At first Mary did not feel at home at Chequers, although she liked the surrounding countryside, partly perhaps because she did not feel herself welcomed by the permanent staff there, many of whom were, she thought, Conservative. Apart from Mrs Attlee, previous wives since the war had all been titled or at least aristocratic and few people are more snobbish and class conscious than the established British servant. The Wilsons' reception seemed cool and polite rather than welcoming, and Mary was sensitive to every nuance of behaviour. It was difficult, too, for someone who had enjoyed the privacy of Hampstead Garden Suburb for sixteen years to leap joyfully into the role of hostess to distinguished strangers.

One of the first tests for the apprehensive Mary was the Defence Conference on November 21st and 22nd. However, she was lucky that a chief delegate, Earl Mountbatten, was her neighbour at the conference dinner, alarmingly handsome, endearingly egocentric with a habit of dropping his voice at the end of sentences, but kindly and diplomatic, a man who always ensured that the lady on his right would not find the evening dull. He was, too, by no means an entrenched Tory. (There is a story that when Conservative canvassers called at his house, Broadlands, he instructed them to go round to the back door, where, he said, they would find their supporters.) The only reported social gaffe at this Defence Conference was caused by Nemo the cat, who, trapped up a tree in the middle of the night, wakened some of the guests and staff with his loud Siamese wails, which sounded like the crying of a deserted baby.

On October 30th *Private Eye* had published its first instalment of *Mrs Wilson's Diary* a satirical imaginary account of her day-to-day life, establishing the famous and erroneous Ovaltine/Sanatogen image just over two weeks after the election. This piece included a poem which began, jumping the gun

> Farewell! Hampstead
> Garden Suburb
> With your friendly
> Bustle and hub-bub.

More unkind parodies of Mary's poetry followed in subsequent editions of the *Eye*. On November 27th the cover of the magazine bore a photograph of Harold and Mary washing up together with the caption, spoken by Mary: 'I wish you would do this when there AREN'T any photographers around.' Another caption at the side read: 'Harold dries up at last.'

The lampooning of public figures is one of the *raisons d'être* of *Private Eye*, but Mary took to heart what she saw as a personal attack. On one occasion, when it was all over, she was unwise enough to declare light-heartedly that she would like to bite the co-author of the *Diary*, John Wells, who reacted with typical quick-witted aplomb, 'I'm flattered. It's long been my sexual fantasy to be bitten by an ex-prime minister's wife — particularly Mary Wilson whom I have loved for many years.'

Private Eye spares no class or section of society. Sir Alec Douglas-Home, as we know, had been satirised as an upper-class Scottish earl, Baillie Vass. Now Mary's lower middle-class background and tastes, coupled with that of a suburban housewife, became the satiriser's punch ball, with as much play on social shibboleths — serviettes instead of table napkins and so on — but always with enough truth at the core to raise the hackles of the sensitive and highly strung. Looking back, after nearly twenty years, Mary wishes she had been less hurt in the beginning by the jokes. Yet in the *Diary* affectionate irony rather than viciousness prevailed and the photographs of her were never completely unflattering. Indeed the first of the regular ones to head the column shows her lying drowsily on a seat, suggesting a vulnerability which engages the reader's sympathy. Later, as Richard Crossman records, Mary tried at times to overcome her resentment and in her more cheerful moods was able to laugh at some of the jokes against herself.

Contrary to *Private Eye*'s assumption, it was nearly Christmas before Mary could bear to leave Southway and then it was Marcia who made most of the arrangements for the storage of furniture and the move to Number 10. 'It was an extremely upsetting period emotionally, not only for Mary, but for the whole family. To some degree this affected Harold as well,' Marcia was to write later in *Inside Number Ten*. It was, of course, the end of the permanent nest dream, and here Mary was less fortunate than Lady Dorothy and Lady Home, who kept their houses when they moved to Downing Street; indeed, Mary's sacrifices always seemed more hurtful than theirs on account of her circumstances and nature. She was never able to make the best of a disappointment immediately; rather she was inclined to wallow sometimes in the awfulness of it all before pulling herself together to see what could be salvaged.

When Harold Wilson became prime minister, Robin was reading mathematics at Balliol, and Giles was still at school in Hampstead. The Wilsons decided not to take on Lady Home's housekeeper as they suspected her cooking might be too exotic for their taste and, when they moved in, a friend provided fish fingers and a fruit pie for their lunch. The newspaper men managed to photograph Robin's harmonium, Nemo in his basket and a few pieces of Mary's furniture as they were carried over the threshold, so emphasising the beginning of the end of privacy.

'It was tougher at first than I thought it would be,' Mary Wilson was to tell a newspaper reporter in 1970. 'I remember the first few days when I was physically sick every morning with the nervous tension involved. But slowly one gets used to it. When you're prime minister's wife you are very much on your mettle.' And then, perhaps with *Private Eye* in mind, she continued: 'Speaking quite generally, I don't think wives are fair game — after all they have to take the husband's job along with the husband. I'm no angel.'

And she might have added, 'the house too'. For that, also, was never to her taste. In 1964 the flat at Number 10 was much as Lady Dorothy had left it. Harold took the small dressing-room to sleep in and Mary the large bedroom which had been used as a double one by the Homes.

The Wilsons' style was to be very different from their predecessors' and much closer to that of the Huyton constituents and the main body of Labour's supporters; instant coffee, bottled sauces, canned beer, tinned salmon, lunch followed by cups of tea rather than coffee, in keeping with the habits of their Irish housekeeper Mary Wright, were all part of the regular menu.

'Nothing could be more deeply petit bourgeois than the way he [Harold] lives in those crowded little servants' quarters up there,' Richard Crossman was to record unkindly in his *Diaries* on May 25th 1965 . . . 'Number Ten doesn't change him. He changes it so that its rooms look exactly like the rooms in his Hampstead house.' But, Crossman added, this suggested that Harold was not corrupted by his new position.

For Mary the intrusion of political colleagues into family life was one of the hardest aspects to endure, an ingredient of public success more easily accepted by the progeny of the rich and aristocratic of her generation. They, like Lady Dorothy and Lady Home, could not readily find solitude at home as children before the war, living as they did in households rather than simply as families. Mary, apart from those few years at boarding school, was not accustomed to people watching her comings and goings, to the servant at the door; nor was she prepared at first to meet, as she dashed out to shop, those who managed affairs of state on their way to a cabinet meeting. She had not grown up with the image of herself as one of the ruling class and as prime minister's wife she never saw herself playing more than a purely 'supporting role'. With this in mind she tried to fix a system of priorities: 'Family and friends first. Labour Party engagements next; then duties concerned with Number 10, and then engagements I would accept for myself.'

Yet when you ask Mary now about those days as prime minister's wife she tells you the years have blurred her recollections. 'It was all so long ago. I will talk about the facts but not feelings.' But even some dates have been forgotten, as sometimes happens with less happy or less personally significant experiences. You are forced to believe that she wishes to forget; that this amnesia allows her to turn freely to today's matters which now seem so much more important. Yet much of wartime remains vivid to her; queueing for kippers for Harold when she was pregnant and liable to pass out; the crash of bombs, the tinkle of shattered glass being swept up, Oxford full of young servicemen. Then, though, she was one of many, an observer, the struggle was more basic, the danger of death highlighting the importance of survival. In war, on those occasions when she toiled and waited and suffered to feed her man, small triumphs like buying kippers took on large dimensions. She was still a woman doing battle in her own right.

The three commonwealth prime ministers' conferences she remembers, however, with affection; the exuberance and totally classless enthusiasm of some delegates brought out the merriment in her, the radiance — shades of the manic side of her nature which normally only close friends are privileged to see.

She worked particularly hard before the first one in 1965 determined to 'get it right'. Her secretary tested her again and again with photographs of the delegates until she could successfully match each face with a name and a country. She loved to see the new prime ministers meeting the others for the first time. She enjoyed being hostess when groups came in turn to Chequers. To most of them she was simply a delightful lady, not middle or lower class, nor with nonconformist or suburban attitudes. Formality was overcome; their response to her hospitality was free from prejudice.

Washington in the spring was another memory which survived the mind's sub-conscious censorship; cherry blossom by the Potomac, President Kennedy's grave at Arlington, 'covered in flowers, his uniform caps lying on the grass wet with dew and the eternal flame burning from a small metal cone'. During her first visit as prime minister's wife in 1965 she stayed in the British embassy with Giles. She found Lyndon Johnson's accent sometimes difficult to understand; 'his Texan lingo', Crossman called it. Under the long dark shadow of the Vietnam War Harold conferred on world affairs, while Mary attended a round of ladies' luncheons and parties, beginning her role as an appendage on the international as well as the national stage, a part she enjoyed when her mood was right and the people interesting. She also made two trips at the other end of the spectrum, to the Soviet Union during Harold's three terms of office and when she speaks or writes of these you realise it is the visual images which caught her imagination rather than the individuals she met: The Red Army goose-stepping at Moscow Airport, 'their curved swords slicing the air'; the Bolshoi Ballet dancers. 'Rivers frozen in Moscow and Leningrad; birch trees heavy with snow. People everywhere in fur hats, fur boots and long fur coats.' 'Did you go to the Hermitage?' you ask. 'Oh yes, we went there,' she says. But the pictures haven't registered in any detail. Duty turned those hours in one of the world's greatest museums into another act, with the kind of conversation she found especially difficult, made even harder because it was expressed through an interpreter. But she remembers Russian children dancing the gopak, and, looking back in 1979, she could still recall vividly steel bands in Jamaica, painted churches in Romania, sleeping in the Grand Trianon in Versailles and driving along the chariot-rutted Appian Way outside Rome. It is now always the children who shine most brightly through the passage of time; standing in the Romanian night to greet the Wilsons with flowers; in Italy, dressed in virginal white; most of all, she once said, the British children: 'Bunches of flowers in their hands, making their little speeches,' as she had once done for less exalted personages. She could identify too with Huyton children as they clamoured for autographs with torn pieces of paper or climbed on Harold's car shouting, 'It's good old Mr Wilson!' For through all the nostalgia, a child-like streak has survived.

Perhaps not surprisingly, a carefree holiday in Israel in 1973, when Harold was out of office and Mary was simply a tourist, remains ablaze in her memory. Giles, who, like his grandfather, learned Hebrew, was working in a kibbutz. Mary went with Harold's sister Marjorie and was captivated. This enthusiasm for the Holy Land must surely reflect back in some degree to Fulbourn; to the loved father in the simple, agreeable chapel with its air of the celestial; the man in the pulpit bringing Christianity alive for the small girl, rolling the Jewish names off his tongue with the authority of a Hebrew scholar. It goes back to the rhythms of the psalms and the Bible's inimitable imagery and prose, the dramatic deeds of the Old Testament, and the gentler morals of the New. 'You see, I was the daughter of a minister who'd always wanted to see the Holy Land, but he couldn't afford to go. So when I went I felt as though I was seeing it for him as well.' She arrived at the point where the river Jordan meets the Sea of Galilee and saw a fisherman mending his net, and felt the tears running down her cheeks. 'It was the Bible come to life,' she says.

But long before that journey into the past, there were scores of traumas to be borne. Crossman suggests that at first the Wilsons were not treated kindly by permanent officials. 'They are bullied and chivvied by Government Hospitality and closed and hemmed in by the ministry of works, and made to feel interlopers in a quite different way than would happen to Alec Douglas-Home.'

Public relations continued to plague Mary throughout Harold's three terms of office and she never overcame her dislike of talking to people she did not know well. 'Making conversation,' she said ruefully in 1977, 'is an art which, in spite of years of experience, I have never properly acquired.' Yet her acquaintances appear to have no such reservations, although admittedly their comments hardly conjure up a picture of liveliness or wit. 'Very nice', they will say, or 'thoughtful, sincere', or, with old-fashioned chivalry, 'a very gracious lady'.

But those who know her better will mention puns and light-hearted gossip, spasms of liberation, a glint of childish devilment in her eyes which does not tally with the reserved and introverted woman she often projects as her true self.

To the general public however, Mary seemed a kindly person ready to lend an ear to the troubles of the underprivileged, misled or duped. A mother-to-mother appeal from a group of women threatened with eviction from their homes for arrears in gas bills was a typical early example of a request for help. Her mail was soon so heavy that part of a secretary's time was earmarked for her use. She had little power but she was glad to sympathise and advise and pass requests on to the relevant departments. A few people wrote regularly because they needed 'to talk to *somebody*'. One man wrote to her every day for several years, then stopped abruptly for no reason that she could discover. At first she had wanted to concentrate most of her time and energy on the problems of the old but other engagements eroded this intention, among them the opening of hospitals and exhibitions, speech days and, more dramatically, the traditional role of launching ships, for which she was once rewarded with a diamond brooch.

Then there were the inevitable public engagements with Harold which she could never treat with Lady Dorothy's light-heartedness. For Mary there was no last minute dash, no barely adequate scrubbing of the fingernails or hasty scrambling into a crumpled dress. With Marcia's advice, she was beginning to choose her clothes with more discrimination, eventually overcoming that suburban look, the fitted coat, the inevitable court shoes and unimaginative permed hair-style. 'And there was Mary coming down the stairs looking elegant and soignée,' wrote Crossman in 1968, after taking her to a party on March 21st when Harold was unable to go. 'Now,' he continues later, 'she is one of the great successes of the government and she's created her own completely personal image. Every interview she's given has been a success and she's hardly put a foot wrong.'

But mention these words of praise to Mary now and, with her usual self-deprecation, she makes a dismissive gesture. 'You know what politicians are like,' she says, lips turning downward. Her one major demand during those first months was that the portraits of previous prime ministers at Chequers should be returned to the stairs where they had hung before being moved to a corridor. She wanted, she says, to be reminded that the Wilsons' position was transitory, that her husband was only one of many, that there was no cause for arrogance or affected grandeur on their part. It was again a very Nonconformist view and yet it is fair to suppose that she also took some pleasure and pride in the thought that one day Harold's portrait would take its place there, just above Lord Home's.

Interesting too was her request at Chequers that a portrait of no particular artistic merit should be brought from a passage and rehung in a prominent position in the hall. This mystified those concerned until they realised that the subject, Admiral Sir Cloudesley Shovell, had been wrecked and drowned off the Isles of Scilly. For Mary the subject of a picture, be it a landscape, still life or portrait, is often at least as important as the painting itself. In this way her taste in art is oddly literary. Association of ideas always plays a strong part in deciding her preferences, which do not include abstract art. She has collected china for years, principally Stafford-shire figures, but also pieces commemorating Victorian prime ministers. So far, however, she has not bought any pictures of note and is not to be seen in the salerooms or dealers' galleries, although she visits the Tate, the National and the Portrait Gallery from time to time.

In 1964 the Garden Girls, who had been so helpful to Lady Home, were considered out of keeping with a Labour government's image. Usually recruited from the same exclusive secretarial college these well-heeled, well-dressed young women were certainly not ordinary. At times their clothes and style upstaged Mary who liked to dress informally and go hatless on all but formal occasions. During his second and third terms of office Harold was to ensure that new girls came from a wider field. The hat and gloves rule was dropped; upper-class accents were fortified or diluted, depending on your view, by more regional ones; homelier-looking females appeared on the scene wearing chain store clothes. Overseas, the girls from Downing Street began to merge more easily into the background.

Now it was Harold who enjoyed breakfast in bed, waited on by the housekeeper. His working day started with the morning papers and a cup of tea at eight o'clock. Breakfast was usually bacon and eggs or haddock and poached egg, but once a year he was sent a crate of kippers by the MP for Aberdeen, Hector Hughes, and then it was kippers every day until they were finished. Mary would begin her day by listening to the farming programme on the radio and later the religious programme, which 'always seemed to set me up for the day,' a renewal of faith sometimes necessary to sustain her in a world of people she did not feel she could always trust. 'People,' she would say crisply, 'tend to let you down.'

But there were of course some who did not, among them John Betjeman, whom she met at the Opera House, Covent Garden, in 1966. Thus began a long friendship which brought her much happiness and inspiration. Here was a poet who took her poetry seriously and, whatever critics may feel about Mary's verse, it had remained a central therapeutic force in her life, giving her, especially since her sons left home, both an identity and a purpose. Poetry was and is far more important to her than the fact that she was prime minister's wife for almost eight years; her character, so full of paradoxes, can only begin to be understood if she is considered as a creative rather than an administrative or academic person. Mary can administer when she is in the right mood; she possesses an academic's pedantry on subjects she knows well; but she has the changeable nature of the aspiring poet. She cannot and will not do the same job day after day; a week of enthusiasm and efficiency may be followed by more helpless days when even buying a piece of furniture seems beyond her. She could have been a teacher because that profession allows a creative outlet and some room for change, but few other jobs would have satisfied the restlessness of her spirit which also ironically desires a permanency of place. She needs friends, but not acquaintances, people on her own terms, people who do not intrude, but can be sought out when her mood needs them. Sometimes when living at Number 10 she would slip out in a headscarf and dark glasses to visit her two friends in Hampstead. At other times she would wander along the South Bank in the evenings, alone or with a friend, drink a glass of wine in a restaurant, perhaps see a play, and walk back often in solitude, loving the lights on the water, the passers-by, struggling with lines in her head for a poem, needing the loneliness with which to renew herself. But which of the many sides of her character represents the real Mary?

There lies the conundrum. There are not only the ups and downs due to the ebb and flow of the body's chemistry, but also the clash of the genetic and the environmental; the deep-rooted puritanism of her upbringing and the giggly, gossipy strain probably inherited from her mother; that old tendency to chatter, which will escape in the right atmosphere after a couple of sherries, and inevitably may have embarrassed her in retrospect in the early days of public life, increasing the guardedness, the fear of saying a wrong word or letting the mask slip long enough to reveal damaging, newsworthy material. There is in her, too, the controlled woman who waited nearly six years for marriage to consummate her love, and the wilder woman who went three times to see the film of *Death in Venice* because she found Björn Andresen so attractive. And there is the woman who will snub those who misquote from sources she knows better herself, where someone else might let the mistake go to save embarrassment. There is the compassionate woman who was so quick to shake John Stonehouse's hand when he came to the Labour conference after his release from prison; the woman who, on the surface at least, has rejected so many of her father's

Calvinistic tenets, without ever entirely escaping their influence.

'I've never worried much about so-called sin in personal relationships,' she told Kenneth Harris of *The Observer* in 1965. 'What I mean is, I don't care for religious attitudes and ideas of morality which seem to depend on intolerance of one kind or another, especially intolerance of personal weaknesses in matters of sex for example. I'm much more intolerant about people ill-treating each other, people of one country bullying the people of another country, employers exploiting workers, or, for that matter, workers exploiting each other.'

But of course, to tolerate and to like are very different things, and, however hard Mary tried, however great her tolerance, she could not be happy with many of the people who surrounded Harold during so much of his working life.

'The only sullen note,' Barbara Castle was to write in her *Diaries* as late as June 9th 1974 about the Labour Women's Conference, 'was produced by Mary who slipped sullenly into the room without greeting anyone. She sat silent throughout our rushed meal, her nose in her plate. I had a sympathetic word with her in the bedroom afterwards. "Of course I hate it," she told me. "But then I always have. But I do my job." Then she added, almost as an afterthought, "But I'm glad for Harold. He needed this. He went through such a rotten time." ' Over ten years later, Mary told me, 'I wasn't sullen. I was silent because I didn't want to interrupt an important conversation.' Sometimes, too, she was homesick for the Scilly Isles.

While she listened to political talk, to speeches that barely interested her, the bungalow stood empty, the June grass was tall, waves broke on pale sands. Allowing conscience to overcome inclination, Mary had been persuaded to spend hours in conferences she found dull and hotel suites she disliked, and, like her mother, she rarely hid her displeasure. After her time as premier's spouse she was to express surprise that people found her tongue sharp, that sometimes in Number 10 the question was 'How is Mary feeling today? How is she taking it?' In 1974 Marcia was looking after her own two children. Peggy Field, Marcia's sister, now Mary's full-time secretary, was sometimes the tactful intermediary between Mary and other members of staff.

During Harold's second term of office Mary became a more commanding figure who could silence the foolish with a withering

Right Harold and
Lady Dorothy
Macmillan with
Catherine, Maurice
and Ann
Far right Lady
Dorothy at
Gleneagles, 1961

Lady Dorothy greets
President Kennedy

Below The 9th Duke
and Duchess of
Devonshire with
some of their children
and grandchildren

Top left Elizabeth Home as a girl
Top right The Homes on the Great Wall of China on an official visit
Above The Homes with children Caroline, Diana, Meriel and David, circa 1946

Mary Wilson holds a charity tea party at No. 10. Seen here with Jessie Matthews, Millicent Martin and Barbara Kelly
Below left Harold and Mary celebrate Mary's 52nd birthday
Below right With Pat Nixon at a White House state dinner, 1970

The Wilsons with Robin and Giles on the Scilly Isles, 1963

Top Jim and Audrey Callaghan celebrate their 40th wedding anniversary with children and grandchildren, 1979
Above left Football with a grandson at Chequers the same year
Above right Performing the 'topping out' ceremony at Great Ormond Street Hospital, 1979

Top left Lady Dorothy in 1920
Top right Elizabeth Home in 1936
Above left Mary Wilson in 1945
Above right Audrey Callaghan as a schoolgirl

Top left Harold and Lady Dorothy Macmillan, April 1920
Top right Alec and Elizabeth when Lord and Lady Dunglass, October 1936
Above left Harold and Mary Wilson, January 1940
Above right Jim and Audrey Callaghan, July 1937

Denis and Margaret
Thatcher at the time
of their wedding,
December 1951

Denis
electioneering, 1983

The Thatchers'
Silver Wedding
photograph with
Mark and Carol

Visiting a Norfolk
factory

In the countryside
near Chequers, 1984

glance. By now she had established herself as a useful and interesting speaker on 'Life at Number 10', talking especially to groups of Labour women and she continued to be in demand for the opening of new hospitals and schools. She floated the idea that her presence as a wife should be exploited more fully, bearing in mind that Edward Heath was a bachelor. But even so, she always seemed to be outside the magic circle, like a small child tapping helplessly on the window pane while inside the adults make arrangements without her. Inevitably the woman closest to Harold when political decisions were made had for many years been Marcia, who was the third strong woman to be his secretary and undoubtedly the most vulnerable.

'I felt at times a bit like his mother and I think he often treated me like one,' she says now.

Marcia found it hard to say 'no' to requests and in politics willing and dependable workers are much used. Her hours had sometimes been excessive; she was often the unofficial chauffeur who drove people home after parties or late meetings. 'Marcia will take you' was a familiar cry: she found staff for the Wilsons, she advised Mary on her clothes, visited widowed Mrs Baldwin in her flat in Wembley, protected Mary from the press, kept her informed on events she would need to attend. She was for some outsiders with Labour sympathies a voice at court, for she was always ready to help and advise people. She brought her own family into the Downing Street fold because when emergencies blew up she could rely utterly on her father, brother, and sister. But that whispering campaign, started by one of the foremost, younger, members of the Conservative Party in 1964, has spread over the years. *Private Eye* was quick to feature Marcia, undermining her reputation by innuendo. Some elements in the media love a villain; they like to see matters and relationships in black and white. Marcia became a victim of that syndrome and a tool too in a campaign to unseat Harold. She was shown as tough, unprincipled and bossy, Harold's office wife, whereas she was in a sense everybody's nanny, a woman who had been working for Harold for eight years before he became premier, so that she naturally knew him better than most of his colleagues. In her strength as an organiser she resembled his mother, but by temperament she was infinitely more emotional, loyal to her boss but easily hurt. If she had a fault it was probably that she cared too much and drove herself too hard. Since she had no personal political ambitions she did not court power; she was given it, because she was reliable and would take burdens on her shoulders which others had abandoned or ignored.

When the Wilsons' housekeeper, Mary Wright, left to be married, Marcia found a replacement in the competent and lively widow, Mrs Pollard, a pleasant plain cook from Coventry, whom Marcia had known since her schooldays. *Private Eye*'s image of Mary Wilson ignored the fact that although she had learned to cook she did not enjoy the domestic side of marital life. She did not see herself as a person who washed and ironed and handed beverages round on a tray to conventionally dressed guests. Sixteen-stone Bill Housden, not Mary, took on many of the tasks performed by Elizabeth for Sir Alec Douglas-Home, checking that Harold's clothes were clean, his shoes polished and his ties pressed. And when the question of menus came up Mary would sometimes consult Audrey Callaghan, who was only just next door while Jim was chancellor of the exchequer, a useful and engaging friend to have at the end of the passage.

Harold was keen to protect his wife from the acrimony and the in-jokes which are so much part of politics. When the stress told, it was better that she was not there to see, for occasionally he could be capable of surprising rudeness — one distinguished museum director remembers arriving at a reception with his wife to be greeted by the prime minister with, 'Who the hell are these people?' But this was not typical. Harold was usually exceptionally polite and kind. Joe Haines, his press secretary, a man not given to paying unearned compliments, worked for Harold for seven and a half years having first stipulated that he would only stay two, largely, he said, 'because of the extraordinary quality he had of making people feel attached to him even when he was not behaving very well'. And Marcia has written of Harold's ability to laugh at himself and his deep basic kindness to those in trouble.

Mary insisted, of course, that Harold was with his family whenever possible, and, with his natural inclination to play Father Christmas, he normally remembered anniversaries. Whatever the problems he tried to take Mary out to lunch, usually to the Epicure, on her birthday and to be at Lowenva with her on their wedding anniversary because that was her favourite place. When the boys were at home there was always a family holiday, usually on the Scilly

Isles, with picnics and boat trips with Harold the oarsman and Mary in the stern.

But Harold's chief recreation was golf, which Mary did not play. Marcia records that in 1968 his most frequent companion on the course at Hampstead was her brother, Tony Field. 'In Tony, Harold had the sort of friend with whom he could chat and talk, knowing that not one word would be transmitted under any circumstances to any outside person, not even his own family.' It was, she added, a close but odd relationship. Odd because Tony was never a member of the Labour Party, and odd because he was a property speculator. Tony Field was very different from the sort of men who became Mary's friends; John Webster, the quiet and sensitive organist, and John Betjeman, whose interest in business affairs and politics was minimal. Ask Mary Wilson whom she liked among politicians and she will mention Lord Home. You can see why, and you can see why the Wilsons found it hard to share each other's friends; they are and were in many ways opposites and although opposites often fall in love, their oppositeness can put strains on a marriage, until its fact is accepted by the people concerned, and appropriate compromises made.

They differed even in their preferences for animals. For thirteen years Harold possessed a golden labrador, Paddy, to whom he was deeply attached. Paddy lived mainly at Chequers, but whenever circumstances allowed he was Harold's companion, a sweet-tempered obedient dog who loved children but was too friendly to be a good guard dog. Harold was proud of his pedigree. 'His ancestry,' he says, 'was impeccable.' But when you ask whether Mary liked Paddy too, he replies quickly, 'She is a cat lady.'

The fact that the Wilsons' marriage — a difficult institution to maintain at the best of times — survived through all the turmoil is a tribute to them both. 'I am sure they are deeply together, but they are now pretty separate in their togetherness,' wrote Richard Crossman in March 1966. 'It is one of those marriages which holds despite itself because each side has evolved a self-containedness within the marriage.'

Yet marriage to any prime minister demands an extra sturdy independence from the wife, if she is not to be intensely lonely whenever there is a crisis which keeps her husband away from her, which causes him to break engagements with her, and leaves her to go alone to private dinner parties, to the theatre or elsewhere. A gregarious affectionate woman needs a surrogate husband at such times, but only Lady Dorothy among my subjects is known to have found one, in Lord Boothby, and society and the media are quick to assume that a male escort is a lover. So each prime minister's spouse must learn early to deal with loneliness in a way which will not arouse special interest or risk either partner's reputation.

In July 1967 Crossman was able to report Mary's success at one of her tea parties for the ladies, to which a few carefully selected men were invited. He had been to a delightful room upstairs, 'open from end to end, with flowers, and all the ladies in their summer dresses and hats;' one hundred and seventy women for Mary to manage. And in October he thought that Mary was happier: 'She quite enjoys going round, quite enjoys her success and her fame.'

That September *Mrs Wilson's Diary*, adapted for the stage by Joan Littlewood, opened in London at the Theatre Royal, Stratford East, and was later transferred to the Criterion where it ran for nine months, another trial to be borne by a woman who found it hard to rise above ridicule. But there were pleasures and heart-warming privileges to counter the miserable times: the meeting with the first men to walk on the moon about whom Mary wrote a poem, and those annual visits to Balmoral. The day the Queen drove the Wilsons quite recklessly down a twisty path to the Duke of Edinburgh's chalet on the edge of the murmuring waters of the loch, stands out unblurred in Mary's memory. Here she assisted the Queen to make tea, and the two of them washed up together, for a while just two temporarily domesticated women chatting over the sink, behaving like equals. It was an event infinitely more exciting and gratifying to the Wilsons than it would have been to the Macmillans or Homes. Undoubtedly Harold and Mary both regarded the Queen with deep affection and unswerving loyalty. They were moved and happy when she and Prince Philip dined with them at Number 10, liking them genuinely as people — flattered that the Queen never failed to ask after Robin and Giles, speaking as one mother to another.

In 1969 Mary's first book, *Selected Poems*, was published by Hutchinson, ending at last the humiliating stream of rejection slips which she had endured since her marriage. It became a bestseller, reassuring Mary who had feared the publisher's offer had been made only because she was prime minister's wife. The royalties enabled her to pay off the mortgage on Lowenva and at last she felt herself to be at least partly independent of Harold. She gave interviews on her own account; she was an acknowledged poet; the boost to her morale would have been considerable if only she had been sure that her work was remarkable. But doubts lingered. She still feels that her poetry, which she hates to read once it is finished, reveals too much of her secret self: hopes, pain, happiness, perhaps the occasional banality of which she is later ashamed; food for the satirist. Reading it, no one would be surprised to know that Tennyson, Keats, Emily Brontë and Thomas Hardy are her favourite poets. She goes back for inspiration rather than forward to hammer out an original style or new approach. But her poems' simplicity is part of their attraction. They can be easily understood; they touch a common nerve, feelings shared by thousands. Their publication was more important to Mary than Harold's struggle and he, in turn, showed little interest in her work, only reading it when she asked him to check facts. For Mary's poems have a strong thread of emotion and Harold's intellectual side has always outstripped the emotional side of his life.

Labour's defeat at the polls in 1970, which caught both the Wilsons by surprise, was a reprieve for Mary. The long drive back from his constituency of Huyton was followed immediately by rapid preparations to leave Number 10. The first person to go was Harold's seventy-seven-year-old father who had come from Cornwall to join in the expected rejoicings and was to die in Perth, Australia, the following year. The celebration breakfast planned by Mrs Pollard for twenty guests became more like a wake. Bill Housden packed a suitcase for Harold to take to Chequers for a last weekend. Tony Field hired packing cases, Marcia started to deal with files and to try to find alternative accommodation for the Wilsons. At such a time Lady Dorothy or Elizabeth Home would have been at the helm organising servants or doing the more domestic jobs themselves, but Mary was insulated from much of the stress by Marcia and Bill Housden. Marcia said afterwards that it was right that she should look for a house rather than Mary, because Mary could not drive. There was also Mary's asthma to consider, a complaint liable to return under tension. The house Marcia found was 14 Vincent Square, on the corner of Vincent Street in Westminster, only a few doors from where Richard Crossman lived. The Wilsons rented the three main floors through Harrods from Jerome

Epstein, the mercurial American film producer, who moved with his wife, Bernice, into the basement. Mid-Victorian, sash-windowed, delightfully compact with well-proportioned rooms and a pleasing staircase, the house was ideal for the Wilsons and their son Giles, and for Mrs Pollard who continued to look after the domestic side of their lives.

The choice of landlord was a happy one. Jerry Epstein was technically outside British politics but his sympathies were decidedly left-wing. He was quick to offer Harold the loan of a chauffeur and car, until Edward Heath reorganised the leader of the Opposition's financial allowances enabling Harold to re-employ Bill Housden. Harold liked show business people, included several actors among his friends and was perturbed by the film industry's problems.

Jerry remembers the day they arrived. 'They were very gentle, kind and polite, but you felt the strain of their election failure.' They were 'thrilled', he said, with the tray of drinks, bottles of whisky and gin he had put out as a welcoming present on the study table. 'It's nice to know we still have friends,' Harold said, still reeling a little from the defeat. To some Mary seemed closer to her husband when life was hardest for him. She could cope more easily with his despair and depression than with success. Her affectionate nature, often frustrated, reached out to meet emotional needs.

At this time the Wilsons were, in Jerry Epstein's words, 'very touching. They clung devotedly to each other in adversity. It was,' he felt, 'the real thing. A couple coming very close together again after the ups and downs of marriage.' One day he found them walking hand in hand like lovers on their way to Westminster and gave them a lift in his car.

For Mary it was also a time of some personal triumph and satisfaction, because of the reviews and publicity which had followed the publication of her book. There were excited journeys to bookshops to autograph copies. She and Giles would go down to the basement to talk about poetry with Jerry and his wife, and once she felt secure in their friendship she allowed the more giggly high-spirited side of her nature to surface, amusing them with witty stories about Number 10 and her life as a prime minister's consort. She told of a Washington visit when Harold was taken straight to see President Nixon and she to Blair House, the official residence for important visitors, where the simple old retainer addressed her throughout as 'Your Majesty'.

Often Mary would sit upstairs in the drawing-room looking out across the square, through the trees to the idyllic peace of Westminster School's playing fields, feeling the words of verse coming, as Sir John Betjeman said, 'kindly supplied by the Management'.

Sometimes the Wilsons invited the Epsteins to parties in the house or sent Mrs Pollard down with plates of party food. This friendship had the rare advantage of being one the Wilsons could share, and when Harold was back in power the Epsteins were invited to Number 10. 'The Wilsons were always approachable,' Jerry says now, 'and long after they left, Mary still came to dinner parties here.'

While living in Vincent Square Harold started work on his book, *The Labour Government 1964–1970: a Personal Record*, for which he had received excellent advances, and which went a long way towards easing the Wilsons' financial position. Indeed comparatively soon after Mary paid off the mortgage on Lowenva they were able to lease 5 Lord North Street and to buy Grange Farm, a fine oak-beamed, five-bedroomed farmhouse in Missenden, not far from Chequers. Soon Mrs Pollard and Paddy were installed in Grange Farm, although the housekeeper came back to London four days a week to cook for the Wilsons, and the adjoining barn was being converted into a workroom for Harold. Now Harold and Mary could escape into the country they loved at weekends, free of all formality, with Mrs Pollard driving to the station to meet Mary if she went by train ahead of Harold. So the Wilsons, out of office, were still nannied a little by the loyal housekeeper and chauffeur whom they treated as friends.

Marcia Williams, who became Lady Falkender on receiving a life peerage in 1974, gives an excellent description of 5 Lord North Street, to which the Wilsons moved in December 1970, in *Downing Street in Perspective*. She writes of the Wilsons' elegant first-floor drawing-room with 'its tall, narrow sash windows', looking out on a beautiful street at the front and a paved garden at the back, its wood block floor covered with Romanian and Persian carpets given to the Wilsons on official visits abroad. She mentions a drinks cupboard built into the bookcase with a door disguised by simulated book spines. But, she tells us, 'this curious and literary-looking cocktail cabinet seldom contained more than a solitary bottle of beer. The drinks were kept on a sofa table by the wall opposite.' Harold had a small room off the dining-room for a study and the largest bedroom to sleep in, while Giles and Mary had two small ones which were little more than attics. The house which had once been occupied by one of Lord North's mistresses was now to be used for many important meetings, a great deal of hard work, and endless discussion. Politics had moved right into Mary's home at last, while she reiterated her resolution never again to live in Downing Street. 'Harold can go if he likes, but not me.'

Six years had been enough for a prime minister's wife playing a supporting role with reluctant sincerity, without the commitment of Lady Home or the zest of Lady Dorothy. When Harold returned to office in 1974, the Wilsons continued to live in Lord North Street; when he needed to be at Chequers, Mary was dropped off by car at Grange Farm unless her presence was essential.

Her greatest joys remained her family and her poetry; in contrast, much of her time as prime minister's wife became increasingly a question of existence and survival rather than an honour or privilege. For by now Robin had married and in 1975 he became the father of twins, Catherine and Jennifer, the subject of several of Mary's poems. The twins created a precedent when they were baptised at Chequers, and drew Harold and Mary closer to each other. They were fair, blue-eyed, clear-skinned, miraculously lovely children in a world which had often seemed grey. Their love of the seaside made Lowenva doubly worthwhile. Paddy, the dog, watched them as a collie watches sheep, snarling with unexpected ferocity when a rough-looking man threatened them. The whole family united in protecting and loving the next generation. The Wilson sons had in one respect filled the roles Mary had wanted Harold to play; Robin was a lecturer at Oxford and Giles, the loner, a schoolteacher. Such family happiness made politics seem dirtier, the machinations and character assassinations less acceptable. Those disagreeable rumours that Harold and Marcia had had a love affair added to the disillusionment. The continuing insinuations and snide remarks only increased Mary's own public stature among Labour Party supporters, and invitations for her to speak on 'Life at Downing Street' to women's societies continued to pour in, while Marcia the superb organiser became more emotional and at times overwrought. 'They can afford to be nice to me, because they have been so horrible to Harold and Marcia,' Mary said.

The two women behaved admirably in public under much provocation. When the so-called scandal was at its height there was a reception at Downing Street, with Mary and Harold receiving guests. When Marcia arrived silence fell. For a few moments everyone seemed to be watching the tall long-legged history graduate approaching the shorter middle-aged wife. Then Mary held out her arms and the two women warmly embraced. They had never felt antagonism towards each other, but to onlookers Mary had made a magnificent gesture. Everyone relaxed, the party went on. It seemed evidence of Mary's new composure, a painfully gained maturity, the public reaction of a woman who felt she was now a person in her own right as well as a wife. And yet Mary had never been more tired of the political life, of being, as she put it, 'public property'. Weary of all the 'pushing', she tried 'to keep at bay the longing, as if for a drug, for solitude and utter silence.'

As that last term of office rushed from crisis to crisis Mary began to worry about Harold's health. He was not ill, but the strain of leadership was telling. He was drinking more, bolstering himself up with extra nips of brandy before speaking in the House. Although still undeniably in command, he was, in his own words, growing stale, and he promised Mary he would retire on March 16th, five days after his sixtieth birthday, one of the few political secrets she knew before anyone else. She pencilled the date in her diary marking it 'D Day'. But in the event he did not retire until April 5th.

Harold Wilson's resignation was a shock to the nation as well as to many of his colleagues. Clearly he was still in reasonable health and quite able to enjoy the farewell parties which followed. Commentators have suggested that Mary persuaded him to step down; a wrong assumption, she says. 'I suggested he should stay on for Jubilee year.'

To the Wilsons' delight the Queen intimated that she would accept an invitation to dine at Downing Street with her longest serving prime minister and there was a dinner for the cabinet and then a luncheon arranged by Marcia to commemorate Harold's last day in Number 10, only hours before his final audience with the Queen at Buckingham Palace.

The move was domestically easier this time, because the Wilsons were prepared for it and living outside Downing Street. They also knew they could expect press harassment and speculation. They were old hands at the game. But if Mary consoled herself with the thought that the worst was over, she had not reckoned with reactions to Harold's honours list, which brought waves of criticism, ridicule and innuendo. What should have been an amicable if unexpected end to a distinguished career as prime minister became a soured finale. Honours had been handed out to friends, some critics claimed, without consideration of their brand of politics or their sometimes dubious business activities; an affront to those who take honours seriously or had been worthy recipients themselves. Marcia, who always aroused strong emotions in one direction or another, received some of the blame. There were suggestions that she had drawn up the list instead of the prime minister himself. Or was the selection a supreme act of cynicism against the whole honours system? Mary remained discreetly silent, keeping to a long-held rule not to make controversial statements.

Now at last she was free of the fetters of political life at one remove. She would always watch her words when with people other than friends, because that had become a way of life, but every day was now her own; she could take off for the Scilly Isles when she wished; catch a train to Oxford to see her grandchildren when the mood took her, travel to Hampstead unmasked by dark glasses, and there were long solitary hours again when she hoped the muse would speak.

In 1977 the Wilsons moved for the twenty-third time in their married life when they sold 5 Lord North Street and took up residence in their present flat in Ashley Gardens which looks out on the side of Westminster Cathedral. They sold Grange Farm, but kept their beloved Lowenva although it was too small for their needs and they were refused planning permission to extend it. In 1976 John Webster the organist died, inspiring Mary to write three poems to commemorate his life. In 1977 Paddy died and the past was raked over again when Joe Haines's potent book, *The Politics of Power*, was published with its attack on Marcia. Mary rose to Marcia's defence, putting her signature to a pertinent and kindly letter to *The Times* which was published on February 21st.

'Perhaps,' she wrote, 'I may be allowed to say a word in the aftermath of Mr Haines's book. I was like a rather unwilling recruit to a group of professional soldiers when I first went to Number 10 and Lady Falkender's help and advice were invaluable to me in all the work I tried to do there. Of course there were tears and tensions, particularly at election times — there must be clashes of temperament in all large organisations — but there was plenty of laughter and enjoyment too. And I should like to add that Lady Falkender's family were also extremely helpful to me over many years.

'Her kindness to so many people in the Labour Party and Number 10 is, or should be, well known. Nobody was refused help if it lay in her power to aid them.'

It was a generous and well-merited letter signed by a complicated woman who now resolutely refuses to talk about her role as Harold's wife.

Indeed anyone meeting Lady Wilson for the first time these days, as an ordinary citizen, would not suspect that her past was so elevated. At her hairdressers she is simply Mrs Wilson, for she likes the identity of a private person, the withdrawn poet, the homely grandmother. She speaks sometimes of a pub she went to one day with a friend, where a countrywoman talked to her about slimming and the weather with 'long gaps of companionable silence'. When Mary finally rose to go she heard this countrywoman say to a neighbour, 'She seemed a nice little person.' 'Now that I like,' says Mary, consistent to the end in rejecting the role her husband won for her, dismissing what glory there might have been as alien and unsuitable for a woman of her character and convictions; yet she is not actually 'little', and is much more unpredictable than the adjective *nice* implies.

Mary Wilson will surely go down in history not only as the first wife of a British prime minister to come from a penurious background *and* live at Number 10, but also as someone who made a success of the job, within the limits she set, and won a place in the affections of the old Labour Party; a woman who never seriously attempted to influence her husband on any crucial national or political decision apart from the date of his resignation.

Yet she remains in a strange way emotionally and socially uncertain of herself, a mixed-up girl in an unkind world.

'You may not think it,' she told John Wells when the Tory Party was back in power, 'but I am terribly thin-skinned and I try to preserve a façade of dignity and calm, because I am very arrogant and proud and not really sweet at all . . . and sometimes bloody-minded. And if anything happens that I'm embarrassed about, I wouldn't let anyone see.' Mary has never acquired the complete self-confidence which buoyed up Lady Dorothy, and esteems herself little. She finds self-examination sometimes a painful experience in the early hours. Her bouts of happiness, laughter and puns, hide the fact that she doesn't like herself. Past hurts needle her from time to time like mild rheumatism. She admits to a death wish that comes and goes. She says, 'If only people knew . . .' life was much worse at Number 10 than suggested in *Private Eye*. 'I am very sorry for Denis Thatcher.'

'She was so frightened,' comments one of Harold Wilson's previous associates. 'When it was all over she was like a different person. I met her at a party and she took my hand and pressed it against her cheek, a warm and loving woman.'

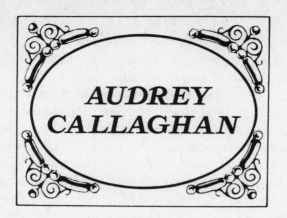

AUDREY CALLAGHAN

When James Callaghan became premier it was Audrey who insisted that they should live at Number 10, because she wanted to be 'at the centre of things'. Jim suggested that they might continue in their Kennington flat, perhaps forgetting briefly that the girl he married has always been a political animal.

Wrapping her arms protectively round her body, she says now that she always thought he would go far, but she 'married for love', after surely the longest courtship by any prominent politician since the war. She is reticent now about her age, more through a sturdy refusal to accept the approach of her last years than vanity. Talking to her you realise that she is still exploring, especially in the cultural field, reading the latest novels rather than turning back to the classics, buying contemporary works of art, going to modern as well as classical plays and to exhibitions, while her husband becomes immersed in writing his memoirs. Changes in her life have often been signalled by a different hairstyle, suggesting that she sees herself as a person open to new ideas, new forms. Audrey Callaghan has never cultivated Mary Wilson's habit of self-analysis nor Lady Home's of self-examination; she looks forward rather than back and loves the Callaghans' present country house more than any previous home. She is always aware that time is running out and she must hurry to catch the best of what remains. Struggling with a full diary, an active woman still expecting to retain the energy of her earlier years, she is surprised to find herself tired. Contemporary politicians will tell you that 'Audrey is a very private person,' meaning that she won't discuss her own character, Jim, or her marriage, that her conversation is normally about everyday life, abstract matters, politics, her children and grandchildren. Believing herself to be dull, she rarely talks about her feelings.

Audrey has remained true to her early loyalties. She always attends the Fabian Society meeting at the annual Labour Party conference, though the Society is nowadays considered a fringe event rather than a platform for new intellectual thought. She accepts this fact with equanimity instead of the regret you might expect from someone who has given the Society her support for half a century.

'She is a very pleasant person,' friends will say, sensing in this lack of anger a rock-like quality, a total integrity rather than dynamite. An intelligent though not a profound thinker, she is known for her practical sense, her enlightened enthusiasm and unfailing support for friends and campaigns; in addition she has always inspired the affection of those who have looked after her security, driven her hither and thither and washed up or decorated for her.

Long-legged, long-armed with a mildly apologetic smile and warm brown eyes, she walks with the slightly awkward grace of a wader bird. When she talks to you she often assumes a quizzical air, head a little bent as though she is accustomed to explaining things to people smaller than herself — a generous woman who has never felt cuddly, a giver rather than a taker who likes to get things done.

After his election as prime minister Jim Callaghan said '. . . I want no cliques. There will be no insiders or outsiders. So far as the past is concerned I shall wipe the slate clean and I ask everyone to do the same, and that includes members of the self-appointed groups in the House. I mean especially the Tribune Group and the Manifesto Group . . .'

In his television broadcast on the evening of his appointment he said, 'I emphasise to you that if we fail to bring down inflation, we shall never succeed in bringing down unemployment.' This is a belief often reiterated by Mrs Thatcher today. Earlier, talking to a close friend, his religious upbringing coloured his language. 'My job,' he said, 'will be to lead the people out of Egypt and into the desert. I doubt if I shall see the Promised Land.'

In April 1976 the public had quite a clear picture of their new prime minister, whose television performances were impressive, convivial and avuncular, but they knew little of his wife.

'What is *she* like?'

'Very nice.'

The banal adjective, like 'pleasant' and 'reserved', means so much and yet so little. Surely someone who chose the music of Dvořak for her wedding in 1938 must have more to her than these descriptions imply. Certainly her gentle but firm character complements her husband's rugger-playing aggressiveness which has been tempered by the years. 'Audrey leads people without them realising it,' he told me. And those who think he bullies her are mistaken. She may accept amicably a certain amount of male bossiness, but nowadays she is quite capable of digging in her toes over more important matters. When she complains that Jim has interrupted her conversation, his 'sorry dear' seems almost a reflex action.

When I mentioned to their daughter, Margaret Jay, that her parents said they had never analysed their marriage, she said, 'That's why it's survived so well.' But both are wiser than that. Both have the essential perception to keep a marital flame alive through all the strains of political life, to mend emotional fences broken by blundering bad temper under stress, or irritable impatience. Talking at the Callaghans' farm on a second visit, I tried to probe deeper.

'Audrey needs a goal,' Jim said. 'Last week it was that new border,' his arm gesticulated in the direction of the garden. 'This week it is the arrangements for the calves she's going to fatten.'

'Which breed?'

'Sussex, because they're local and look so pretty, but farming is a business. They won't have names,' she said.

'Audrey is a very private person,' Jim said. 'Even I don't know all the sides of her character and all the things that have happened in her life. But she's proud, too. Oh, yes,' he gave his rumbly laugh, 'she's proud all right.'

'I don't see why I should talk to people who say, "we *do* want to meet your husband," ' commented Audrey. 'They are quite polite, but all the same . . . It is rather trying.'

'She doesn't always appear confident on the surface, but deep down she's very confident, very confident indeed,' added Jim.

'But she thinks she's dull,' I pointed out.

'That's because she is married to such a brilliant man,' joked Jim.

I suggested that his skill as a raconteur might be one cause. She couldn't compete, I suggested.

'He always says I've got the story wrong,' she said.

'It's a matter of timing. Timing is everything,' Jim said. 'And she never gets it right.'

For a moment there was a companionable silence, no resentment. We were eating shepherd's pie in the kitchen, which was light and white and blessedly cool on a sultry August day. Then Jim said, 'She's the most selfless and hardworking of all the consorts, so you'd better make her piece the best. She's always busy. Sometimes she makes me feel guilty. I can be very aimless, but Audrey never stops. She's constantly working towards something.'

I mentioned some of Denis Thatcher's problems. Were hers in any way similar?

'You don't want to compare her with *him*,' said Jim. 'Compare her with Elizabeth Home.'

'Audrey's more political,' I said. 'The most political consort.'

'But Lady Home, with her political background . . .' Jim argued.

'She wasn't a councillor, a politician in her own right,' I insisted, marvelling again at how much the Homes are admired for one reason or another by so many different people in the political field.

'I come from a very ordinary family,' Audrey said.

Later she showed me a photograph of her maternal grandfather with his wife and ten children. 'He used to joke,' she said, 'that a penny bun always cost him a shilling. He always bought twelve.' The handsome bearded grocer looked almost embarrassed at the size of his family. 'That's my mother, looking glum,' Audrey says, 'because she had been told off for cutting her hair short.' Under the fair and faintly frizzy hairdo, her pale, slightly stubborn face showed character rather than beauty.

Audrey Callaghan's upbringing was typically provincial middle-class, Nonconformist, respectable and unadventurous. Charity was taught at home and at school, which sponsored three places for boys at Dr Barnardo's Naval School from money raised mainly by the pupils' efforts with plays, collecting boxes and an annual bazaar. She longed for a brother, but only one sister, Jeanne, four years younger than herself, rivalled her place in the warm-hearted family home.

She was born in a house built for her parents, Runswick, 4 Boughton Lane, on the outskirts of Maidstone; semi-detached, three-bedroomed, red brick, with gable and bay, part tile-hung, part pebble-dash. 'A nice comfortable small house,' says Jim Callaghan, a touch of nostalgia in his voice, 'very attractive cherry orchards in front, lovely trees.'

She went to the junior establishment for the Maidstone High School for Girls. There she surprised herself by always being among the top three of her class. Her teachers' names had a ridiculous ring which seemed to escape her notice: Kidd, Hook, Harmer, Hewitt and Higg. Kidd the head mistress had close-cropped grey hair. She lived with two other teachers and was 'fierce but fair', a martinet about grammar. Her temper was shortest when girls failed to parse properly, and Audrey remembers a wretched Scottish girl who could not understand the head mistress's accent catching the lash of the Kidd tongue.

But the girls' heroine was pretty Dorothy Higg with her bobbed hair and whimsical manner. Miss Higg — they were all Misses — played hockey for the county and taught geography. There was a fine laboratory in the high school, good playing fields, dedicated teachers and, inevitably, an element of lesbianism which, although never named, seems to me implicit in Audrey's description of the teachers. It was a single-sex school run by manless women, typical of the 'twenties and early 'thirties, which so often concentrated the girls' thoughts on work and games rather than men, often delaying consciousness of their own feminine attractions. Certainly, the high school instilled in Audrey an interest in learning, so that more than any other prime minister's spouse she was to continue her own education formally and informally over the years. Inspired surely by the attractive Miss Higg, she played hockey in the First XI and won a distinction in geography in her school certificate exam; she also went twice to France to improve her French, once with a school party to Paris and then, before taking higher school certificate, with a friend to Fontainebleau. And French, she says, has been useful to her as Jim Callaghan's wife.

Fellow pupils at school included Ann Brookfield and Ella Margaret Tiley, who were to marry William Golding, the Nobel prize winner, and Lord Beeching. Mrs Alan Bullock, Audrey's junior by two years, remembers the future Mrs Callaghan as 'elegant rather than pretty and very distinguished looking', with a father who was well known in Maidstone.

'But rather withdrawn,' says Audrey. 'His work came first. He never arrived back before seven in the evenings and looking back now I think my mother must have been lonely sometimes because he was away from home so much. Even when we went on holidays, he would telephone the works daily and insist we returned after twelve days.'

Tall, brown-eyed with smoothed-down black hair, Frank Moulton had come to Maidstone when he was twelve and immediately joined the Knightrider Street Baptist Church where he excelled as a Bible class 'scholar'. Educated at Cambridge County School, he gained his first job through a deacon named Frederick Ball who owned the Lead Wool Company, which was part of the non-ferrous metal industry. He married, at twenty-five, thirty-year-old Watford born Clarie Kempson, who nearly matched him in height. She had blue eyes below hair which had darkened with the years like seasoned oak, and a narrow nose. Clarie was one of the ten children in the photograph, seven girls and three boys. 'If grandfather had not been a grocer,' Audrey says, 'I don't see how he could have afforded to feed them all, but it was rather nice because I had lots of aunts and cousins.' Clarie came to Maidstone to work in a draper's shop after a broken engagement. 'She was tough,' said Audrey, 'and when her employer offered her a small rise she asked for more. She had kept the books so efficiently that she was able to point out how much she had increased his turnover.'

Clarie and Frank Moulton remained dedicated Baptists all their lives, with the Knightrider Street Church their social centre.

Audrey found home a quiet place, very domesticated, with simple and healthy food. 'Roast beef always on Saturday,' says Audrey, 'and then cold on Sundays, because of church, cold with lovely creamy mashed potatoes.' Her emphasis is on creamy, as if she remembers them with special relish after the hymns and the long sermon, and the chat that followed. And there were delicious tarts and pies too, made from soft fruit grown in the Moultons' ninety-foot garden, which was tended by an uncommunicative jobbing gardener called Mr Harvey, who, unlike the Homes' servants, did little to brighten the life of those around him.

Life passed slowly while Audrey read Angela Brazil and wished from time to time that she was at boarding school. There were walks in the Kentish woods to find wild irises and orchids, picnics, summer holidays spent at Dymchurch, Hythe, Folkestone, Broadstairs and later, Devon and Cornwall and happy days spent with her mother's sister Bertha who had lost her fiancé in the war and lived in a little house in Watford.

On to this staid provincial scene came Leonard James Callaghan in 1929, a seventeen-year-old inland revenue tax clerk fortunate, his mother thought, to have a safe job in Maidstone in the midst of the Depression. He took lodgings, attended the same church, taught a Bible class and, within days, was invited to tea at Runswick.

From the first this fatherless youth was captivated by the house and hospitality, as well as the elegant girl. 'She had a steady home,' he explained later. 'Mother, father, motor car. I'd had a life of moving around. I had one, two . . . nine houses and I can remember them all.'

For Audrey, at first he must have been the brother she had always wanted, a fellow Sunday school teacher and tennis partner.

'She was very good,' Jim told me, 'an excellent player.' But when I asked whether she had beaten him, he hesitated, perhaps through a trace of male chauvinism, and, coming quickly to the rescue, Audrey said, 'We always played *with* each other not *against*.' Indeed, they soon became a formidable pair at doubles.

In those days Jim was slimmer than now, tall with strong shoulders, black hair, black-lashed blue eyes under black brows with a small cleft in a strong chin. His father and maternal grandfather had both been naval chief petty officers. His father, who was of Roman Catholic descent, changed his name from Garoghan to Callaghan to disguise his identity when he ran away from home to join the navy as an under-age volunteer. An honest God-fearing Irishman, CPO Callaghan had volunteered both to serve on the royal yacht *Victoria and Albert*, and to go with Scott to the Antarctic. His wife, a Devon girl, persuaded him to take the first option. They already had a daughter, born in 1904, and since the yacht was rarely used she hoped to see more of him that way. In consequence it was Petty Officer Evans who perished with Scott, Jim Callaghan was conceived, and his father lived to fight in the Great War. Wounded at the Battle of Jutland, CPO Callaghan was invalided out at the end of hostilities and moved with his family to Brixham, Devon, where he became a coastguard. His wife, Charlotte Cundy, known to Jim Callaghan's children as Grandma Lottie, was a dauntless woman, previously married at twenty to another sailor who drowned in Plymouth harbour. The baby of that union also died, but Lottie was one of those stalwart characters who are strengthened by disaster. She was, Audrey says, a great raconteuse, merry-hearted and, in today's terms, a 'survivor'. A devout Baptist with a sharp tongue, she insisted that grace be said before meals, and believed implicitly in the importance of honesty and hard work. Lottie Callaghan was destined to suffer loss. Jim's father died at forty-four of stomach trouble and a heart attack, the after-effects, it was said, of his war wounds, leaving Lottie with only a small lump sum of money on which to live.

Back in Portsmouth, she struggled to survive, moving from one set of rooms to another with her two children, while Jim went to Portsmouth primary and secondary schools. He has since said that he was an idle scholar, but when he reached his teens he was always in the top three in the class. Lottie's request for a pension was refused by the Tories under Baldwin, but granted during Ramsay MacDonald's first Labour government at the rate of ten shillings a week, a fact which left an indelible mark in Jim's mind and turned his mother overnight into a Labour supporter. Those who have been deeply affected by poverty never forget and today Jim cannot bear well-placed patronising people with silken tongues. 'I was conscious we were poor,' he said in a much quoted interview with Terry Coleman of *The Guardian* in 1970. 'That led to one or two things I shall not describe to you . . . I hate injustice. I hate people not getting their rights. I will go out of my way to help any inarticulate man who doesn't know where to go for help, who comes into my committee rooms . . .' But not, he said, the 'smooth people' who can help themselves. The toughness of the man who has fought his way up remains. Out of old habit, one suspects, he will sometimes brace himself, stand four square, and look belligerent. This is a stance that has survived the better years, which neither Macmillan nor Lord Home would ever take. There is something of the bull about it, the fighter, not the actor, although in milder moments, Jim will promote the avuncular image by which most of his public know him.

By 1930 his years of poverty were over. Securely employed, he was earing 33/6d a week, and slowly falling in love with a slightly directionless middle-class girl whose expectations of marital happiness were fortunately practical and realistic as well as romantic, a girl who wasn't sure of her own mind as school life ended and adulthood arrived.

'I had no idea what I wanted to do,' she says now, still conscious that she finds personal decisions difficult. 'But a friend of mine was doing domestic science and seemed to enjoy it, so I followed suit.' She laughs a little disparagingly at herself for taking the soft option, the safe, tried path. She trained at the Battersea College of Domestic Science, lived in its hostel, joined the Fabian Society and went with Jim, who travelled up from Kent, to lectures by most of the Labour thinkers of the day, including Harold Laski, who became a friend, and George Bernard Shaw. At nineteen, Jim had passed the necessary examinations to become a junior tax officer and was soon to become an official in the Inland Revenue Staff Federation, because, he said, no one else wanted to travel to Canterbury for the meetings. With customary zeal he read Beatrice and Sidney Webb's book on trade unionism so that he would know more about the job than anyone else.

Politics were now a frequent subject of conversation at the Moultons' house. Audrey and Jim championed the Labour cause while Audrey's parents stood up for the Tories. Feelings ran high but good nature prevailed through all the arguments. Jim and Audrey continued, like the Wilsons, to play tennis together — though more expertly. These were the days before the mini-skirt when the game provided one of the few occasions, apart from swimming, when a young man could see almost the full length of his girl's legs — Audrey's were enviably slender. Jim has always enjoyed the sight of a well turned-out woman and Audrey never lacked a certain style. She might not feel cuddly but she was athletic and graceful. Photographs of the time show delicate features, wavy brown hair, and that wide disarming smile which reveals unusually short teeth, looks which suggest that Jim was lucky she waited so long. From the first she must have seen a lovable and admirable side to him not immediately recognised by many of his colleagues; he was a friend, who turned into her young man with much assumed and little said, a state of affairs a more neurotic and highly charged girl might have found impossible to sustain. Her parents seemed unable to find out how matters stood from Jim Callaghan as the years passed, such were the middle-class inhibitions of the 'thirties, that half-way house between the Victorian formalities of courtship and the liberated habits of today. Nonplussed, Frank Moulton vainly asked Douglas (later Lord) Houghton, Jim's colleague and friend, whether he knew what the young man's intentions were, but canny Jim had kept his own counsel, while Audrey characteristically left him to make up his own mind.

'I often ask his advice, but he never asks mine,' she says now with disarming simplicity.

Although Jim was clearly English, someone somewhere must have made the obvious joke about 'an Irish engagement'. But Audrey's parents dealt delicately with their daughter's sensibilities; good manners dictated that emotions were private, personal questions taboo, and Audrey is vague now about when the relationship was formalised. 'I can't remember,' she says. 'Perhaps we got engaged on my twenty-first birthday. I think he bought me a ring then. It is awful how much one forgets.'

He was certainly a handsome man, not to be overlooked. In photographs of members of the church tennis club he is the dominant figure, so that in any circumstances you might ask, 'Who is that man?' Burly and strong, with just a touch of arrogance, he towers at the back, while Audrey, hair centrally parted, sits smiling demurely at the front. Frank Moulton, the captain, smiles earnestly, pleasant-faced, a little solemn, with the spare figure of a sportsman. Frank Moulton belongs to this small-town, Nonconformist scene, but Leonard James Callaghan does not. Knightrider Street Baptist Church had only briefly provided a link for Jim with childhood and his mother, the undemanding cosiness and the strict guide lines he knew so well. When a fellow Labour Party member said in 1976, 'Jim cares about the Labour movement, those dreary committee rooms, the bad teas, the duplicating machines that get ink everywhere, the old ladies writing notices with exasperating slowness. Jim *likes* all that,' he had perhaps forgotten that Jim had grown up and found his wife in an atmosphere of earnest endeavour, chapel socials, ladies in cardigans, struggles that were often essentially local but also, the workers believed, for the greater good of the world. So when Jim and Audrey later visited committee rooms during campaigns they were on familiar ground touched with nostalgia, only this time it was the idea of the Labour philosophy and manifesto rather than God that spurred on the workers.

So the young Jim, new to Maidstone, had sensibly found his way to the church of his youthful beliefs, and captured the love of the prettiest girl in the congregation. When promotion came he left for

London, never to return to the Baptist fold except for his wedding. By 1932 James Callaghan and Audrey Moulton were a modern couple unhampered by the mores of their parents' generation, breaking away early from the constraints of home. Audrey became a domestic science teacher in Eltham, where she lived in a rented room. In 1935, at this stage always a little doubtful about the wisdom of choosing a practical rather than an academic subject, she enrolled in a four-year evening economics course at Eltham Hill School, where one of her lecturers was Hugh Gaitskell, who became a friend.

A companionable summer followed when Jim and Audrey drove around the countryside in a Wolseley, which they bought for £8.10s and sold for thirty shillings as winter approached.

In 1937 they went on holiday together to Lucerne, a try-out before the leap into matrimony the following year, at two o'clock on July 28th, Audrey's birthday.

They were married in Knightrider Street in the rather severe grey stone church where they had met, which stands just across the road from the grander, older All Saints Church. Many of the congregation had watched Audrey grow up and the wedding was almost a family affair, for Frank Moulton had been superintendent of the Sunday school, captain of the tennis club and, in 1938, church secretary. In 1919 he had been elected as a deacon, and it was through the Bible class and the Nonconformist network that he was offered a post in the Lead Wool Company where he worked until retirement. The presents were quite conventional. Audrey gave Jim an Omega watch which he still wears: he gave her a fur wrap, which was later stolen. Family and close friends presented cheques and furniture. The combined generosity of the officers and executives of the Inland Revenue Staff Federation of which Jim had become the full time assistant secretary in 1936, produced a canteen of cutlery and a cheque; and other presents predictably included kitchen equipment, china and glass.

Jim and Audrey were married by the minister, the Reverend Robinson Brunskill, assisted by the Reverend Sidney Carter, husband of Jim's sister, Dorothy. Audrey wore a white slipper-satin gown with a train and a long flowing veil held by a wreath of orange blossom. She carried a sheaf of white lilies. Jim wore morning dress. The bridesmaids, pale in ice-blue silk crepe, were Sonia, Jim's niece, Audrey's sister Jeanne, and a cousin, Eileen Cross, chosen partly for her height, for Audrey was always conscious of her own tallness. The best man was Jim's friend Archie Clark.

In a church decorated with pink roses and white daisies, guests took their seats to the rousing strains of Purcell's 'Trumpet Tune and Air' which was followed as Audrey walked up the aisle by the Bridal Chorus from Lohengrin. The hymns were old friends, 'All Creatures of Our God and King' and 'O Perfect Love', but the music to accompany the signing of the register was significantly modern for the time, Dvořak's 'Humoreske'.

Unlike the Homes, the young Callaghans look totally relaxed in their wedding photographs; well turned-out, middle class and happy, they could have been the children of bankers, stockbrokers, land owners. Only the relations, Jim's mother a little grim in her edge-to-edge coat and Audrey's parents, suggest lower steps on the social ladder. Still Christians but no longer weekly churchgoers, Jim and Audrey had grown out of their backgrounds, moved on to what they must have seen as wider fields. Audrey mentions no teenage rebellion, only occasional irritation towards her parents, but in several ways she had already rejected some of their beliefs, as she mixed with atheists and agnostics, equipping herself to fight for the rights of the poor. The churches seemed to accept the poor as part of God's plan, in need of alms and succour rather than the peaceful, legitimate social revolution desired by Jim and Audrey.

Few of the guests can have suspected this dilution of faith and change of endeavour as they crowded into Great Danes, a Tudor restaurant in Bearsted. After champagne and a sit-down tea, the future prime minister and his wife, whose dress was a shade of rust, left by train to Folkestone en route to Paris and Chamonix.

'We had proper boots,' Audrey says, 'but we didn't actually climb. We walked.' This decision was somehow typical of two people known later for a moderation which has infuriated the left wing.

They came back to a white three-bedroomed house, 18 High View Close, Croydon, up on a hill with a pleasant garden and integral garage. It was a nearly new house in a wholly respectable cul-de-sac, whose solidness added to the sense of stability Jim Callaghan needed after his penurious nomadic childhood. So his marriage started properly, as he wanted, on a secure financial footing with his wife living in the circumstances to which she was accustomed. Jim was often away attending meetings and conferences, so that, although he was not yet a politician, Audrey grew used to these absences, for which her father's industriousness had prepared her. But it was a time when nobody could plan ahead; as Hitler's armies grew, Poland trembled and secure domestic happiness seemed suddenly as temporary as a trip down the river. And when it came, war found Jim Callaghan impatient in a reserved occupation.

In 1940, after the bombing started and after the birth of Margaret, the Callaghans' first daughter, Jim's office was moved to Llandudno in Wales, and a maisonette at the top of Winchmore House where he worked was made available to the Callaghans. Here, high among the tree tops, Audrey looked out to sea from the front and to Mount Snowdon at the back. At night she could hear the bombs falling on Liverpool and sometimes see the sky glowing red and gold from the flames of the incendiaries. Maidstone had been designated a security area, so she rarely visited her parents, and when her sister married an engineer in London she felt unable to go to the wedding. So, although spared the actual horrors, she was stamped, as all the spouses discussed in this book are, by some of war's deprivation, a greater divide between her and future generations than years alone can create. Yet life was made easier by the Nonconformist church upbringing that taught that happiness is to be found in the soul rather than in the pursuit of material things.

She is remembered differently by those who knew her in Llandudno; as sensible and kind, a generous woman, politically committed, who always saw that the babysitters were given a meal despite rationing — a feat in wartime.

One of these, a girl in the typing pool who married a man much older than herself, to her mother's disapproval, remembers how Audrey bolstered her morale and guided her hand. 'She lent me her veil for the wedding. She fed my guests afterwards and looked after my mother. She was a person who would always lend anything to anyone. A good manager.'

Such praise seems banal to Audrey.

'Someone came to talk to me about my writing a book on my life as prime minister's wife,' she told me. 'Jim wanted me to do it, but I would rather be outside picking beans in the garden any day than writing a book about myself. I mean what could be more boring?' So perhaps after all Jim's joke was closer to the mark than either liked to admit; perhaps the tentative schoolgirl was overwhelmed by the dominating brilliance of the young man who became a notable orator and was to be prime minister, and has ever since measured herself against him. There is no trace of the performer about Audrey; she is absolutely genuine and incapable of putting on an act.

But in insisting on her ordinariness, Audrey has overlooked the fact that ninety-nine per cent of the population might appear dull if measured against the leaders of the land, that performance is not everything, that sometimes the deepest and most complex characters erect around themselves the stoutest defences. 'No one could ever write a biography about my mother. There wouldn't be enough to say,' Margaret Jay told me, accepting Audrey's own assessment of herself. And yet at the same time Audrey is expressing a state of mind which must affect all the spouses of prominent people, which results in part from the constant inevitable relegation to second place. Eyes will always look away from you to the greater being, your spouse, reinforcing over and over again any feelings of inadequacy, the sense that 'I am only here because I am his wife, not because I am myself,' which, however strong the personality of the consort, will rise like a spectre at so many feasts. In earlier times when a woman was expected to marry well and make her way through her husband it mattered less. Lady Dorothy Macmillan and Elizabeth Home who moved in such circles could accept the position more happily with light-hearted irony or pride, but for Audrey, whose friends were often professional women known in their own right, it continued occasionally to demoralise.

Even in those early days in Llandudno when she and Jim formed a branch of the Fabian Society, inviting left-wing speakers which included John Parker, Harold Laski and the 'red' Dean, Hewlett Johnson, Jim could take over an argument she had started and make it seem more pungent, his personality overshadowing hers. Heads would turn when he spoke, a man with a future, while Audrey remained simply a wife. He disarmingly describes himself now as indolent, without expecting to be believed, but in Llandudno even the most exhausting rugby football matches (he played for the staff federation) did not work off all his aggression or pacify his deep discontent at not fighting for his country. He is recalled by some of his colleagues of the time as an angry young man, who would continue reading the newspaper when Audrey's friends came to tea, and also paradoxically as a 'cold fish' with a 'limp handshake', descriptions which do not fit the warm-hearted grandfather we know today, or the bullish man who can be blisteringly critical of his social equals, but is undoubtedly a good listener and has his mother's gift as a raconteur.

Before Dunkirk he had volunteered for the navy, only to be told to join the army. Never one to take 'no' for an answer, he wrote again saying it was 'monstrous' considering that his father and grandfather had both been chief petty officers in the navy.

'That's one of the nice things about the navy,' he said later. 'I got a letter from the admiralty from a lieutenant-commander RN, retired, saying yes, I was right; to go and ask to join the navy again, and show them this letter.'

The ploy worked, but the staff federation refused to spare Jim until 1942, after the birth of the Callaghan's second daughter Julia.

When Jim finally left to become a sailor, Audrey started the loneliest, hardest years of her life, as head of a one-parent family with two children and sixty-seven steps to climb up to the maisonette.

'And Julia was a very plump baby,' she recalls, wearying at the thought. 'It was very hard.'

But she shored up the Llandudno branch of the Fabian Society, while Jim started his naval life on a mine-sweeping trawler in the North Sea and was later commissioned, as legend has it, after a sharp-eyed censor had noticed he was carrying on an intelligent correspondence with Harold Laski. Drafted into naval intelligence, Callaghan served in Iceland as a liaison officer with the Icelandic government. Then in January 1945 Audrey moved with Margaret and Julia from Llandudno back to Maidstone, where the Callaghans rented 13 Ashford Road, a long, low, white house, tile-hung with the special charm sometimes found in places near the sea. It stood above the town by the girls' high school, catching the sunlight, a lane at the side, a long garden in front. From here Audrey, with her usual political drive, ran yet another branch of the Fabian Society and became chairman of the local Labour Party. May, the daughter of Jim's old landlady, baby-sat when the Moultons could not. May was known as Auntie to the young Callaghans, and became Audrey's standby over the years, especially when the clash came between politics and children.

'She wasn't really a baby-sitter,' Audrey explains. 'She was *in loco parentis*. She lived in when I had to attend party conferences and that sort of thing. The children loved her.'

And because Audrey was not tuned in to child psychology in quite the same way as Mary Wilson was, because she was not so possessive, but quite low-key, the arrangement worked; she could leave and not expect tears and tantrums from the youngest on her return. Her life was always made easier on such occasions by the matter-of-fact approach which was to be the hallmark of her life; her assumption that things would turn out all right, her lack of unnecessary anxiety.

In 1945 Jim put himself forward for selection as a Labour parliamentary candidate, backed by John Parker and Harold Laski. His first hope was Reading which he lost to Portsmouth schoolmate, Ian Mikardo, because he was at sea when the selection conference met. But later he won the candidature for Cardiff South beating George Thomas, the future speaker of the House, by one vote. It was the year their son Michael was born, and the year of victory, when Jim was out in the Indian Ocean chasing a Japanese cruiser while others celebrated VE day.

With three small children and no servants Audrey could not, like Lady Dorothy Macmillan, keep her husband's constituency warm, but the Labour Party saw to it that he was flown back six weeks before the general election to contest the seat. He was actually one of those who had promoted the Labour cause during the war, when so many men and women, who had never before strayed far from their own villages and towns, mingled with more sophisticated and politically educated colleagues, hearing the Socialist message of fair shares for all, equality and justice, a quiet campaign waged in mess rooms and barracks, on ship and shore, wherever a committed Labour man had the will and the audience. A cabin mate in Iceland later recalled how Jim converted him. 'After a couple of weeks I was enquiring what steps I should take to become a Labour Member of Parliament.' At home Audrey continued with Fabianism and the Conservatives at large seemed complacent in the belief that the British nation would rally behind the victorious Churchill.

Callaghan won Cardiff South with a majority of 5,944 beating Sir Arthur Evans who had held the seat for nineteen of the previous twenty-one years. He had the full and unequivocal backing of his wife, who would never grudge the long hours he spent away from home because his cause was her cause, and she had never expected him to be anything other than a politician.

'Audrey,' he was to say, with measured modesty, 'gave me middle-class stability.'

So, with marriage and love settled, three children born, reasonable financial security, he was free to push ahead, and in those heady days of 1945 opportunities for the young and talented in Parliament seemed to abound. He was not only a member but also, within weeks, appointed by Clement Attlee to be parliamentary private secretary to his friend and fellow Fabian, John Parker, now undersecretary of state for the dominion office. Hugh Dalton also invited Callaghan to join a small group of able Labour men with experience of finances. Although Callaghan was later to resign his parliamentary private secretaryship, it was a favourable beginning.

Audrey, however, says, 'That was the worst time, when Jim was commuting and I was in Maidstone with three small children.' The idea that she is a very motherly woman fades. She loves children; in feminine company grandchildren are her most frequent topic of conversation, but she is not a woman who can lose herself in motherhood, she needs a certain degree of freedom. Her sense of identity, although never formulated in her own mind, refuses to be submerged. Despite domestic science studies, she is not a person who would ever be a slave to the sink, and has usually managed to employ someone else to do the rough work. When I put it to her that I was shocked to find that a robust Russian children's author, whom I knew, employed a fulltime maid to look after her in Moscow, Audrey mildly remarked that it gave someone employment, while I fretted about inequality in a communist state.

But behind that gentle aspect there is a stubbornness which will always resist exploitation when she sees it, the strength of will which anyone married to a man of Jim Callaghan's calibre and temperament needs.

'Remember you're not playing for the second eleven any more,' Clem Attlee advised Jim when he appointed him parliamentary secretary in the ministry of transport in 1947, 'you're playing for the first eleven. And one thing: if you're going to do business with somebody don't insult him the day beforehand.' The advice was heeded. The public may well remember Callaghan best in that job for the extension of cats' eyes to British roads — a life saver rather than a vote catcher. In 1950 he was moved as the junior minister to the admiralty, and appointed Labour Party member of the Consultative Assembly of the Council of Europe. Unlike Harold Macmillan, he could not take his wife and while he struggled to improve his French and fought against the setting up of a European army, Audrey canvassed and campaigned in local government elections. 'A cheerful companion,' Hugh Dalton said of Jim, 'and,' he added, 'a very capable and self-confident young man.'

Soon the Callaghans moved back to London, settling high above Lewisham where the wind blows free and large Victorian houses look at one another across Burnt Ash Road. Behind these and new developments runs Guibal Road, where the Callaghans bought Number 83, which in several ways resembled their earlier homes. It stood on top of a hill, part pebble-dashed with a timbered elevation and leaded panes, the only one of its kind in a street notable for duplicates. Built in 1925, it had five bedrooms, kitchen, dining- and sitting-room as well as a small study overlooking the road. The verandah at the back led to a long garden with an old apple tree for the children to climb; there was a garage and parking space at the front. From the first-floor back window the Callaghans, who like views, could look across a residential valley to White Horse Hill, Chislehurst, Kent, a scene which gave the illusion of wooded countryside.

Now the Callaghans definitely belonged to the professional classes, as Audrey employed an au pair and took a part-time job as a dietician at a local clinic for expectant mothers.

'We used to help her draw the charts, specifying which vitamins were to be found in which foods,' Margaret Jay says. 'She was very good with the au pairs, going to great lengths to find them friends, looking after their social life and putting them in touch with the right churches if they were religious.'

Margaret and Julia belonged to the local Brownies, a movement which still holds Audrey's regard. Their education and upbringing Margaret Jay described as totally middle-class: kindergarten before school, ballet and music lessons, swimming, everything you might expect for that section of the community except riding.

'Mother was always very supportive,' Margaret says. 'My father is the one who pushed. But we were very protected and when I went to

Oxford I was incredibly naive. I knew nothing about life.'

The girls were educated at Blackheath High School and Michael went to Dulwich College as a direct grant pupil. For, whatever his Labour convictions might be about equality, Jim was determined that his children would be well educated.

'He was the efficient one, the tidy one,' Margaret says. 'He has always been able to put his finger at once on anything he needs. Mother was less organised. She didn't file her letters. Her methods were different.'

Jim was having to temper his ideals a little, and in 1950 he voted in support of the introduction of prescription charges, a decision he probably would not have contemplated for a moment a few years earlier.

When the Tories regained control in 1951 he kept his seat. 'Yes, I helped canvass,' Audrey says. 'I always help. We all do. We should hate to miss it.' And the next year she stood unsuccessfully in the LCC election as Labour candidate for Lewisham North polling 14,110 votes against her nearest rival's 16,190, while Jim was elected to both the national executive of the Labour Party and to the shadow cabinet. Over the next twelve years he was to be remarkably successful.

A table in *Callaghan, The Road to Number Ten* by Peter Kellner and Christopher Hitchens shows that Callaghan was elected to the shadow cabinet every year from 1951 until 1963, winning the most votes in 1960 and 1962 and coming second the following year. For Audrey, his success must have been a source of great pride and satisfaction. But now maturity and success had persuaded him to see even more clearly the shades of grey that lie between black and white. In 1955 he wrote in a *News Chronicle* article, 'I want a classless society — even though we are going to take longer to get there than I used to think. I am against a centralised state machine that would control all our affairs. It degenerates into tyranny. On the other hand, I don't want private enterprise to rule the roost — it is irresponsible.'

Unlike Alec Douglas-Home, he was impressive on television, a sensible, well fed, well balanced person. 'A good man to be in a shell hole with,' is how one of my octogenarian friends described him. And on the farm, in a heavy dark sweater he does have the aura of a coastguard about him, he is the reliable-looking man you would run to if your child was lost or your boat drifting out to sea, the stalwart sailor you would ask about tides.

In 1953 on the day of King George VI's funeral the Callaghans moved to 40 Maze Hill, an early Victorian house with a walled garden and bay window looking directly across Greenwich Park, from which they planned a new abode, on land facing Blackheath, bought jointly with their architect friends Gordon and Ursula Bowyer. Here the Bowyers designed two houses, one for themselves and one for the Callaghans, 17 and 17a Montpelier Row. From the oustide the houses looked more like maisonettes because of the integral garages, but inside they were spacious and light, with a study for Jim on the ground floor. Each house still reflect the needs and tastes of its first occupier. The Callaghans wanted a more traditional interior than the Bowyers whose ground and second floor are open-plan. Audrey asked for an old-fashioned sink and eschewed a fully fitted kitchen. The position was idyllic, the long room upstairs with dining area and kitchen off, looks both ways, into the lush garden and right across the wide heath. Despite its newness, the house was in keeping with the Callaghans' spirit of moderation.

The Bowyers are close friends of the Callaghans, a couple in partnership. Their first big commission was the sports section for the Festival of Britain Exhibition in 1951, and others, in a long and distinguished career, include Peckham Methodist Church, Charlton Assembly Hall, a home for handicapped children in East Dulwich, the treasury at Gloucester Cathedral and most recently the War Cabinet Room Museum under Whitehall. The Bowyers are an example of the kind of people the Callaghans like, hard working, talented professionals, and Ursula Bowyer describes Audrey as 'a very pleasant, and extremely intelligent person.'

In 1958 Audrey, while still at Maze Hill, was elected Labour councillor for Lewisham North on the LCC along with the distinguished Conservatives, Christopher Chataway and Norman (later Sir Norman) Farmer, so becoming the only prime minister's wife ever to have followed her own political career. She was steered, as most women are, to the committees dealing with children and health, two interests which were to be amalgamated in her work when she became chairman of the Hospitals for Sick Children. From the first she made her mark.

'She was,' says Christopher Chataway, 'one of the few people you always listened to with respect and care. She made no Party speeches. She was outspoken and actually tough, forthright. You knew she was sincere.' He says she lost her seat in 1961 because of a general swing to the Conservatives. 'It was nothing to do with her own performance.' But talking to her about this you scent a faint air of depression, suggesting that she feels otherwise. 'I was there such a short time,' she tells you, as though those three years are not now worth discussing.

In 1959 Jim Callaghan was appointed a visiting fellow at Nuffield College, Oxford, and in 1961 he turned as shadow chancellor to his university friends for help and instruction in the study of economics, frequently travelling down to Oxford on a Friday evening in term time to adjourn after dinner at high table for informal seminars with Ian Little, Thomas Balogh and Roger Opie. Dons of the time, quoted in *Callaghan, The Road to Number Ten*, remarked that he was 'eager — almost pathetically eager'. He showed a 'bluff common sense', and he was 'quick on the uptake'. 'My verdict,' one said 'would be that he was worth a good second class degree, but needed to learn more.' The search for self-improvement was an indication of the visiting fellow's lack of arrogance, very much in keeping with Audrey's old Labour Party's concern for self-education. Both Callaghans remain prepared to pick other people's brains on subjects where they feel they are less than knowledgeable, a rare and rather endearing trait in people who might be expected to throw their weight about, and one which perhaps reveals a sense of security strong enough to allow a confession of ignorance. But deep down there lies still a remnant of regret that Callaghan has no degree, a gap which ensured that Margaret, academically the most gifted of their children, should be steered to Oxford.

It was again in keeping with the Callaghans' characters and temperaments that they should support Gaitskell, with Jim voting for him rather than Harold Wilson for the Party leadership in 1960.

Audrey's father had died in 1956 with his Bible at his bedside and Mrs Moulton followed five years later. By this time the Callaghans were taking regular holidays on the Isle of Wight, where they had bought a cottage. Sometimes they went sailing with Reggie Paget (now Lord Paget), MP for Northampton and a naval lieutenant in the war.

'The three of us used to take out my Swedish boat,' Lord Paget says. 'John Strachey, Jim Callaghan and me. We used to have a lot of fun. In fact I think I gave Peter Jay his first sailing lesson. Audrey never came, so I never got to know her well, but she was awfully nice.'

'But I did sail sometimes,' Audrey says.

Lord Paget was a barrister, an Old Etonian who went on to Trinity, Cambridge. His upbringing was very different from Jim's, but he was now a fitting friend for a man who could no longer be described as working-class; Callaghan by now exuded authority, wore well cut suits, drank wine and was one of the more popular Labour members among the Conservative voters who knew him. Audrey's own tastes fitted in very well with the more trendy, youngish couples who had settled at Blackheath, shopping at the new boutiques, delicatessens and stores full of stripped pine furniture, cane baskets and pottery.

After Labour's return to power in 1964 under the leadership of Harold Wilson, Jim Callaghan became chancellor of the exchequer. The Callaghans let their Blackheath house and moved into Number 11 Downing Street which they found more spacious and convenient than they were later to find Number 10. In the same year Audrey became an alderman, partly, cynics might say, because of her husband's position, but in fact she had already been co-opted since 1961 on to committees concerned with children in care and was chairman of one which dealt with 3,000 girls at risk in south-east London.

'Women,' Jim Callaghan told me, 'like serving in local government because they see the tangible results of their labours: they like to get things done.'

I replied that it seemed to me that men like theorising and that there was an awful lot of talk in the House of Commons.

'You are suggesting that I've spent my life exuding hot air, thank you very much,' he said laughing.

Unsurprisingly, success evaded Jim Callaghan as chancellor, struggling for the right answer while the government moved from one financial crisis to another.

His budget in 1965 put up taxes on drink and tobacco and brought in capital gains tax and other deflationary measures, all on a tiny Labour majority, tiny enough to allow the clauses in the subsequent Finance Bill to be thrown out. In 1967 the most serious crisis arose when Callaghan, against his earlier judgement, felt forced to devalue. 'This,' he said in parliament, 'is the unhappiest day of my life.' On the actual evening of devaluation he resigned.

'I was very conscious,' he wrote to Wilson, 'that I was going back on pledges that I had given in good faith to a number of overseas countries about the value of their sterling holdings. No chancellor of the exchequer can escape this dilemma.'

Shortly afterwards Susan Crosland, whose husband was tipped as Jim's possible successor, met Audrey at an official lunch, 'dignified as always, discussing with Mrs Mulley something sensible like curing dry rot.' Mrs Crosland asked Audrey how she was. 'How can you get through a week like this?'

'I can't sleep,' Audrey said. 'I wake up and I can't make my brain stop. I would never advise Jim on politics, but I can't make my brain stop.' Susan Crosland replied that she had hoped experience 'would make it a little easier to deal with terrible anxiety'.

'It gets much worse, because the responsibility increases,' Audrey told her, with the calmness of a person who has learned complete self-control.

The Callaghans sold 17a Montpelier Row and in 1968 they bought Upper Clay Hill Farm near Lewes in Sussex and rented a flat in Kennington, deals which caused unpleasant rumours to circulate about their apparent financial prosperity, a hazard for any Labour politician. True or otherwise, the allegations did not suggest impropriety, but it is perhaps worth remembering that Audrey's family were not without resources and some of these were left to the Callaghans.

Upper Clay Hill Farm's house is Elizabethan with a Georgian addition, combining the best of two worlds, part pink-washed, part tile-hung, with two staircases, sash windows looking on to the lawn, lattice windows elsewhere. Audrey and Jim's bedroom is in the Georgian part, with his study leading off, above the drawing-room. The colours that greet you are predominantly yellow and springlike, with touches of red. The open fireplace in the dining-room was decked out in flowers the first day I went, because Audrey's birthday had just passed; the old chimney piece was thick with cards. Upstairs in one of the bedrooms used by grandchildren there is a bedside rug woven with a picture of Jim's head and face, on which the guests of the moment will trample every morning.

'Were you upset by cartoons and caricatures? Did they embarrass your children?' I asked Audrey.

'Come and look!' she said, pointing to several on the passage walls. 'Our children framed them and gave them to us for Christmas.' There were drawings by Hugh Casson too and a Rupert Shephard landscape and prints by John Bratby and Keith Vaughan, mixing with the efforts of grandchildren. Downstairs there were presents from friendly governments: an exquisite picture of a polo game painted on ivory, given to the Callaghans when they visited Iran, with other gifts in specially-made glass-fronted cabinets. The white walls give this house an air of spaciousness and light. Lots of polished wood adds a contrasting mellowness. Audrey's kitchen, white too, looks out on to a little courtyard and lawn and beyond are the farm buildings where her pigs lived. She took their breeding seriously, worried about the barley and laughed when I fed them titbits on my first visit as though they were horses. She liked, she said, to be around when they farrowed, but she refused to be sentimental. Some of them lay flaccid on bare concrete. 'Most of them have to go for bacon,' she said. 'If a sow fails to produce the goods she will soon be pork sausages.' There was just one part-time man to see to the sows. Audrey never actually mucked out the sties.

Any suggestion that she might have done so took Jim aback. 'No,' he said, at once, 'that is a very muscular job, man's work.'

It is the country garden Audrey really loves, scrambling around with trowel and fork, cherishing flowers and shrubs when there are no other calls on her time. Above all perhaps, she takes pleasure in gathering the soft fruit and vegetables, up there above Lewes, where once again a wind blows and the air is fresh with the tang from the sea less than ten miles away. And yet Audrey was never carried away with even this enthusiasm, as Lady Dorothy Macmillan was. She calmly kept a balance: time for the grandchildren, the social work, the duties as prime minister's wife.

Upper Clay Hill Farm was a refuge for Jim when he shouldered the arduous duties of home secretary, the office to which he had been appointed after he resigned as chancellor.

The story of his struggles to solve the Irish problem are told in his book *A House Divided*; and in this he writes on page two:

Another interest of mine was the care of children, which I learned about from my wife's activities in this field. It seemed to me that reform was long overdue and should take place on the principle that the care of children and the control of children should go hand in hand, instead of being divided between the courts and the local authority.

He tells of a talk with the Reverend Ian Paisley, especially significant because as we know Jim is part Irish, with both Roman Catholic and Protestant forbears. The passions he saw in Belfast between what were, in his own words, basically the same people, deeply shocked him.

'You know, Mr Paisley,' he said, 'we are all children of God.'

'We are not, Mr Callaghan,' replied Paisley, 'we are all the children of wrath.' And Paddy Devlin remembers the impact Callaghan made on the Falls Road. 'He has a great smile and a great wave and a great way of approaching people: the crowds came from everywhere to see Callaghan . . . and the atmosphere was dead right because he represented everything that was totally different from the sort of politicians that we had met before.'

But for Audrey it was a particularly worrying time. 'I think what shocked me most,' she said, 'was the strength of feeling of young children and old ladies, the hatred, the way they shouted at us. It was in awful contrast to the beautiful countryside.' There was an occasion when Jim was low with influenza and she was consulted on whether or not he should be wakened during a big disturbance; one of those moments when a consort is called upon to make a decision which is part wifely and part political. 'There was nothing he could do, so I said let him sleep on,' she recalled. And there was always the thought that he might be killed, brave or foolhardy Jim who walked amongst the crowds shaking hands, refusing a bullet-proof car.

Fortunately Audrey's own activities kept her increasingly busy and in 1969 she was appointed by the then minister of state for health, Baroness Serota, to the chairmanship of the board of the Hospitals for Sick Children at Great Ormond Street. As chairman herself of the GLC children's committee Baroness Serota had been impressed by Audrey's contribution to juvenile welfare. This prestigious and important appointment was to enable Audrey to give notable public service over the next thirteen years, and it would be no exaggeration to say that she throve on it. She had of course been brought up to believe in charitable work, but in a way this was more than that. It was a position of power as well as trust.

An album commemorating the service she gave records special events during her chairmanship: the opening of the Hayward Building at the Queen Elizabeth Hospital and the Mildred Creek Unit, and the computerised tomography scanner in the presence of the Queen; royal visits from the monarchy of several nations; nurses' prize-giving ceremonies; the foundation stone and topping out ceremony for the cardiac wing and so on. She is always cheerful in these photographs, as she was in those early tennis club groups; sometimes laughing outright, leaning forward a little as she walks as tall people often do. Sometimes the image is different — with a particular hat, she occasionally almost resembles the public's idea of a Tory woman.

'She wasn't a tiresomely dogmatic chairman,' comments Mr R.G.B. Milchem, house governor of the time. 'She cared more about the matters being discussed than the form of the meeting, and because she was gentle she could be misjudged, because in fact she was very astute. She did not particularly like being in the chair. She was there to further a cause.'

That cause became undoubtedly a major factor of Audrey's life, which, partly because Callaghan did not seek her political advice or help except at election time, also helped their marriage. She became a public figure in her own right with her own worries and commitments. She had the joy of travelling abroad with her husband not simply as wife of the foreign secretary or prime minister, but as chairman of one of the world's most famous hospitals for children.

'She always consulted heads of department and groups, within the hospital, with interests abroad so that she could find out for them the latest developments in their field,' said Miss Betty Barchard, the chief nursing officer. Yet during her chairmanship she probably met occasional opposition from the medical staff.

'But,' says Miss Barchard, 'in this hospital she was chairman first and prime minister's wife second, and when one or two militant strikers tried to use her position in the winter of discontent, she resisted.'

'During those trade union troubles in 1979,' explained Mr Milchem, more prosaically, she never let politics come into it. She was very vulnerable but her tremendous loyalty to the hospital and hospital needs was outstanding. She was looking always for the fair answer. She could not condemn the unions, but she did condemn the militant stance some members took. It was not like the old Labour movement. After a pause, Miss Barchard said, 'We all hold her in the greatest affection. I think it is important to say that. Of course she was occasionally absent-minded, she mislaid her glasses sometimes or her papers.'

'Sometimes when parents are not satisfied with the treatment of a child,' explained Mr Milchem, 'we arrange for them to meet the chairman, Miss Barchard and myself, and I have seen the tears come into Mrs Callaghan's eyes when the case is sad, that is a measure of her compassion.'

'A kind endearing lady,' summed up Miss Barchard, 'with the interests of the children at heart, a great concern for the staff and a great sense of humour.'

These loyal officials must certainly cast doubt on Audrey's assessment of herself, but she feels she could have done more. She does not seek praise; she has no wish to be honoured for her work. Knighthoods and peerages, she says, are 'all right for other people if they want them.'

Callaghan's years at the foreign office from 1974–6 were marred by his problems with Cyprus, the cod war with Iceland, South Africa, the black states in the commonwealth, Rhodesia, and inevitably the common market. Although he largely kept his own counsel he worked closely with Henry Kissinger who became a friend.

He preferred to have his own supporters around him, and when Joan Lestor asked why she had been moved from the foreign office to be parliamentary under-secretary, department of education and science he replied, 'You see, my dear, the trouble is that I like to have people around me who are *friends* of mine.' 'Jim,' she said later, 'is a very kind man and very pleasant to work with until you cross him.'

Audrey became hostess to diplomatic wives and president of their association. 'It was a serious organisation,' she explained, 'we looked after the new ones, but we also discussed conditions, schooling arrangements for the children, allowances and so on.' Like Lady Home and Lady Dorothy Macmillan, she also met world leaders. In the Soviet Union she was impressed more by the restoration of bombed palaces and churches, which she loved, than the style of life.

She visited the Gulf States, and six African countries in twelve days. The Victoria Falls were a 'rainbow of splashing water'. Parts of Malawi reminded her of Scotland and she remembers with affection a great banquet there, African-style, with the women sitting on one side of the table, the men on the other and everyone clapping loudly and obediently at the right moments. Hastings Banda's garden she found 'very tidy and flourishing'. In Nigeria there were horrific traffic jams, which the policemen tried to break by kicking cars that were in their way. She particularly loved Gamborone, the capital of Botswana, where the popular woman British high commissioner won her regard and admiration. She looked at the cattle with a farmer's eye and found them beautiful. Ruth Khama became a friend and Audrey conceived a great respect and affection for the British diplomatic corps.

High commissioners and ambassadors found her pleasant and homely; her interest in schools and hospitals made it easy to arrange trips for her. 'I always did my homework,' she told me. 'It is much more fun if you know something about the country before you visit it.' She studied the schedules she was given before planning her wardrobe. She drew on her domestic science training to supervise the menus and to deal with caterers and cooks when entertaining at Dorneywood. She felt, in her own words, that she could 'speak with knowledge and experience to the staff'. The foreign office was more fun than the home office or treasury.

Although Jim had advance notice, the Callaghans were as much surprised by Harold Wilson's resignation as anyone else, and although Audrey had always known that he might go far, Jim's elevation to the leadership was sooner than either expected. Overnight he became the first man ever to have held the four major offices of state. A *New York Times* reporter described him on April 6th as 'blunt, ambitious, politically cunning with an almost genuine yearning to serve as a unifier of the party. He is deeply conservative, distrusting, even hating extremes.'

One of Audrey's first tasks as premier's wife was to speak at the opening of an exhibition of American furniture and furnishings, when in a 'rather tart speech' (said *The Times* correspondent) she expressed a hope that Britain would also sell furniture to America. Later in the summer she wrote as chairman of Great Ormond Street Hospitals to the South African Ambassador expressing deep concern about the arrest of a seven-months pregnant woman on conspiracy charges.

From now on Audrey was determined that she would use her position as prime minister's wife to help her charities. She was anxious, too, that as many of her friends and colleagues as possible should see 10 Downing Street. Great Ormond Street nurses were invited to help with her annual party for handicapped children. A cocktail party was given for all senior members of staff. Officials from the hospital often came to the flat for discussions when Audrey could not spare time to go to the hospital. A delighted Miss Barchard found herself on a list for diplomatic parties when an extra single woman was needed.

Audrey loved the views from the sitting-room in the prime minister's private flat. 'St James's Park one way and Horse Guards the other.' But she describes the flat as rather like a 'railway carriage.' The dining-room and kitchen were 'small and inadequate'. 'You could,' she said, 'entertain downstairs if you wanted, but even then the kitchen was too far away and too small.' She hated having no back door. 'It is ridiculous that everything has to come in and go out by that one entrance.' She believes is is time the prime minister's residence caught up with modern technology. But all this is not to say she was unhappy. There was much that she loved about the job. If she had her life again she would still like a spell as premier's wife. Unable to make structural alterations the Callaghans left the décor as it was because Audrey said, 'Edward Heath had had it beautifully done up by Colefax and Fowler.' Heath had also turned his mind to Chequers where a swimming pool had been installed and a smaller room turned into the second drawing-room the Homes had wanted for entertaining.

Jim had spoken of his aims on a television broadcast on April 26th. 'I want our administration, not only to make Britain economically healthier, but to make it a society with greater fairness and greater social justice.' These words could equally well have summed up Macmillan's aspirations, which is not surprising; both appeared to want to lift up the proletariat rather than pull the rug from under the feet of the capitalists. Indeed, there were Labour left-wing members who regretted Callaghan's previous connections with the Italian International Bank and the Commercial Bank of Wales, along with his alleged friendships with Lord Cobbold, Sir Charles Forte and Sir

Julian Hodge, whose firm had provided loans for a pyramid-selling operation. Peter Kellner and Christopher Hitchens comment on the fact that Callaghan did not specifically deny *Private Eye's* information on his links with Hodge, but everything about the Callaghans suggests that, unlike the Wilsons, they are not inclined towards libel actions. Audrey, who would certainly have hated the publicity, has not even read *The Road to Number Ten*.

She was at Callaghan's side whenever he needed her, but kept her own identity and friends and he, in turn, remained interested in her life as a committee woman. Margaret Jay, with a sharp eye for significant detail, remembers her father going up to Number 10's flat after a day when events had come close to toppling the government. Most husbands, she reflects, given the circumstances, would have brought their worries with them, but Jim Callaghan turned to Audrey and immediately asked after the meeting she had been chairing at Great Ormond Street. He suppressed a politician's essential egoism, stored away for the moment his own mind-bending problems to think of hers. It was an action symptomatic of how he feels a political marriage should be. A prime minister's wife, he says firmly, should have a life of her own. And, in many ways, Audrey Callaghan is the most modern of the spouses since the war. Her press has been good. Her image does not lend itself to caricature, being without those strands of absurdity, those quirks of character or class distinctions which bring light to the satirist's eye. Stories about her life as a politician's wife tend to stress her altruism or sometimes an occasional loneliness.

'I can't exactly remember where I met her,' said close friend Roshan Horobin, a distinguished Pakistani probation officer, 'but soon after I came across her at a reception at the Pakistani embassy sitting alone, I went over and we had a long talk, and she was very interested in my work.'

'Sometimes,' Audrey says, 'I go into my shell. I become quiet when everybody else is chatting. I withdraw. It depends whether the company is sympathetic to me.'

'She is so good to her friends,' Roshan continued. 'When I mentioned to her that the publication of the report I wrote for the home office was delayed, she promised to do what she could, and I learned later she had written a note to the people concerned, with immediate effect. She was always writing little notes for other people. A very kind, a very warm person. And when we went together to Wisley Gardens, she moved to the bottom of the queue for the ladies' loo when a coachload of old age pensioners turned up. She was prime minister's wife then, but she said, "let them go first".'

When Jim became prime minister he was four years older than Harold Wilson, who had retired largely on account of age, but although they accuse themselves from time to time of laziness, the Callaghans were and are notable for their energy; they want to survive to see the year 2000 unless senility or painful illness intervene. Undoubtedly they belong to the 'never say die' category, as did, of course, Jim's parents.

This staunchness after thirty-eight years' marriage, stood Audrey in good stead when 1976 (especially memorable for a visit to Canada where a mountain trail was named after Jim) was followed by twelve months which were by any standards remarkably exhausting for a prime minister's consort. In this Silver Jubilee year there were four international conferences held in London, in addition to traditional celebrations in the Queen's honour. There were days when Audrey sped from place to place with such testing schedules to keep that there was barely time for a change of clothes or a mental adjustment to a new set of circumstances. Politicians, of course, are accustomed to pressures of this kind, with (for the men) less worries about clothes. Female consorts, on the other hand, must learn as Mrs Thatcher has, to fit in hairdo's and to switch quickly from morning to evening wear. Many tours require clothes suitable for the mountain path as well as the smart luncheon and the evening reception or banquet. Audrey, who looked after her own clothes, with advice from her dressmaker on the dresses she needed, had perhaps inherited an interest in costume and a feel for fabric from her mother, whose work in the draper's shop had included buying accessories.

Studying a veritable snowstorm of schedules, programmes and appendices supplied to her by Jim's devoted and efficient personal assistant, Ruth Sharpe, Audrey determined to make the delegates' wives she was about to meet feel relaxed and at home. In May she appeared for the first time on television when she presented the Nurse of the Year award in Birmingham. In the same month she dined in Holyrood Palace in Edinburgh and President Carter made his fleeting wifeless visit to Newcastle, Newtown and Washington, near Durham, where he planted a tree. But it was in June that Audrey experienced, as consort, the most hectic week on home ground. The pressure started on the 9th after a meeting of the Commonwealth Prime Ministers' Conference at Lancaster House with a daring drive, with police escort, at eighty miles an hour to Tower Bridge to lunch with the Queen and Prince Philip on the royal yacht *Britannia*. 'Of course,' Audrey said, 'you can't keep royalty waiting. I thought he would never make it, but we got there just in time, only to find that the Queen had been held up, too.'

That royal lunch was followed in the evening by a formal dinner in the state rooms at Number 10 with Audrey hostess to sixty guests, before a visit to the Shell Building to watch Jubilee fireworks. The next day she was in country clothes at Chequers entertaining the commonwealth delegates' wives to lunch. Her task was made easier by a guide to the place which she had written with Miss Vera Thomas, the curator, who had also made lavender bags (out of material used to drape Churchill's bed) to be presented with flowers to the guests. After tea, it was back for Audrey to Number 10, to receive the secretary general and heads of delegations and their wives next morning before they took their seats in the prime minister's stand to watch the Queen's birthday parade and the Trooping the Colour. This over, the less formal side of entertaining began as the conference members and the Callaghans piled into a coach for Heathrow whence they flew to Edinburgh for a weekend at Gleneagles Hotel and a hefty slice of Scottish tradition. That Saturday night began with a sumptuous dinner in the banqueting hall and finished with a display of Scottish country and highland dancing. It had been a long day, but there are rarely lie-ins after such occasions for the consorts of the great and early next morning the wives, hosted by Audrey, were once more in a coach, this time en route to Scone Castle and a Scottish fashion show. On return to Gleneagles they faced cameras on the lawns for official photographs before a buffet lunch, followed at last by a break for those who wished to escape from bagpipes or people, until dinner and a reception by the secretary of state for Scotland. This was followed by a programme of Scottish musical entertainment and, finally, the beating of retreat on the lawns.

Next morning they caught the eight-fifteen high speed train to

London with meals provided on board, for this was Monday, a working day, and on Tuesday Audrey (by now a grandmother) had to chair an important meeting at Great Ormond Street. On Wednesday 15th there was an end of Commonwealth Conference reception at the Royal Academy; on Thursday a Museum of London meeting (Audrey is a trustee), and on Friday morning the Callaghans left for Cardiff where they lunched with the directors of Aeronca Ltd, before presenting awards at Greenway Junior School.

On June 28th the Callaghans were back on the royal yacht for a Jubilee review of the fleet at Spithead and the next day they attended a Buckingham Palace reception for the council heads of government of member countries of the Council of Europe.

For several days without respite Audrey, who has always doubted her skill as a conversationalist, had to make polite conversation, while further up the table Jim might be raising his neighbours' blood pressure with stories told with an expertise she could not achieve. How does a very private person compete, manage, entertain, while keeping so much of herself behind drawn curtains? Audrey, the least egocentric of women, managed partly by unconsciously feeding the egoism of others. Genuinely interested in them rather than in herself, she asked about their lives, their national problems. Because she had done her homework, the questions were usually well informed and intelligent, and the guests she sat next to were often flattered by her concern and the trouble she had taken to understand their countries. Rather than promote her own image, she gave them every chance to shine, so that they remembered her as a 'very kind lady'.

Typically, given the see-saw of life, the day after the reception at Buckingham Palace Audrey paid a humbler visit to Brent Knoll School for Delicate Children, where she was able to talk on a subject after her own heart without expecting her hosts to look over her shoulder to see what the prime minister was doing. She was now dealing with people at the other end of the social spectrum. These children were disadvantaged by nature, let down by their genes, as well, perhaps, as by society; victims of chance who would continue to arouse her concern and compassion long after Jim had left the centre stage. On July 5th she was an enthusiastic guest at 'An Evening in Indonesia', an event organised by the Indonesian Women's Association in Great Britain in aid of Save the Children

Fund. Soon after that there was a party in honour of a retired cleaner, Mrs Rose Pilcher, who had worked for eight prime ministers, followed by a Lambeth Palace ecclesiastical garden party.

Great versatility is demanded of prime ministers' consorts, who must move charmingly from queens to cripples, from cleaners to clergyman, dictators to labourers, bankers to bishops, and appear to take it all in their stride. Any false move may sow the first seeds of a legend. Audrey's behaviour gave no such opportunity. Concentrating on the matter in hand, quickly stifling any minor hurt she might feel, she gave no clue to the chinks in her armour and, as Susan Crosland has pointed out, would fasten on subjects such as dry rot in order to steer the talk away from sensitive issues or her own feelings.

The unease aroused when Peter Jay was appointed British ambassador to the United States of America, and the suggestions of nepotism, posed another problem. 'It was David Owen who wanted him,' Audrey says, 'and in the end Jim felt he could not stand in Peter's way.'

The annual visit to Balmoral was, however, pure joy. 'One of the nicest things we did,' Audrey says now. 'The high tea and all the young people gathered around reminded me of home on the farm.' She loved the walks through the Scottish countryside and the barbecues. Above all the Callaghans' stay was without strain; they were simply and maturely happy.

Their audience with the Pope in September 1977 was less relaxed. Audrey, feeling a little odd in a black dress and mantilla, was surprised by His Holiness's small stature and benign air. She had expected to be more awed than she was. For a man who held the devoted goodwill of millions in his hands, the Pope seemed astonishingly ordinary rather than divine.

Life throughout Jim's premiership was full of contrast. There was the excitement and noisy rumbustiousness of question time when Audrey always tried to be in the House to hear Jim's answers, and the solemnity of presenting the *Woman's Own* Children of Courage Awards in Westminster Abbey, and less inspiring but rewarding visits to the Age Concern Pop-in Parlour for the aged in a Peckham café. Then there was the unforgettable and more dramatic inspection of an oil rig where photographs show Audrey looking remarkably young in orange helmet and waterproofs, smiling broadly and totally undeterred by the possibility of danger.

She continued to make friends through the job; the Canadian Prime Minister Trudeau and Prime Minister Lee Kuan Yew of Singapore were two among many from all walks of life. Typically, when Bryan Organ was later commissioned to paint a portrait of Jim Callaghan for the National Portrait Gallery he was invited for a weekend in Sussex. 'He looked and looked at Jim across the dining-room table,' said Audrey.

The Jays' marriage broke up, but Peter remains a friend and frequent guest; it is all part of the Moulton family tradition, the habit of hospitality which originally brought Jim to tea at Runswick all those years before. Lady Dorothy Macmillan was equally kind, notably providing chauffeurs with sandwiches at midnight after they had driven Macmillan home from Bromley after a constituency evening, but it was not her hands that cut and buttered the bread. Audrey is usually cook as well as hostess when home fare is offered. Because of this she must rank highest in any hospitality stakes among the spouses. Her support could be useful too, and, although she might think otherwise, sometimes her opinion counted politically.

Leo Abse in his book *Private Member* makes this point. Abse came seeking Jim's support as home secretary for a proposed change in the adoption laws, and he says the response to his 'importuning' was 'generous'. 'I was fortunate too, in having a good ally in his wife, Audrey, who had for many years brought an informal interest in her local authority work to the fate of deprived children . . . She is an eminently sensible woman,' Abse continued, 'and when I visited her when she lived at 11 Downing Street, or dined with the family in the top flat there, insulated from flunkeys and officials below, I was gratified by her warm realism and her lack of pretensions: she stood out from some of the other ministers' wives who lost their silly heads as they found themselves temporarily with more money and status than usual.'

Anthony Holden, the well known author and journalist who travelled with the Callaghans to India in 1977, also has reason to be grateful for Audrey's sympathy and insight. Having journeyed with the prime ministerial party across Pakistan and Bangladesh, he woke up in Delhi with face ache which was subsequently diagnosed as mumps. The climax came, he says, as they flew on to Bombay when Callaghan's advisers grasped the fact that although Callaghan was sixty-four he had never contracted the complaint. Taking note of his doctor's anxiety, they decided Holden must be left behind at Bombay, to protect the prime minister from risk of infection. Holden, miserable and feverish, had visions of himself lost for ever in that hot and teeming city. But Audrey objected to the decision; a sick man must be nursed not abandoned, she said with great firmness. A little hospital must be made for him at the rear of the plane, where he could be cared for. Jim agreed. As the long journey continued the prime minister and his wife frequently visited Holden in his isolation, bringing him books. The three of them joked that he must have infected half the leaders of the Indian sub-continent for he had shaken hands with several at every meeting. He has always felt since that it was Audrey who saved him from abandonment, in the face of stern opposition, inspiring his admiration and affection as well as his gratitude.

He recalls her poise when, dramatically dressed in cream silk, she corrected Callaghan when he muddled the Indian dynasties on their visit to the Taj Mahal, quoting Indian poetry. 'She knew it all. She's a very bright intelligent lady,' he says. 'And when we meet now she always jokes about the mumps and the way they might have damaged my fertility. But she knows that I've fathered another child since then, so all is well.'

Audrey remembers with delight, as so many British visitors do, the Lutyens Government Buildings in Delhi, but was saddened by a stone commemorating a vast number of birds shot by a particular Rajah, hating the thought of such carnage, the torn feathers, the spilled blood, the pleasure in death.

She remarks wryly now on contrasting safety cover. 'When you fly by helicopter to Chequers an ambulance and a fire engine stand by. But in some places abroad you might find just two men, a stretcher and a bucket of sand.' Safety and health are two considerations to which consorts sometimes have to turn a blind eye. After that visit to India, Pakistan and Bangladesh, Audrey suffered for six weeks from an unspecified virus, a sad, sick figure long after Anthony Holden had recovered from his mumps.

Nowadays she views those ministerial trips with a cool eye. 'Israel,' she says, with none of Mary Wilson's Biblical excitement, 'should be enjoyed on three levels: religious/historical, political and sociological.'

Sometimes Audrey's good-natured level-headedness is in direct contrast with Jim's carefully controlled but more volatile nature. In many ways Jim is Audrey's opposite, a man whose persona can change in a flash from the avuncular to the sharp, from the humble to the lofty, from the humorous to the deadpan. Perhaps more than any other prime minister, he learned in boyhood to make his way through quick wits, compromise and dogged perseverance. As he grew older he acquired the ability to shift ground, to tailor his ideals to the attainable; as he saw it, to put aside dogma to further his aims, to play a balancing act — the true characteristics of the conciliator. It was not enough. Few prime ministers before him had struggled with so many different factions within their party and among their supporters.

He was, it has been suggested, too fluid, and, perhaps partly because he was fatherless from nine years old, he appears to have no solid picture of himself as a person in the manner of Lord Home, for example, or Margaret Thatcher. Even his name has changed from Leonard to Jim and now James. Now too he has capitalist friends; he is a landowner, part of the property-owning democracy promoted by Macmillan. He moves in high circles. And Audrey, whatever she may say, is sometimes the voice that brings him back to essentials.

In office he could count on her absolutely for support when times were bad. Nothing was ever easy or straightforward for Jim Callaghan during his premiership. His majority, diminished even further by lost by-elections, was too small. The Lib-Lab pact helped for a time, but old problems continued: inflation, rising unemployment, high wage claims, industrial strife, the common agricultural policy, immigration, devolution, Rhodesia, Northern Ireland, a rising bank rate.

In late summer 1978 some Callaghan advisers urged him to go for an October election, but he decided to hold on until the spring, hoping to find solutions which did not materialise. 'I think he was right to stay on in the hope of reaching agreements on a pay policy with the unions,' says Audrey. But the winter of discontent followed. Thousands who refused to settle for the 8.8 per cent pay rise enforced by the government came out on strike.

For Audrey, caught up, too, in her problems at the Great Ormond Street Hospitals, it was another time to lie awake at night worrying, not only about her husband's setbacks but also about the endless strife in the Labour party. The young Fabian was still there under the lines of middle age and the persona of the top woman at 10 Downing Street, prodding tardy officials with little notes, working quietly on committees and behind the scenes in private conversations where her views counted. She was a force never acknowledged by the media, perhaps partly because she does not *look* forceful, because her warm smile and eyes suggest only the reticent half of her personality. In this way she differs from her paternal grandfather, from whom she believes she has inherited much of her political zeal, a paper-making engineer who campaigned so fiercely in Sawston, near Cambridge, for the abolition of compulsory religious education in local schools that his wife thought he would end up in gaol.

Jim's attempt to peg prices and wages was undermined. Loyal by nature and hating disloyalty in others, he had supported Harold Wilson absolutely, and it hurt to find the unions against him. He had no kitchen cabinet. His chief press secretary, Tom McCaffey, and his personal assistant, Ruth Sharpe, were perhaps closer to him than his fellow ministers, for in a sense he has walked alone, often jovial and friendly, but not clubbable like Harold Macmillan nor having in his nature the sing-song, all-together Boy Scout element which was once so much part of Harold Wilson. In early February 1979, with local and health authority workers still out on strike, he began to admit that he had 'stumbled'. Troops were on ambulance standby. It was alleged that he had suggested the pay rise for local authority workers could go above the stipulated 8.8 per cent to 10 per cent so long as the rate payers met the difference. The next day he said his speech had been misinterpreted. While negotiations collapsed, the weather became colder, snow fell, rats scuttled in the rubbish piled up at street corners. Some underground trains stopped running. Older people began to recall the General Strike of 1926, and in a television interview Jim admitted that he had misjudged the level of wage demands. 'But I am not an archangel,' he said. At the beginning of March matters seemed to improve. Council workers went back to work and the bank rate dropped again. *The Times* strike, however, had driven many people to read the *Daily Telegraph*, imbibing in this way a largely Tory slant on the news. In the middle of March the leader of the Scottish Nationalist Party told Callaghan that unless the Scotland Bill was put before the Commons for a vote within two weeks the Party would seek a general election despite the perplexing result of the referendum. Two days later volunteers were called to work in hospitals as the health workers' strike continued and Jim admitted that inflation would rise to double figures that year. For a man who had started his political career working for a union events now had an ironical twist.

A few days later the Scottish nationalists signed a no confidence motion, then the next day backed Mrs Thatcher's own motion of no confidence. Callaghan's appeals for all party talks on Scottish devolution fell on deaf ears. Meanwhile Audrey was fighting her own battles within the Hospitals for Sick Children, going on ward rounds at night to give support to the nurses who were still working, and continuing to give help and support to the administrators and doctors. She refused to be led into political discussion by left-wing strike leaders, who demanded a meeting with her which ended in failure. For both the Callaghans it was a desperate time, and not surprisingly Jim's patience shortened so that he became harder to live with. On one occasion he lost his temper with a television interviewer.

On March 27th Healey's budget was threatened by a walk out by civil servants. Everyone and everything seemed to be conspiring to bring down the government. The balancing act which Jim had so skilfully maintained since his appointment as prime minister had fallen apart and paradoxically the unions with whom he had once been on such good relations were contributing massively to his downfall. On March 28th Mrs Thatcher put her motion of no confidence. At 10.19 pm the government was defeated by a majority of one. Jim was the first prime minister since Ramsay MacDonald to be led into an election by a vote of the Commons. After he had stalked out of the House a clutch of Labour MPs stood in the gangway on their side of the House and, led by Mr Neil Kinnock, sang the 'Red Flag'.

The next day Jim went to the Palace just before lunchtime to ask the Queen to dissolve parliament, while Audrey prepared herself to fight the election.

The fight was on, although there were still a few matters to be covered in the Commons, including Healey's caretaker budget. Jim was sixty-seven, but even a correspondent on the *Daily Telegraph* remarked that he looked years younger. If genetics, as the experts tell us, have much to do with longevity, it is worth noting that his mother lived into her eighties despite the hardships of her life, and he has inherited from her that capacity for survival which old-fashioned people still call *grit*. It was a very personalised campaign. Denis Thatcher's face appeared frequently in the newspapers, because he was, as a male consort, a new phenomenon. Audrey's appeared so rarely that readers must sometimes have wondered whether she existed.

Callaghan's programme for the week before Easter gives some indication of the pressures on Audrey who accompanied him everywhere. Monday he opened the campaign with a press conference at Transport House, followed in the evening by a speech at a Glasgow rally. Tuesday found him in Manchester where another press conference was followed by visits to two Conservative strongholds, High Peak and Stretford, and then Labour Moss Side, with an evening meeting at Stockton where he spoke. Wednesday, back in London, included another press conference, a visit to Ilford and a speech in the marginally Tory seat of Upminster.

On Maundy Thursday he appeared at Transport House, and visited Oxford and West Gloucester where the Labour Party's majority had slipped to a mere four hundred votes. Good Friday was a day off and Easter Saturday was spent mainly at Portsmouth with a rally in the evening at Southampton.

The deep if usually unrecognised influence of religion on both the Callaghans was noticeable again when, in a jolly mood in Bury's shopping precinct, surrounded by warm-hearted Lancashire women, Jim declared, 'We're all lovely. We're all God's children.'

Jim's troubles were manifold, however. Audrey had to sit silent while his speeches were interrupted by the odious heckling of the Troops out of Ireland Movement, whose activities ensured that his Sussex house was still under police guard five years after he left office. Inevitably the strain told and Audrey had to cope with a husband's irritation increased by the disloyalty or tactlessness of those he had once deemed sympathetic members of his Party. Lord Robens, for example, former chairman of the Coal Board and an ex-Labour minister, wrote to a national newspaper calling for a return to Tory rule, describing Mr Callaghan's ministers as pygmies compared with the giants in Mr Attlee's government. An article by Lord George-Brown in the *Daily Telegraph* was less than sympathetic.

The Liberals decided to throw their weight behind the Tory candidate in Jim's own constituency. And the *Daily Mail* reported Harold Wilson's alleged comment that Mrs Thatcher, with the appeal and charisma of a successful woman, would win his wife Mary's support. Meanwhile the left-wing element in the Labour Party continued to press for policies which were often unpopular with the general electorate and with the IMF, on whose bounty the country still depended: import controls, greater nationalisation, increased social services, abolition of the House of Lords, measures to cut unemployment rather than control inflation. Skilfully Jim persuaded the Labour Party national executive to accept that the Labour manifesto should be drawn up by a small group dominated by experienced ministers.

Certainly there were no eggs thrown at Jim, none of the dangers that frightened Mary Wilson. 'But,' Audrey says mildly, 'the press can be very tiresome at election time, very persistent.'

Jim Callaghan lost the election. At Cardiff the incoherent shouting of Miss Pat Arrowsmith, the anti-nuclear arms campaigner, denied him the statesmanlike speech conceding defeat which is every losing prime minister's right at his constituency count.

He returned to Number 10 at seven o'clock on Friday morning 4th May 1979 where he talked with Party officials, awaiting the final outcome, while Audrey started to pack, and disconcertingly bouquets of pink and red roses arrived for Mrs Thatcher. When every vote had been counted he tendered his resignation to the Queen and went with Audrey and Michael to Transport House to thank party workers, where he was greeted with cries of 'Good old Jim!'

His final interview on television was traditionally dignified and generous. 'I congratulate Mrs Thatcher on becoming prime minister. It is a great office, a wonderful privilege, and for a woman to occupy this office is a tremendous moment in the country's history.' He went on to wish her well.

On that day, caught in a melancholy moment by a press photographer, Audrey looks disconsolate, mouth turned down, eyes sad, weariness apparent in every line that gives character to a face still young for its years. But broad-shouldered Jim came out of 10 Downing Street with a wide smile, his demeanour showing little sign of deep and undoubted disappointment. After a few words to journalists he left with Audrey in his Rover laden with suitcases, for Upper Clay Hill Farm for a well-deserved rest. His three years at the top were over, but unlike Harold Macmillan and Harold Wilson, he was not slipping away into retirement.

After fifty-five years (as a boy of twelve he had run messages for the Labour candidate for Portsmouth) politics were in his blood; in religious terms they were his life's mission. This was not the end of Audrey's work either. In 1982 she resigned her chairmanship of Great Ormond Street Hospitals after thirteen years, partly because Jim wanted to spend more time at the farm, but mainly because she felt it was time that someone younger took on the job. But she remains involved. She is at present chairman of the special trustees for the Hospitals for Sick Children and president of the Sick Children's Trust, which has recently raised enough money to purchase and furnish a hostel near the hospital for use of patients' relations. She is also a member of the Friends of Great Ormond Street Hospitals, a vice-patron for the Society for All Speech Impaired Children and vice-chairman of the National Children's Bureau. She looks after the house at Upper Clay Hill Farm with the help of a daily woman, the flat at Kennington Park Road, and to a lesser extent the Callaghan's Cardiff flat where Jim's constituency secretary lives. She is the fond grandmother of ten grandchildren.

She is still primarily a politician's wife. A typical week in April 1984 started with a visit to Cardiff to see a factory Jim had officially opened a year earlier, followed by celebrations for the hundredth anniversary of a local school and a National Children's Homes' concert in St David's Hall. The journey back to the farm on Friday was followed by a special lunch on Sunday for daughter, grand-children and friends, then off with Jim to Vienna with presents for the British ambassador to Austria and his family. In between times she still manages to read the early novels of Ivy Compton Burnett, the work of Antonia Fraser, Paul Scott, Muriel Spark, V.S. Naipaul, Ruth Rendell, P.D. James, and many others. Jim hates ballet, but orchestral and choral music, opera and straight plays interest them both, their recent favourites including *Children of a Lesser God* and *Beethoven's Tenth*. Audrey admits to being 'rather embarrassed by four-letter words'.

She has twice been in hospital during the last ten years, once for a hip replacement operation and more recently for the removal of a serious ulcer on her leg. On each occasion she has made a remarkably quick recovery, and those experiences have been pushed firmly into the background.

Ask her about life at Number 10 and, no name dropper, she does not mention the day Prince Charles came to lunch or dwell on her visit to Balmoral. She greatly admires the Queen, but has no inclination to join the ranks of the rich and would not fancy living in Belgravia. Her one-bedroom home in south London looks through trees to the car park behind; the small grey painted sitting-room is rich in potted plants by the window. There's an Utrillo reproduction by the door and modern prints and pictures, several by friends, on the walls elsewhere, but the furniture is unremarkable because most of the inspiration and money has been expended on Upper Clay Hill Farm. This modest flat is just for convenience when parliament is sitting or Audrey is needed on her committees.

'But it's warmer than the farm,' Audrey says, 'because the heating is in with the rent. In Sussex we have it off all day to economise.' Thus she makes it clear that she is not a privileged person. They may have a farm but the Callaghans have to count the pennies just like the rest of us; it's not a pose, it's more or less true. Perhaps she seems a little haphazard. Perhaps sometimes she is a trifle absentminded, but when she pulls herself together all the good sense is still there. Here is a woman who has known Ernest Bevin, John Strachey, Clement Attlee, Hugh Gaitskell, Harold Laski and so many more, who numbers ambassadors among her friends, yet her conversation does not harp on past glories; she still questions people about themselves and their professions. She discusses current problems without the nostalgia which is so much part of Mary Wilson. It is the people who are arriving now who capture her attention: mention authors and she will immediately talk about Public Lending Right; mention artists and she will be up-to-date with the latest art exhibition or scandal.

She has never been Jim's right hand when it comes to political work; she would probably drive him mad if she tried. Sometimes she may have put people before politics, because in her mind politics are for people. She seeks no power for herself, but whatever happens she will remain a Labour woman until the end. And the end is not in sight because Audrey has not been able to retire with her husband like Lady Dorothy Macmillan or take life more easily with a spouse in the Lords like Lady Home and Lady Wilson. She still has a constituency to help look after. She expresses regret that she was not younger when Jim was at Number 10. She is six years older now, but she will not shirk the calls on her time as a Member of Parliament's wife.

'I wouldn't like him not to be in the House,' she said on my visit to the farm in 1984, 'although I wouldn't mind if we never had to fight another general election. What I dislike most is being a book widow.' She looked up to where Jim was ensconced in the little room above us off their bedroom, writing his memoirs.

Their life is still full of excitement. Their happiness in the company of their grandchildren is evident. Margaret, who works on *Panorama*, has two daughters and a son; Julia, a trained secretary, married a doctor with a practice in the Lake District and has three sons and a daughter. Michael is employed by the Ford Motor Company, and has two daughters and the heir, Joe Callaghan. In summer 1984 Jim and Audrey were looking after Michael's cross-bred bitch, Polly, just one symptom of a family bond which is deep and lasting. Margaret and Jim, two of a kind in several respects, often argue about politics and life, prompting Audrey to quieten them with a 'now, now, calm down'. But Jim doesn't play the heavy father and debates are waged on equal terms. Sixteen guests came to lunch to celebrate Audrey's 1984 birthday, fourteen members of the family and two friends. For several days thereafter, she will tell you with pleasure, there were eight people for every meal.

So life, official and unofficial, goes on in Sussex, in London, in Cardiff. In October 1984 Japan was the next stop, where Jim was to lecture at Tokyo University. In the meantime there were meetings connected with Audrey's new and special concern, the National Children's Bureau, an organisation whose success depends largely on a knowledge of politics, sociology, psychology and above all, child care, as well as an understanding of education, all interests near to Audrey's heart.

Whatever you may think of their politics or achievement, the Callaghans' vigour and commitment have survived blunders, traumas and disasters and are still alive and well. In many ways they may not be in step with the Labour Movement as we know it today, but their voices will continue to be heard and for Audrey the struggle to help the underprivileged continues. She remains politically and personally committed to the causes she has supported and advanced for more than half a century.

DENIS THATCHER

For Denis Thatcher, valiantly smiling like a clown through days sometimes littered with minor embarrassments, the pleasure at his wife's triumphs has been tempered by an increasing awareness of the shackles that bind him. To the public he is a familiar and usually popular figure on television, a hard-working man who walks as though he has just dismounted from his horse after hours in the saddle, who keeps his chin up, enjoys a drink and tries not to let the side down. Some are sorry for him because although by no means hen-pecked, he has had to take second place to the stubbornly ambitious wife who won his admiration and love thirty-five years earlier with her sharp blue-eyed good looks and her astonishing drive. Denis, who applauds efficiency, has married the world's most efficient woman and sometimes her capacity to manipulate, manoeuvre and impress makes him seem a trifle mediocre which is a totally false impression.

A man as intelligent as Denis Thatcher has to possess a philosophy of life to survive good-temperedly a situation which has curbed his tongue and destroyed his expectation of a mellow marital old age. Curiously, perhaps because he does not strike one as a poetical person, the most interesting buoy that keeps him afloat is the ethos of that often underrated patriot, Rudyard Kipling. Denis was cast in an heroic mould; he aims high. Kind and remarkably well-meaning, he wishes to be a good and noble person, and, if we think of 'If ', we see one reason why he doggedly tries to ride the storms of life, fortified with a drink now and then, with such resilience, always bouncing back after the sort of disasters which befall the consorts of the great with a determination to do better next time.

If you can keep your head when all about you
    Are losing theirs and blaming it on you,
If you can trust yourself when all men doubt you,
    But make allowance for their doubting too;
If you can wait and not be tired by waiting,
    Or being lied about don't deal in lies
Or being hated don't give way to hating,
    And yet don't look too good, nor talk too wise:

'If ' sums up so much of Denis's attitude to life: his modesty, loyalty and integrity. He has 'walked with kings' and yet not lost 'the common touch'. He is a man in a million. His position leaves him wide open to ridicule, but he is mature enough to refer jokingly to the world-famous wife with the bit between her teeth as 'the boss'. To accommodate her political advisers and to save her any embarrassment which a characteristically spontaneous comment might cause, he has, in his own words, kept his head 'below the parapet for many years', at the risk of appearing 'even more an opaque non-entity than (I think) I am'. But it is worth reflecting that he might not have kept so silent had he not been convinced that Margaret was leading Britain along the right road to national recovery and respect. He is said to support her on every major issue except capital punishment; he is against the death penalty. His background is as solid as the British countryside, for despite a barely discernible south London accent he comes from a long line of Berkshire farmers, whose bones rest in Uffington churchyard, which is now in Oxfordshire.

His father, Thomas Herbert, was, however, born in Wanganui, New Zealand, in 1885, the son of another Thomas (they were all Thomases or Johns) and of a formidable horsewoman with a strong fine face, bold eyes and a good leg for a boot. 'The last of the Edwardian snobs', is how Denis once described her, a stickler for manners whose influence has been passed down two generations. Although Denis rarely mentions it, the New Zealand Thatchers were important enough to have a street named after them in Wanganui to commemorate their services to the town. Denis's grandfather was a go-getter and an entrepreneur, a successful sheep farmer and brewer, who realised that the sheep dip, sodium arsenite, could double up as a weed killer, particularly useful to the railway companies. In 1898 he visited England with this in mind, bringing the twelve-year-old Thomas Herbert. In 1901 he formed Atlas Preservative Ltd to market his weed killer in Britain and America. Seven years later Denis's father returned to England determined to make money by managing and expanding the British branch of the firm. When the authorities refused to accept his trade mark depicting a man holding up a globe because the symbol was already the mark of another company, Tom Thatcher seized a pen and wrote his own name across it. 'Will that do now?' he asked, knowing that in one stroke he had made his design unique.

Tom Thatcher settled in England. A likeable and open-faced man who made friends easily, he became a freemason, devoted to rugby football and the Kipling Society. His insistence on fair play 'towards the other man' made a lasting impression on a son who shared all his father's interests except freemasonry. On 21st May 1912 at the register office, Camberwell, London, Tom married Lillian Kathleen Bird, whose father was a south London horse dealer and jobmaster who had inherited the astuteness that profession demands. Lillian rightly considered herself a good businesswoman. Her other relations were in trade, so genetics ensured that Denis would not lack business acumen and his eye for a good deal has rarely been in doubt. Nevertheless, apart from that old cavalry man's walk, nothing about him immediately suggests horsey or farming forbears. He was brought up in the surburbs, surroundings which have left their stamp on his personality.

Down leafy Southbrook Road at Lee, Lewisham is the pleasant double-fronted Victorian house where he was born on May 10th 1915. Number 26 is unpretentious, well-proportioned, and has a feeling of tranquillity about it. He was registered as Dennis with two 'n's'. The later alteration may have been due to parental error in the first place or a change of mind, but he is said to attribute it to his own bad spelling. His sister Joy was born two years later, but as a boy Denis had his generation's attitude towards the other sex, and they were not very close until middle age. Although Joy's existence spared him some of the drawbacks of being an only child, it did not prevent him from developing that somewhat old-fashioned attitude which inclines him to talk of gracious and charming ladies where other men might speak of nice women. His parents kept themselves to themselves, so that no surviving neighbours appear to remember the family at all in the house at Lewisham Park where they subsequently lived, and Denis, unaccustomed to chit-chat, has battled with shyness from time to time all his life.

Prep school, in his father's milieu, was considered essential if a boy were to grow into a full-blooded man with high morals and a sound education, so when he was eight Denis was sent to Holyrood School, Bognor Regis, where he was prepared for the public schools' common entrance examination, and presumably suffered a normal boy's intense loneliness and homesickness at being separated so early from loving parents and a happy home. But with a well-developed eye and a sure hand, he had the inestimable advantage of being good at games, and found his salvation through cricket, becoming captain of the school XI, a top person with all the glamour and opportunities for leadership that such a position brought in a small school with the British sense of values of its time.

Public school followed with the usual upheavals when a successful boy suddenly finds himself again at the bottom of a ladder, struggling to find the right rungs in a world which can be both ritualistic and cruel. Denis, more sensitive than his public persona suggests, needed good companionship, religion or a supportive philosophy to prosper and at school he found not only lifelong friends but Christian belief. He was sent, like Mary Wilson — although his parents never went to church — to a Nonconformist school, but for him the ethics were less puritanical, perhaps because men were in charge. He looks back to his school days with apparently unqualified gratitude.

Mill Hill School, to which Denis went in 1928, was founded in 1807 and is pleasantly situated high above London. The 'plan' of the 'institution' was originally to 'combine on an extensive scale the advantages of a religious education with solid and correct erudition and general knowledge.' Each resident master was to 'watch over the morals of the boys, as with parental solicitude, and to take every opportunity of inculcating sound principles and good dispositions.' It catered for middle- rather than upper-class children, who were mainly destined to work in trade and business and the professions.

Maurice Leonard Jacks, who was headmaster in Denis's time, appears to have kept assiduously to the plan, and the books he wrote afterwards suggest a concern for the whole man in society rather than for simply academic achievement. The titles have an old-fashioned but worthy ring today: *Education as a Social Factor* (1937),

God in Education (1939) and *The Education of Good Men* (1955). Still in his early thirties when Denis arrived, Jacks had read classics at Balliol, before breaking his studies after Moderations to enlist in 1915 in the King's Royal Rifle Corps. He had, therefore, one must suppose, the logical mind of the classicist, the courage of the soldier and the spiritual devotion of a religious man. His influence through the school still impinges on Denis's life.

The British empire was in Denis's formative years a subject for national pride, shared by many boys of his age. The influence of heroic poetry and fine patriotic prose on educated children of the 'twenties and 'thirties has remained a potent force, the role of the recited words, the calls to duty and honour, the brave tales hauntingly told — Macaulay, Newbolt, Henley, Masefield and so many more all reinforcing Kipling — caught young imaginations. The high flyers might mock later, but there was a hard core of middle-of-the-road young who incorporated much of its ethos into their philosophy of life. They became the dedicated soldiers, the workers and patriots who would always follow the flag without cynical asides. Denis Thatcher belonged to that category as a young man, and although time and experience has watered down the enthusiasm and complicated his outlook, he has always been a staunch supporter of his wife's calls to the nation to return to old-fashioned virtues and heroic endeavours. He is as a result an encouraging consort for our most right-wing prime minister since the war.

But at Mill Hill the practical side of everyday life included the experience of finding one's own level, so that Denis was soon well aware of his limitations as well as his talents. He learned, as did millions like him, not to blow his own trumpet. Even today he speaks of being a 'not unsuccessful businessman' rather than a 'successful' one. Though he was only an average scholar, he was happy enough at Mill Hill to want to become a schoolmaster himself — a compliment surely to members of staff — once he realised his short-sightedness would bar him from a military career. But deep down he knew that, like most of his school contemporaries, he was destined for the family business.

Basically a conformist, outside his schoolboy fantasies he was prepared to accept authority and look up to his elders without being too staid to make a splash or play the fool within the limits authority imposed. Now Denis is remembered as a good mixer and friend, a boy who believed in 'decency' and 'fair play'. He is to this day a loyal member of the Old Millhillians and sometimes after a drink or two the old schoolboy humour bubbles up. Other traits remain from his time at school. He played with great enthusiasm in the 2nd rugby XV, the 2nd cricket XI and the 2nd hockey XI. 'Thatcher,' wrote a school magazine reporter of a house cricket match, 'with complete disregard for the barracking spectators brought the score to forty before he was out.' An early example of that stubborn streak, which makes him speak his mind when those around want him silent and turn a deaf ear to critics when he believes what he is doing is right, which is one reason why his tongue can be a risk to political harmony.

Elizabeth Home, Mary Wilson, and Audrey Callaghan were so careful that they could sometimes be dull. Dorothy Macmillan's heyday came when newspaper reporters were less inclined to leap like ratting Jack Russells to exploit any provocative statement a prime minister's spouse might make. Moreover, she possessed that inborn political sixth sense. Denis, who lacks this, is actually the only consort to have decided against speaking publicly except at sporting events.

But in the Mill Hill days politics was just a small part of history lessons rather than a science. Instructed to take up a hobby, Denis became unsuccessfully interested in the printing press, first as an assistant then as chief printer, without actually printing anything. He also learned Spanish but never quite mastered the language. At home there were the usual middle-class pursuits; seaside holidays, weekend expeditions by car to picnic in the Kent countryside and, more excitingly, occasional days and nights on a cruising yacht in which Tom Thatcher owned a share — an experience which started Denis's interest in sailing.

In 1931 the Thatchers moved from Southbrook Road to 46 Lewisham Park, into an exclusive estate built in the shape of a horseshoe on ground owned by Lord Dartmouth. This estate was started in 1840 but Number 46, bay-fronted, part pebble-dash over red brick, is more like a turn-of-the-century house. Standing on the curve of the shoe it looked across a private unmade-up road to the residents' private gardens, now open to the public, where Denis and Joy played tennis. The Thatchers' tall privet hedge gave extra seclusion. Inside their house the doors were varnished dark brown, the walls papered in sober patterns, the general air one of respectability. There were five bedrooms and three reception rooms, a spacious hall, but no living-in maid. At the back the eighty-foot long garden ran down to a narrow road from which a track led to the side of the house where a lean-to provided shelter for the old bangers Denis was to drive while taking a course in industrial training after leaving school at seventeen.

One of the most enduring influences in Denis's life as he moved into adulthood was the Duke of York's camp to which he first went in 1932. This rousing annual event, permeated with a sense of patriotism, comradeship and healthy living, was the brain child of Robert Hyde (once a parson serving in London's poverty stricken east end and later Sir Robert Hyde) founder and director of the Industrial Welfare Society. Its venue had changed from Romney, Kent, to Southwold, Suffolk in 1931. From the first its prestige had been assured by the presidency of H. R. H. The Duke of York, a slight, spare figure sometimes glimpsed among the tents wearing shorts and smoking a briar pipe.

Margot Strickland in her short history *The King Comes to Southwold* explains that each year four hundred young men were sent personal invitations from the Duke to attend. Robert Hyde wanted a good social mix and among the establishments from which the chosen boys came were a Bradford clothing works, a Norfolk shoe factory, a jam factory in the midlands, Westminster School, Eton, Harrow, Queen Mary's Grammar School, Walsall, and Mill Hill; two hundred schoolboys, two hundred workers and apprentices from industry. Hyde's dislike of snobbery was implicit in the camp's motto, 'Abandon rank, all ye who enter here.' And a public schoolboy who became too uppish had a bucket of whitewash tipped over him, a corrective which he apparently took with good humour. The one rule of this remarkable camp is reminiscent of the 'thirties, easy meat for the cynics but inspiring for boys of the day: 'Play the Game'.

Denis loved the camp, whose tie he still wears proudly from time to time. The hardness of the straw-filled mattresses and pillows didn't matter because the organisation was superb and every day up on the common above the sea he found happiness in a programme filled with activities from seven in the morning till half past ten at night. The boys were divided into twenty sections, each of twenty boys, with a letter to represent their section and a colour their group. A bugle summoned them to bathing and meals. There were games galore, morning and evening prayers with the leader, Captain J.G. Paterson, reading the lesson, a cross-country race, a concert put on by the boys, songs round the bonfire. Chefs from Harrods, the Savoy and the Kit-Kat Club cooked the meals. 'Everything,' Margot Strickland tells us, 'was organised with the meticulous attention to detail of a military operation.'

The camp lasted seven days; normally boys were only invited once, but Denis was one of the honoured ones to be asked back twice as a member of staff serving under Noel Halsey, from whom he felt later he had gained experience of leadership which was to stand him in good stead during the war.

The Duke of York's camp also reinforced spiritual beliefs not to be found in the Thatchers' home; four hundred voices singing hymns Denis loved (in particular *The Day Thou Gavest, Abide With Me* and Hyde's favourite, *To Be a Pilgrim*) inspired and strengthened lofty ideals. The example of Captain Paterson — Pat to the boys — was unforgettable. Young Thatcher was such a success that in 1934 the section under his command won the coveted flag. For two years the camp provided a break from work, for in 1933 when Denis was eighteen he joined Atlas Preservative Ltd, which his father had extended to include other chemicals besides weed killer, and paint.

Denis Thatcher was now six foot and half an inch tall, bespectacled, brown-eyed, lightly but well built with a face that was agreeable rather than handsome. He played squash, rugby, football, hockey and cricket, but loathed tennis — perhaps, he once said jokingly, because of those early days when he played with Joy. After leaving school he had continued to read history for pleasure, adventure stories, whodunits and thrillers, with John Buchan and C.S. Forester among his favourites. He was later to enjoy works by Nevil Shute, le Carré and Helen McInnes, as well as historical biography. By now he had slipped into the use of sporting and business terms to explain everyday reactions or more solemn matters, an eccentricity which remains with him today. He will speak sometimes, for example, of unattractive propositions that present a 'large downside risk' and 'no upside gain', even when talking to women who cannot be expected to understand such jargon.

You can tell a man's attitude towards his religion by how he addresses his priest. Denis says Padre. War found him characteristically already a territorial officer, despite his eyesight, in the 34th Searchlight Regiment Royal Artillery (Queen's Own Royal West Kent Regiment), which he had joined in 1938. He was young enough to enjoy danger, although later he was to feel deeply the futility and wastefulness of combat.

From the beginning Denis Thatcher appears to have been earmarked as an organiser rather than an active soldier in the field; and in 1940 he was sent on an anti-aircraft staff course at the School of Military Administration. He served during the Battle of Britain and became a staff captain in the 9th Anti-Aircraft Division the following year. Service in the 45th and 34th Brigades followed, and some time in these first years of war, he fell in love with 'a stunning girl in a blue silk dress' to whom characteristically — for he was fond of dancing — he had been introduced at a Grosvenor House officers' tea dance. Margaret Kempson, slim and blonde with a notable nose, had been brought to the dance to make a foursome by a friend called Barbara, whose surname has escaped her memory. Barbara was a friend of one of Denis's brother officers, and the evening passed very pleasantly with dinner following the dance. A few days later Denis telephoned Margaret Kempson, who bore an uncanny resemblance to the second Margaret Thatcher, to arrange another meeting. She was indeed a fine featured and high spirited girl and Denis, as we know, has always liked strong, courageous women. At this time she was in her own words, 'working terribly hard driving lorries, tearing about delivering Mosquito parts from the factory to dispersal points around the country'.

It was, of course, a time when no one could plan ahead. Moments of happiness were snatched like ripe peaches from a wall. Time was short; love urgent; the chance of sudden death very real. Dancing on Sunday evening, a dinner out, the uncertainties of war led to an impetuous and joyful wedding on March 28th 1942 at Monken Hadley Church in Hertfordshire, and a commitment for which neither partner was ready. For twenty-six-year-old artillery officer number 77300, Denis Thatcher, it was perhaps more the idea of marriage to the lovely girl whose appearance so well matched the accepted view of female beauty at the time, than the actuality that attracted him. Or, maybe, the simple fact that in those days an honourable man was expected to marry a respectable girl before he slept with her. They were, his first wife says, very happy. But they never set up house together and the war prevented the sense of permanency and shared experience that cements many marriages. Margaret lived with her parents and stayed with Denis in hotels when he was on leave. It was a racy sort of life which brought no long term feeling of security to a partnership which eventually became, after it ended, like Denis's war record a subject that was never discussed. A close friend of thirty-odd years told me that in all the time he had known Denis he had never once mentioned his first marriage, his parents, his background or his war service, even when they visited together one of France's most notable war cemeteries.

Of course, since Denis was sometimes concerned with future operations, secrecy had been essential during the war — 'careless talk costs lives' — and the habit stuck. Perhaps also he felt the disappointment of a man with heroic tendencies who was kept on the staff rather than thrown into action. Nevertheless he enjoyed working with other people towards a set goal, while typically not expecting anyone to be the slightest bit interested afterwards in the part he had played; a part which called for courage, dedication and efficiency. In July 1943 his father died, two days before Denis was sent abroad with operation 'Husky', code name for the invasion of Sicily. Denis's admiration for Tom Thatcher has never diminished, but at the time there was no opportunity to mourn; death was a constant reality. As a staff captain Denis was never, he has been known to say when pressed, close to the action. Success in Sicily led to the mainland of Italy and a mention in despatches for 'gallant and distinguished service'.

In February 1945, Denis, now a major, played an outstanding part in operation 'Goldflake', an organisational feat which exactly suited his own particular talents. He was sent to Marseille as a backroom boy, and worked night and day at British headquarters to arrange the movement from Italy to Belgium of the 5th Division and thousands of Canadian troops. The task was especially difficult because the Canadian units in Italy were so widely scattered, while the 5th Division was spread along the coast for thirty miles from Cervia to Cattolica with troops of its 12th Infantry Brigade stationed inland at Camerino, thirty miles south west of Iesi.

Accommodation was provided in Marseille for 10,000 troops in tents and two hundred vehicles. The 5th Division consisted of 20,000 troops who brought with them 5,600 heavy vehicles many of them tanks, travelling via Salerno to Naples where they were shipped to Marseille to be reloaded in flat cars and cattle trucks to be hauled to Ath or Renaix (now Ronse) in Belgium — a four- or five-day journey. The Marseille transit camp, one soldier reported, was the most exposed in the world, but the rough sea journey was made easier for those lucky enough to travel in modern American ships with a plentiful and unexpected supply of coffee and food. The schedule allowed for a daily discharge at Marseille of forty tanks, 650 wheeled vehicles, fifty carriers and 3,700 personnel. Secrecy was largely ensured by operation 'Penknife' which saw to it that various ruses, such as the continuation of the publication of the Canadian forces' magazine in Italy after they had left, fooled the enemy. 'Penknife' was so successful that the Germans were not aware of any troop movements until they met these hardened soldiers in battle in north-west Europe.

For Denis, who values efficiency and hard work so highly, it was a challenge to be met with the enthusiasm which won him the MBE (military). The citation for this award tells its own story.

AT MARSEILLE on 14 Feb 45, H.Q. 203 Sub-area assumed responsibility for dealing with the very urgent and large scale operation called 'Goldflake'. The timetable available for preparation was so short that all concerned had to work day and night to ensure adequate arrangements in time. Maj THATCHER set an outstanding example of energy, initiative and drive. He deserved most of the credit for the very fine message of appreciation which has been conveyed to me from Field Marshal MONTGOMERY as to the excellence of the work done. The operation is still in progress at the time of writing.

By the end of March 3,535 officers and 54,638 men had been transferred from Italy to north-west Europe, and later that year Denis was again mentioned in despatches. He did not, however, see service in Germany and returned home to be demobilised in 1946, while keeping his name on the reserve. He threw himself enthusiastically into his work as general manager of Atlas Preservative, and started proceedings for an amicable divorce.

'It was,' the first Mrs Thatcher said many years later, 'one of those war-time marriages, which never really got off the ground.'

'I was away so much,' Denis explained. In between those brief meetings both had changed, matured, branched out in different directions. The decree became absolute in 1948. That same year, Margaret Thatcher the first married Sir Howard Whitby Hickman, and Denis became managing director of Atlas.

Now Denis, while working in Kent, took an active part in the Dartford division of the Conservative Association and joined the Erith Rotary Club, an interest which soon waned as he found himself out of sympathy with the movement. More exciting was his standing as a Ratepayers' Candidate for Dartford and Belvedere in the 1949 Kent County Council elections, a typical act of good-natured bravado since he knew he could not win so safe a Labour ward and had no intention of making a career in politics.

He continued to play cricket, a lasting love, and started his outstanding career as a rugby referee. In the words of Mr Geoffrey Fenn, honorary general secretary of the London Society of Rugby Football Union Referees, Denis became 'one of the leading referees in the country, refereeing most of the senior clubs in England, county championship matches and representative games'. It was a job which suited his restless energy and quick decisive mind. And, although a slipped disc in 1960 brought his active refereeing to an end, he continued to help the society, first on the committee and then later, as treasurer. He is now a lively vice-president, who attends meetings whenever he can and is usually at the annual dinner.

But in those years immediately after the war, work came first, as he built up the family business. His liking for cinema, music and theatre did not prevent him from putting in twelve and a half hours most days in his Erith office. Without pretensions, although very conscious of his position as a director, he was popular with the work force, a boss who never passed the factory doorman without exchanging a few words. Mindful of his father's dictum of fair play and fair dealing, he yet possessed a certain saloon bar humour and sense of bravado which saved him from priggishness. Indeed he dislikes 'stuffy' people, the pompous and the grand, and is sometimes uneasy with typical products of the more prestigious public schools (by and large they don't like him either). Certainly Mill Hill did not brand him with that special stamp which makes one ex-public schoolboy recognise another anywhere in the world, and his general demeanour and choice of words are not theirs. But in 1949 he definitely had his own style and was not a man to be overlooked. As managing director of Atlas Preservative Ltd, whose turnover rose dramatically under his leadership, he drove a Jaguar, lived in a small flat on the sixth floor of Swan Court, Chelsea, and added sailing to his other regular activities. He took girls out from time to time, but sport remained the paramount interest in his life outside business.

In 1949 all this was to change, when he was asked to fill a gap at the dinner held to mark the adoption of Margaret Hilda Roberts as prospective Conservative candidate for Dartford. Margaret had impressed the local Conservative Association chairman at a conference, but the selection of this twenty-three-year-old Lincolnshire woman was in some respects influenced by the popularity and success of the fiery red-headed candidate for neighbouring Chislehurst, Pat Hornsby-Smith, who was at that time one of the young stars in the Conservative Party. It is to Denis's credit that he immediately recognised that Margaret was, whether you liked her or not, an exceptional woman. Who could meet her, he was to ask later, 'without being completely slain by her personality and intellectual brilliance?'

That night after dinner Denis drove this daughter of a Grantham grocer back to London in his Jaguar, from where she was able to catch the train to her Colchester digs. It was a good beginning and they were soon to see each other again at a Rotary meeting, but from the first there was another contender in the field for Margaret's hand which would ensure that Denis could not be too slow in pressing his suit. Dr Robert Henderson, the Scottish superintendent of Dartford Southern Hospital, was a notable rival; prematurely grey-haired, but slim and personable. Views on him differ now. 'A confirmed bachelor, I thought he would never marry, but he fell heavily for Margaret,' one friend of the time says. 'A wicked, lively man, great fun,' comments another. While Henderson, who was not to marry until retirement, says, 'Margaret and I were very close.'

Views of Margaret at that stage differ too: 'She wasn't very good looking'; 'She dressed badly'; 'Rather mousey really with a bad complexion and as a speaker she couldn't compare with Pat Hornsby-Smith.' But looking back, in October 1970 Denis loyally told *The Times*, 'She was beautiful, gay, very kind and thoughtful.' For him her brilliant analytical mind was never in doubt.

Soon after her adoption as Conservative candidate, Margaret left Colchester, took a job with J. Lyons at their Hammersmith laboratory and found lodgings in Dartford, from which she commuted to London daily leaving her digs just after half past six each morning. Her evenings were usually taken up with canvassing, public speaking, meetings or speech writing, so if her suitors wanted to see her they had to go along, and an Erith businessman was probably more often available than a busy medical superintendent of a large hospital. Denis soon fell into the habit of chauffeuring her to meetings, while she told a friend that she doubted whether she could fit marriage into her life as a politician.

With two men to advise her, Margaret's style of dress changed dramatically. Until her adoption she had been the sort of girl who turned up at a party wearing a long evening gown when everyone else was in simple cotton. There is a story of her visiting the Harwell Atomic Centre with her friend Airey Neave, and others, wearing a see-through chiffon dress more suitable for a wedding or the stewards' enclosure at Henley Royal Regatta. The distinguished physicists were astonished to see this extraordinary girl among their visitors. What, they wondered, could such a frivolously dressed young person know about atomic energy? It was only when Margaret began to talk that they realised she had a far greater grasp of physics than the people accompanying her.

Plainly aiming to be glamorous, but needing direction, she began to appear in expensively cut classic suits and matching accessories, promoting a clean, upper-middle-class, professional image. She cultivated a look belonging to the town rather than the country where the well-heeled can be seen in relaxed moments wearing scruffy jeans or tattered sweaters, which would be intolerable to Margaret. Nor would she in any circumstances allow herself to take on Shirley Williams's rumpled, academic, mind-above-clothes look. From 1950 on, Margaret was to be unfailingly well groomed.

'Denis changed her,' says Edward Moore, for many years chairman of Chislehurst Conservative Association and deputy lieutenant of the county. 'He gave her greater style and confidence. Her complexion and skin improved as well as her dress sense. He made a lot of difference.' In fact his influence turned Margaret into a woman whose dress was absolutely right for the wife of a wealthy businessman, although she retained a hankering for the exotic, which occasionally surfaces in a dramatically attractive outfit — the dress worn in a television interview with Newsnight on July 28th 1984 being a notable example, a choice which lifted Margaret into the alpha class.

When her schedule allowed, Denis took her out to dinner in London and to theatres and cinemas. She met his mother, whom Edward Moore described as 'a very nice, stout, homely, grey-haired lady, friendly and very much in control'.

Soon Margaret's lean, self-disciplined father came to Dartford to speak in support of his daughter, and later Margaret took Denis to Grantham to meet her parents, where he saw the shop which has since become famous, and their Edwardian house, Allerton. Alfred Roberts, a born teacher thwarted by circumstances, was six foot three inches tall, a striking man with well-chiselled features, white hair, once flaxen, and astute bright blue eyes behind thick-lensed spectacles. His wife, Beatrice Stephenson, was plain, with a wide, open face, the daughter of a railway cloakroom attendant and high-principled, proselytising Phoebe Cust, a farmer's daughter. Margaret and her sister Muriel, four years older, had been born and reared in the rooms above the shop, which stands in North Parade at the shabbier end of Grantham. There was no piped hot water in those days and only one lavatory, in the back yard, to serve the household. The front windows looked across to a busy road, noisy with horse-drawn and motor traffic, and all day long the children could hear the hissing and shunting of steam trains in nearby sidings. But Muriel and Margaret never felt underprivileged because there were so many worse off than themselves. Once a week, when Beatrice Roberts baked, they were despatched to deliver the pies she had made for families on the bread line. Alfred Roberts had left school at twelve to be a grocer's assistant, and had saved and worked long hours to raise enough money to run his own shop which he eventually extended to include a post office. A committed Methodist and lay preacher — known in that branch of the church as a local preacher — he had toured the countryside, like Mary Wilson's father, spreading the gospel. Sponsored by the chamber of commerce as a councillor, he had become Grantham's youngest alderman. He was a teetotaller and led the campaign to keep Grantham's cinemas as firmly shut on Sundays as his own children's toy cupboards.

Life was a serious affair in those rooms above the shop, where widowed Phoebe Stephenson ruled while her daughter Beatrice helped to serve customers below. Margaret's penchant for delivering homilies can be traced back to Grandmother's proverbs and endless advice which were daily medicine. 'Cleanliness is next to Godliness.' 'If a thing is worth doing it is worth doing well.' 'Waste not, want not,' and so on and on.

The shop was the hub of small town life. Politics were discussed with Alfred Roberts as he cut the ham or measured the groceries. Problems were brought for him to solve across the counter. Everything was done with a purpose; the importance of education, largely because Alfred had missed out on it, took on enormous proportions. And Margaret, whose exceptional intelligence was soon obvious, became in one sense the son the Roberts never had, the vehicle through which many of Alfred's frustrated ambitions would come to life, a burden she was happy to shoulder. When she was eight he started to send her to report back on meetings he could not attend himself. She became a runner at local elections and was frequently sent to fetch books from the library, learned ones for her father, light novels for her mother. Meanwhile Beatrice Roberts taught her daughters to sew, housekeep, and less conventionally to paint and wallpaper a room. But it was Alfred whom Margaret adored as she strove to be the woman he wanted, and, when she won a scholarship to Oxford and he arranged elocution lessons to drown the last remnants of a Lincolnshire accent, she happily complied.

Whatever her doubts eventually, Alfred Roberts, who later became mayor of Grantham, was a big noise in her childhood and that early imprint is what mattered; the father who lectured, exhorted and knew best was a hero to the pretty girl with the hooded blue eyes, and the remarkable mind. He was her kind of person and she was his, and from him and Phoebe Stephenson she inherited the desire to proselytise and an extraordinarily deeply held conviction that her own views were fundamentally right. Closer to her father than her mother, she would never make deep friendships with members of her own sex. The relaxed give and take of comradeship, the banter and the warmth somehow eluded her. She could relate to female colleagues in a struggle shared, but not often simply in friendship, and her elder sister Muriel, who was more like Beatrice Roberts, was never very close to Margaret. In contrast to many of the figures of her youth, Denis, with his jolly, off-the-cuff remarks and obvious admiration for her must have been a tonic.

'Denis is so kind,' his first wife remarked, when Margaret became prime minister, 'one of the kindest men I've known. He's a very gentle person. It must be lovely for Mrs Thatcher now to have someone like that to lean on, to go home to.'

Margaret lost in the 1950 general election to Norman Dodds, the sitting member and Labour and Co-operative candidate, by 13,638 votes, cutting the Labour majority by a third, and was immediately reselected. Characteristically she threw herself back into the job with great vigour, making it clear to Henderson and Denis Thatcher that they must convince her that their careers would in no way hinder her own political ambitions before she was likely to consent to marriage. Both were mature enough to understand her needs and to remain unperturbed by her forcefulness which might well have put off a younger man. Yet endearingly her political drive and certainty sometimes contrasted oddly with an emotional and social naivety which was more lovable. A young woman of very limited means, living alone in digs, spear-heading a campaign in which both men believed was obviously a subject for advice and protection as well as admiration.

Margaret, the rationalist with the inborn capacity to weigh up the odds ascribed to Librans, must have assessed both her suitors. In many respects she had more in common with Denis: hard-working English forbears, an interest in financial and business matters, spiritual links with the Nonconformist Church, a reverence for efficiency and hard work, and a love of Kipling so strong that at one time she wanted to join the Indian civil service and she later bound a set of his books for their house in Flood Street. Physically, Denis resembled her father in three respects: he was tall, athletic and bespectacled; but, unlike Alfred, he possessed the outwardly more light-hearted approach to life of a man who had started with money behind him. In 1950 he exuded a friendly and relaxed self-confidence on home ground only disconcerting when he exploded into bad language, the natural outlet of a man who is more strung-up than he cares to admit. The swear words, which still shock Margaret, are sometimes the comparatively harmless sparks from the volcanic temper which he likes to think of as mere impatience, and at other times, as when he makes a poor shot on the golf course, simply high-spirited expletives. They are all part of the ebullient side of his nature.

If Margaret did weigh up those two basically agreeable men to calculate coldly, as one of Henderson's friends has suggested, which would best help and accept the demands of her career, Denis's wealth and London home must have been one consideration, while Henderson's professional commitments must have gone against him. In the end, a doctor's patients must come first and a doctor's wife needs patience and forbearance if the marriage is to survive. Whether Margaret's choice was based on love, chemistry, cool assessment, instinct or opportunity or all five scarcely matters now.

On October 15th 1951, as the general election approached with alarming rapidity, Denis, chairing a meeting at Bedonwell School, Erith where Margaret was speaking, introduced her as a girl with 'unlimited beauty, brains and charm; three qualities,' he added, 'with which we can do in the House of Commons.' They were effusive words, which most of the audience must have supposed were spoken in admiration, flattery, or merely in an attempt to bolster the Conservative cause rather than in genuine love. In fact the chairman and speaker were already engaged, lovers sitting side by side on the platform, trying to keep their secret until after election day, a scheme thwarted when the *Erith Observer and Kentish Times* printed the news as a scoop four days later. But while Denis has always spoken lovingly of the match, Margaret was only to comment later, 'We had a lot in common. He was on the financial side, I was interested in economics. He was in the paint and chemicals business, I was a chemist.'

The official announcement of the Thatchers' engagement was made by Denis from the town hall podium after Margaret had again conceded defeat to Norman Dodds, whose majority was reduced to 12,334 while their friends William Deedes and Pat Hornsby-Smith held Ashford and Chislehurst. The Roberts cannot have been happy about Denis's previous marriage, which after some initial hesitation Margaret totally ignored, but inevitably their influence over their second daughter had declined as she began to make her way in a larger field. For a woman who wanted to change the political climate of Britain, provincial Nonconformism and local politics were small beer. By now she had started to read for the Bar, seeing the law as a career which would provide opportunities for a politician.

Impressed by her single-mindedness and knowing her character, Denis expected her to go far, but the idea of a British female prime minister never entered his head.

Margaret wanted a religious wedding which meant a church had to be found whose clergy would not mind consecrating a second marriage. Finally the Thatchers plumped for the distinguished Wesley's Chapel in City Road, London, where Margaret arrived looking magnificent on December 13th 1951 '. . . in a long brilliant sapphire blue velvet dress, the exact replica,' Penny Junor tells us in her biography, 'of an outfit worn by Georgiana, Duchess of Devonshire, in a painting by Sir Joshua Reynolds, complete with a little sapphire hat and ostrich feather.' She carried a muff. Denis wore black morning dress, a white carnation in his buttonhole, his dark spectacles lending a slightly serious air to his smiling rather fleshy face. His mother came from her flat in Buckingham Court, Kensington Park Road with Joy; and Muriel, who had trained as a physiotherapist, was there too, with her Scottish farmer husband, William Cullen.

This small London wedding was also very much a Kentish political Conservative affair with prominent guests from the county and many presents from the Dartford area, including a solid silver tea service from the Heath Ward. The chairman of the county council, Sir Alfred Bossom, lent his splendid house at 5 Carlton Gardens for the reception and the toast was proposed by Kent builder John Miller, who was chairman of the Dartford Conservative Association. Even the name of the best man, Kent Green, fitted the picture.

Margaret tempted providence and broke with tradition, marrying on December 13th and leaving for a honeymoon in Madeira and Portugal with a few days in Paris, wearing a black fur-trimmed coat. While abroad the Thatchers decided they would like two children, one of each sex, which would satisfy parental instincts and give them a stake in the future while leaving them time to follow their demanding careers. For theirs was to be a marriage between two totally professional people, not a cosy liaison where one would exist through or depend entirely on the other. Now, living in Denis's flat in Swan Court, they saw less of each other than is usual among newly-married couples of their generation. Denis departed early in the morning to drive to Erith while Margaret left later to study law, arriving back in time to greet him at eight o'clock, a well turned-out wife with a swiftly cooked meal waiting to be eaten. He was the dominant male and she the domesticated female, but during the day she had been competing with men. In several ways the Thatcher partnership belonged more to the nineteen-eighties, than the nineteen-fifties. Although Margaret Thatcher, unlike Mary Wilson, achieved independence while remaining married, without ever aspiring to be a feminist, to a large extent her success was made possible, as she freely admits, by Denis's salary, interest and support. It is perhaps worth considering how much further the brilliant Pat Hornsby-Smith might have travelled politically had she possessed a wealthy, loving husband, who tried unfailingly to offer sound advice and sympathetic encouragement.

In August 1953, Margaret produced twins by Caesarean with only a two-minute interval between them, thus achieving her maternal ambitions in one go, instead of waiting years as many women do. 'Just like Margaret,' Denis commented later, 'Bar Intermediate in May, produced twins in August, and Bar Finals in December. I would like to meet any other woman who could equal that.' By no means a chauvinist, Denis basked in Margaret's success, which reflected also on himself for having made so admirable a choice.

Denis commemorated the arrival of Mark and Carol by presenting Margaret with a double string of cultured pearls, which she frequently wears to this day. After the birth the Thatchers took the next flat in Swan Court for a controlled rent of seven pounds a week. They put a communicating door between the two flats and installed a nanny in the new one with the twins, while they remained undisturbed themselves in the old, a typical example of one of Margaret's practical ideas which could not have been carried out without Denis's money. It was she, however, who, following family tradition, wallpapered and painted to ensure that both flats were clean and sparkling and, although Nanny was often the one to comfort the twins if they cried in the night, Margaret made sure that she allowed time each day to play with them, to educate her progeny from the first moments of understanding.

When, after being called to the Bar, she followed Denis's advice and became a tax lawyer, she always left her chambers at five-thirty to be back before the twins' bedtime. Denis's interest in the children was not fully aroused until they were old enough for ball games, when Mark became, in Denis's words, 'a very good games player, I may say'. Looking back when the twins were fourteen, he reckoned that the Thatchers had been 'pretty indulgent parents'. He had, he told *The Times*, 'only once raised his hand to each of them . . . Margaret bends over backwards at holiday times to make sure they've everything they want.' He defended himself against the suggestion of their school teachers that two successful parents might put the twins under strain. 'I don't myself know that it affected them, bless their little hearts. They certainly know what hard work means, there's no doubt about that.'

By 1957 Denis was well established as chairman and managing director of Atlas Preservative Ltd and had joined the boards of the Educational Supply Association, and, as befitted the father of young children, the Nursery Schools Workshops. Two years later the *Directory of Directors* listed him as a member of the board of the Chipman Chemical Company, on which he served until 1985, and in 1965 he made news when he sold Atlas Preservative Ltd to Castrol for £560,000. Obtaining a seat on the board of the larger company for himself, he became a member of the Institute of Directors; and when Castrol was taken over by Burmah Oil, he was appointed Burmah's divisional director of planning and control. 'It was,' says present director Keith Wilson, 'a senior position in a very thinking role. He stayed and was extremely successful.'

As prospective Conservative candidate for Dartford, Margaret had already acknowledged Denis's tremendous help on 'the economic and industrial side of politics', and since then he has undoubtedly advised her also on talking sensibly to the lower-paid workers on factory visits, with an ease which had entirely escaped her in her days as a laboratory assistant.

Business took Denis frequently to Europe and America and also to the middle east, South Africa and Japan. Denis's ill-chosen remarks at the time of the disputed rugby tour of South Africa must be seen in that context. South Africa was a country he knew and rugby was *his* game and almost certainly he sees black people in the same light as do the majority of Englishmen of his class and generation, regarding them as people often but not always on a different wavelength from their more stable and sophisticated white brethren. Added to this deep-rooted attitude is a belief in amateurism in sport which many of the older generation hold dear. Games are games and money should not necessarily be paid to the players. So when Denis spoke at a rugby referees' dinner on sporting links in 1979, it was from the heart. 'I might be sticking my neck out,' he allegedly said, 'but we are a free people, playing an amateur game, and we have got the right to play who we like. As sure as hell we can play our game in South Africa.' Such freedom is, of course, easier for the rich man to exploit than the poor man; lack of money is a great inhibitor, and the freedom of speech denied Denis Thatcher in certain areas since his wife's premiership (albeit by his own choice) contrasts oddly with this sentiment.

When not abroad promoting business interests, Denis tried to be with Margaret at every crucial point in her life. Understanding her ambitions, he encouraged her to find another constituency to represent, fully aware that she had read law mainly because it opened doors to a political career. In 1954 when she was one of three short-listed for Orpington in Kent he drove her to the interview, knowing how much she needed a calm and steadying companion. In those days intensely nervous before such occasions, she was quickly depressed by failure, and when she found she had been passed over her morale slumped. 'Denis,' she said, on the verge of tears, 'I will never try again.' Of course she did, and how much of the trying was due to Denis's special brand of encouragement will probably never be known. 'He bolsters her up,' a close Thatcher friend told me, 'he says "Pull yourself together girl," and that sort of thing — that's the way he talks to her.'

She failed again, at Beckenham, Ashford and Maidstone. It was always harder for a woman to make her way than a man, and unlike Pat Hornsby-Smith Margaret was a mother with young children. Quite apart from male chauvinistic attitudes, she was unlikely to receive support from the females representing the Women's Conservative Association on the selection board. There were other constituencies to which she applied where she was not even short-listed. Meanwhile she continued to speak when she could at meetings in support of her party, accompanied when possible by Denis. Edward Moore remembers an occasion when she was supporting Pat Hornsby-Smith at Chislehurst. 'Just as she was about to begin, a bell at the Church of the Annunciation started ringing,' he says, 'and Denis was in quite a state. He said the bell would upset Margaret. It had to be stopped. I went out, had a try just to please him, but nothing could be done. Now Pat would have raised her voice and carried on, but in those days Margaret Thatcher was easily put off, and Denis worried about her welfare, worried all the time.'

Denis is in fact a fussy man underneath that deceptively bluff exterior; he pays great attention to detail, rewriting his business reports over and over again until he considers them perfect. Always respectably dressed himself, he loathes untidiness and is the sort of person who could not bear to have a clock in the house that does not work. His children were not allowed to keep pets and a sloppier more absent-minded wife might have fared rather less happily as his partner, provoking the irritable and impatient strain in his nature.

Loving sport largely for the companionship and exercise it brings, he took up golf, which has given him years of pleasure. A left-handed player with a handicap of twenty-one, he is a good loser and those expletives which leap from his mouth like demons when he makes a poor shot are directed at himself rather than anyone else.

In 1956 Lillian Thatcher, who was always known by friends as Kathleen, left Kensington to live in Barnes with Joy, where she stayed until her death in 1976 at the age of eighty-three. In 1984 Denis arranged for an oval grey slate plaque in memory of his parents to be fixed to the east-facing external wall of the south entrance of Uffington Church, next to six stone memorials to other Thatchers going back to 1789.

Early in 1959, when, owing to a Conservative Act of Parliament, rent control was removed from the Swan Court Flats, the new asking price seemed too high so the Thatchers bought Dormers at Farnborough in Kent, a four-bedroomed house with an acre of garden, and moved out of London. Farnborough is a place much favoured by commuters, many of them belonging to what used to be known as the 'gin and jag' set. Out there to the south of London despite fields and woods the atmosphere is not really country or county. The quality of a man's car is probably more important than that of his horse, and wellington boots are not essential for survival. In the pubs the talk is more likely to be about the air show or the stock exchange than the harvest or swine fever. Still cared for by Nanny, the children now lived a more suburban life, mixing with other families in the immediate neighbourhood. Denis was on the right side of London for Atlas Preservative, while Margaret, who was selected soon afterwards as Conservative candidate for Finchley when Sir John Crowder announced his retirement, commuted from Bromley Station.

Thereafter the children took second place in the Thatchers' schedules unless they were ill, and when Nanny left to marry the gardener, an older woman known as Abbey was employed as both nanny and housekeeper. Bearing in mind that the excellent local hospital was within easy reach, the Thatchers felt that they could concentrate on their careers with easy consciences, and the separateness of their lives was firmly established, with Margaret, who was elected to parliament in October 1959, staying at the House until at least ten most nights and Denis frequently going to sports meetings and/or dining out with friends. Family meals became a rarity except at weekends and during the week the children relied heavily on neighbours for daytime company, but on Sundays Denis at least was often available for ball games. He looked after their sporting activities and tried to promote good manners, while Margaret continued to seize every opportunity to further their education and stimulate their minds with homilies, questions, lectures and demonstrations, her attitude to her children deeply influenced by her father and Phoebe Stephenson. Tidiness, hard work and self-improvement were encouraged. As a dedicated Member of Parliament her time, when she was not at the House, was largely taken up with bazaars, fêtes, socials, speeches, school visits and all the activities which make up so much of political life, so Denis, like the children, continued to enjoy his leisure without her, an anticipated sacrifice which was in the end to make his role as prime minister's spouse a little easier than it might otherwise have been. Paddi Victor Smith, Margaret's part-time secretary remembers Denis as 'the perfect consort, like the Duke of Edinburgh.' He was, she says, very supportive to his wife, and was always ready to bat or bowl for his son.

When he was eight Mark was sent to Belmont, the preparatory school for Mill Hill, in keeping with Denis's enthusiastic membership of the old Millhillians. When it came to a final decision, however, Harrow, which has more kudos, was chosen as his secondary school. There seems to have been no question of Eton being considered; since the Thatchers had no connections there, it is unlikely that Mark would have been accepted. Indeed the Thatchers would not then have felt at home at Eton and were destined always to move in different circles from the Homes or Macmillans. Their background was much closer to that of the thousands of young people who joined the Young Conservative Associations during their heyday in the 1950s, organisations supported largely by people from trade and business. Denis, Penny Junor tells us, used to say that the twins were spoilt; Mark was given more leeway than Carol, who was always academically the brighter of the two, but both parents insisted rather obsessively on good manners and cleanliness, and old-fashioned virtues were extolled both by them and Alfred Roberts who was a rare but loved visitor.

In 1963 the Thatchers sent Carol to the Queenswood School, near Hatfield and, disenchanted with building developments at Farnborough, sold Dormers and bought a flat in Westminster Gardens, a mansion block in Marsham Street. Denis has always hated London at weekends so they also rented a cottage in Horsmonden near Tunbridge Wells, while they looked for another country house to buy. Margaret, who occasionally suffers from hay fever, has never been a country person, and in her spare time was more likely to stay indoors tidying or decorating the house than walking across the fields to look at local cattle. Denis thrives on fresh air and exercise, and for him the main attraction was usually the nearest golf course, where swiping balls helped him to keep his mental equilibrium. It cannot be easy for a man to be married to a relentlessly ambitious politician, who, despite a domestic side to her nature, always puts her career first. For Denis, male decisiveness has often to be put aside, while loyalty and a sense of duty rule out any chance of psychological relief by grumbling. But a blossoming business life had its compensations and by 1965, after the Atlas/Castrol deal, Denis, bowler-hatted, with the obligatory rolled umbrella close at hand, drove a Daimler with the registration number DT3. Soon the Thatchers left the cottage when they bought their largest house, the Mount, Lamberhurst, Kent, an eight-bedroomed mock-Elizabethan place built in 1914, standing in three acres of garden with tennis court and swimming pool. Although the style was to their taste, it was a surprising choice for professionals whose children were both at boarding school. The garden was magnificent, the countryside gloriously wooded, but Denis as we know loathed tennis; Margaret played only very occasionally and neither could be described as keen swimmers. Nevertheless Denis predictably became attached to Lamberhurst Golf Course and on Saturdays patronised the local shops when Margaret was too busy to look after the housekeeping. The Thatchers' well-stocked store cupboards, deep freeze and larder were due more to Denis's organisation than Margaret's. From now on he also ate occasionally in the Lamberhurst hotels' restaurants.

'He came in the first time with several friends wanting dinner at half past nine at night,' one manager told me. 'He was quite brusque and we nearly refused, but I spoke to the wife and there weren't many people around so she said all right, she'd cook them something. The next time he phoned first very politely and booked a table.' And that is typical of the man. He is very reticent about many of his feelings, but he watches himself and, if in his view he has slipped up, he tries to put things right the next time. He is prejudiced in many respects, occasionally dismissive of other peoples' attitudes and often opinionated, but never arrogant, and, although he expects people to respect Margaret because she is prime minister, he does not want any reflected glory for himself. In an odd way he remains totally separate from what he sees as the political circus, while never ceasing to admire his wife for her achievements and leadership.

By 1967 Margaret's advance had been remarkable by any standards. Six years earlier she had succeeded Pat Hornsby-Smith as parliamentary secretary at the ministry of pensions and national insurance, a job she carried out with energy and commitment though not the efficiency and intelligence of a likely future prime minister. In 1965 Edward Heath, as leader of the Opposition, gave her shadow posts in housing and at the treasury, before appointing her shadow minister of power in 1967 and the following year shadow minister for education, the job which gave her the most scope to make her name. Since she was a dedicated constituency MP her time at home became even more limited, and the family were soon able only to enjoy each other's company fully on holidays. The earlier summer ones had been spent usually at Seaview on the Isle of Wight where Denis could sail or race boyishly over the waves in his speed boat. Here the Thatchers met John and Tricia Stebbings (later Sir John and Lady Stebbings), two of their closest friends. For five years the Thatchers also took their children annually to

Lenzerheide in Switzerland to ski — the only sport which Denis and Margaret shared.

In 1970 Alfred Roberts died, a few months before Margaret became secretary of state for education in Edward Heath's government. Alfred Roberts' demise, a devastating blow for Margaret who is always shattered by death, cast a shadow over her new appointment, but if anything it strengthened the ambitions fostered by the father who had been her greatest mentor. Margaret now needed more time in London, so the Thatchers sold The Mount, for £185,000, and their Westminster flat, and bought 19 Flood Street, a pleasant small red-brick house built in the Georgian style, large enough for the whole family, just off King's Road, Chelsea.

Over the years Margaret was to redecorate that three-storey house several times, with Denis often painter's mate. Light, sunny but never garish, its décor and furnishing in 1948 reflected a mature taste. It was touched with the mood of the time (cartoons in the downstairs lavatory, modern abstract prints here and there, a dining-room clothed in orange watered silk, a brown, orange and white kitchen), but also with overtones of the 'fifties in suburbia: candlewick bedspreads, floral chair covers, green brocade curtains, a washed Chinese rug. It was a house which admirably suited Margaret's way of life, but eliminated Denis's regular country weekends, although, of course, he could always travel forty miles for a game of golf at Lamberhurst. This time his sacrifice was hard to bear for he has never particularly liked the Flood Street house, which he immediately gave to Margaret. Chelsea is not really Denis's scene, and the special attractions of the King's Road, which appealed at that stage to the twins, meant nothing to him. For a year he suffered before finding a flat in Court Lodge, on Lamberhurst Golf Course, only two minutes' walk from the first tee. In those days he rose at six-thirty every morning to drive from Chelsea to Burmah Oil in Swindon, while Margaret's taxing job as secretary of state for education created tensions which sometimes made an escape to the country all the more welcome.

Her difficulties were highlighted by the angry response to her withdrawal of free school milk which provoked the jibe *Thatcher Thatcher School Milk Snatcher*, which hit hard at a time before she had steeled herself against vicious attack. 'That milk episode shook her,' said Mark, 'she almost went the colour of shamrock.' From

Gardiner's biography of her we learn also that she seemed at one moment so close to despair that Denis said, quite uncharacteristically, 'To hell with all this, why not pack it up?' to which Margaret is reputed to have replied, 'Not bloody likely.' But Denis was back now in the company of Lamberhurst friends and his business commitments continued to provide the occasional foreign trip which he loved. More than any of the spouses in this book Denis continued to remain his own man, stubbornly refusing to play second fiddle until his wife became leader of the Conservative Party, for him a traumatic transition when he suffered agonies of shyness for the first time as consort. 'They say I'm the most shadowy political leader of all time,' he modestly commented. 'I intend to stay that way and leave the limelight to my wife.' Escaping when he could, he joined for ten pounds a year the Island Cruising Club in Devon, pottering about in converted naval vessels and old trawlers. He washed their decks and polished the brass, and found new friends, a man making his way on his own, desperately trying out new things, restlessly energetic. But he remained totally loyal, allegedly telling a *Daily Express* reporter that Margaret was 'one of the most brilliant brains in the country, she is a barrister and a scientist too. She has enormous singleness of purpose. Margaret sets herself a programme and it is done. At the same time she is tremendously thoughtful about everything and everybody. Nothing is too much trouble.' Such statements suggest a basic self-confidence, but the degree of Denis's poise depends on where he is and what he is doing. 'Dad had a rough time,' Mark told Tricia Murray in 1977, 'because of the demands on my mother. He's a very strong personality. He was successful in his own sphere. Now he has to sit back and play second division. That's naturally very hard for a proud man and takes an awful lot of doing. But he's totally one hundred per cent for mum. He does and would do anything he could to help her.' But Denis, never a smoothly social man, lacks wide topics of conversation: business, travel and golf are his passions, small talk his bugbear. Women placed next to him at banquets are apt to find his sporting and business allusions difficult to understand. His manner, especially on the telephone, can be abrupt. 'Thatcher' he will say, snatching up the receiver, for he still sees himself, public school fashion, as Thatcher rather than Denis, and Thatcher was in his field a name to be conjured with, well before it became synonymous with

Britain's most famous female politician. Speed and efficiency are also evident when he canvasses for Margaret. With Carol's help he can, Penny Junor tells us, canvass a thousand houses in one and a half hours. At sixty, Denis's early morning week-day drives to Burmah's offices in Swindon were over, and he had more energy with which to look after his wife. When Margaret became leader of the Opposition in 1975 he realised she was taking on too many of the engagements previously arranged for Edward Heath as well as her own. It was too much, testing to the full even her exceptional stamina. 'Like most people,' Mark said of his mother, 'when she's very tired small things irritate her. The degree of anger or irritation is related entirely to how hard she's working or what pressures she's under, which is natural . . .' Sensing the strain, Denis strode into Margaret's private office. 'Unless you get her diary under control,' he told her staff, 'you're not going to have her as leader much longer.' It was an action which none of the other spouses in this book would have taken (except perhaps Lady Dorothy) and was a male rather than a female symptom of protectiveness.

Denis was to learn later that he could not always throw his weight around in this way, that there were some matters which had to pass through certain channels. He had on an earlier occasion perceived, too, that he must be a little cautious when providing his wife with information. He realised this after he had written a detailed report for her on the rather parlous financial state of Rolls-Royce, to help her advise, he thought, a constituent who wished to know whether to sell shares in the company. This seemed an innocent enough request, but afterwards when Rolls-Royce crashed Denis heard from Sir Keith Joseph that Margaret was the only member of the cabinet to have the details of the firm's finances to hand. Yet although misled he merely said, 'Never do that to me again,' for it is the small irritations rather than the serious ones which fire his temper. He is without malice, and hates certain attitudes of mind — laziness, jealousy, callous stupidity — rather than individuals. 'Any damn fool can be unkind,' he says. 'It's much harder to be kind.' And kind he is; for example, he replies at length in his own flowery hand to many letters, often from complete strangers.

Like Mary Wilson Denis did not have the very useful run-in as foreign secretary's spouse before the premiership, a position which actually would not have suited him, because of those spontaneous comments which still very occasionally delight journalists hanging around the corridors of power. Of China, he once commented after an official visit, 'I've seen it all before. Yugoslavia, East Germany, China, all the bloody same, grey, drab conformity. I don't care where it is, socialism, communism, the lot. Doesn't bloody work.' During one of the last interviews just before Central Office suggested he curb his tongue, he said, 'I don't pretend I'm anything but an honest-to-God right-winger. Those are my views and I don't care who knows them.' Some people in consequence would describe him as a man without hypocrisy, others would feel him to be a liability. In fact he is simply too honest to be a politician, and lacks the self-restraint which has controlled Lady Home and Audrey Callaghan and the caution which has always inhibited Mary Wilson. But where his wife's cause is concerned he equals Lady Home every time; his praise is undiluted; in public his support is absolute. Just occasionally he is inclined to clap at the wrong moment, so that he once told Robin Day in a TV interview he sometimes has to say to himself, 'Watch it Thatcher, watch it.'

Certainly Margaret's elevation to the premiership must have triggered off dismay as well as pride and triumph in this complex man as he surveyed his future, for experience has taught him that gains in life are usually countered by losses. As the first male spouse of the first British female prime minister he was meat for the media. Was he hen-pecked by the Iron Lady? Did he give her political advice? Who were his friends? What were his business interests? How much money did he earn? The questions would be endless. But in those anxious hours on May 3rd and 4th 1979 when, fortified at one stage by champagne, the Thatchers waited after an arduous campaign, every inch of Denis must have wanted success. There was a moment in Flood Street when Margaret tidied her drawers and desk; a natural outlet for stress. There were frightening minutes of tension in Finchley when it was found that one of the ballot boxes for Margaret's own count was missing. There were cheers from enthusiastic crowds as the Thatcher family arrived in two cars at Conservative Central Office at three o'clock in the morning of the 4th and when they went home two hours later, their victory assured, to find blue-ribboned cheering flag-wavers in Flood Street. Margaret stayed up for the rest of the night making telephone calls. Denis, more somnolent by nature, slept. At noon the Thatchers returned to Smith Square for more champagne and slices from a huge chocolate cake made overnight in the shape of Number 10's door. They lunched in Central Office, where the children and Margaret waited afterwards for the call from the Palace, while Denis dozed. After it came, Denis straightened his tie, Mark, who was always to feel the reflection of her position on himself, put his arms round his mother and proudly said, 'Prime Minister'.

'Not yet,' said Margaret.

'The car may break down,' suggested Denis.

He waited downstairs with Palace aides, the first man to do so, while his wife was with the Queen. Like Prince Philip he was now to take second place in the public eye, a position for which, unlike the Prince, he had not bargained when he married. The two men had little in common, apart from a love of sailing. The two women upstairs had perhaps even less except for their positions of power, the one calling for deviousness, dedication, a sharp tongue, a quick wit and a crafty nature among other attributes, the other for innate graciousness, patience, good manners, serenity and resilience.

Now Denis was to lose even more of Margaret, not simply to politics but to a group of men who would make up her cabinet, who would advise and flatter, argue and console, take her orders and cues, thus removing a small part of his marital role. But he would remain the ultimate crony; the one man to whom she could turn who would not consider his own political position in any way when he offered advice or consolation; the person outside politics, but with some knowledge of them, which every premier needs. Lord Whitelaw and Norman Tebbit among others would undoubtedly play a large part in keeping Britain's first woman prime minister as calm and collected as possible, while in no sense diminishing the sense of mission which drives her forward. But Denis would be witness to the real emotion, the tears the others must not see.

As early as 1970 he had said, 'Well, we all get depressed sometimes don't we? I mean sometimes one does sit down and think "Jesus wept" — excuse my language — "is it all worthwhile?" ' He was still watching her with an understanding which sometimes belied his hearty manner. 'Don't stop her cooking,' he would say. 'It's her form of therapy.' And in campaigns and at meetings he was increasingly the man just behind her, stepping forward to elbow people out of her way, ready always to produce a Biro and piece of paper should she need it and to urge haste when she was running late.

There was an earlier stage when Denis was asked to submit his speeches for approval by the prime minister's political office. 'I did my best,' he told a meeting in Canberra, Australia. 'I prepared a draft. It was very polished, with quotations from Shakespeare and Livy in the original.' But he says he was told, 'This is all mumbo jumbo. Please confine your remarks to plain jumbo.' And that, he explained, was why these Australians would find him silent.

Now his country weekends were assured, for although the Court Lodge lease had expired there was Chequers, a place Denis particularly admires for the exemplary efficiency of its staff, and also a belfry flat which the Thatchers had rented for a rumoured sixteen pounds a week in the New Scotney Castle, part of which was occupied by friends. This early Victorian mansion, owned by the National Trust, was build in stone quarried from the extensive gardens and designed by Anthony Salvin in 1837 in the Elizabethan style. Its views across the gardens which drop steeply down to the moated Old Castle are spectacular, particularly in the spring and autumn when the rich tapestry of the trees' foliage is a feast for the eyes. There is so much variation, so much that is romantic and dramatic in these gardens that it would be impossible to become tired of them: the winding paths, the great trees, the massed shrubs, the ferns, the Japanese maples, the buddleias, the rhododendrons, the water lilies on the lake, the charming bridges, the sweet-scented herb garden and much more — everything is here. And the joys of the Lamberhurst Golf Course are close at hand. At Scotney the Thatchers have found seclusion, for the New Castle, divided from the main gardens by spacious private lawns, is reached only by a long drive, open to the public only at certain hours. Birds sing, cows low in the nearby fields, but no traffic passes their high flat.

Although no longer a nine-to-five man, Denis's business interests had widened in the 'seventies. In 1972 he had been appointed a director of Edwin Cooper, manufacturers and distributors of lubricant additives, part of the American firm Ethyl Corporation. By 1974 he had joined Quinton Hazell, another subsidiary of Burmah Oil which was mainly concerned in the manufacture and distribution of motor vehicle components and also of ultrasonic equipment, radio, electrical and cycle goods. For some time he had also been chairman of Chipman, a subsidiary of Staveley Chemicals, suppliers of weed killers and fertilisers involved in the construction and maintenance of sports turf. In addition he was for many years a director of Halfords, a useful retail outlet with its string of High Street shops. In 1982 he became a non-executive director of Pitney Bowes plc which is concerned with postage meters, printing, folding and copying equipment and similar products. A year later he took on the deputy chairmanship of Attwoods, which had recently become involved in waste disposal and sand extraction. 'He will be advising on business and financial matters,' managing director Ken Foreman told *The Times*. Mr T.J. Gilligan, chairman of Pitney Bowes, was more expansive. 'He regularly attends our meetings and participates in other combined social and employees' events,' he wrote to me in August 1984. 'His extensive personal business experience is of great value to us and he has made a valuable contribution to critical analysis of current operations and future planning.'

Planning is indeed one of Denis's greatest strengths, be it in war or peace, and any analysis he makes will be meticulously detailed and accurate. But despite his diligence there were embarrassments highlighted by his wife's position which, an *Observer* correspondent suggested in 1983, might have mattered more in the Party if there had been a less right-wing regime. Chipman, for example, was found to be manufacturing the weed killer which contained the harmful and subsequently banned 2,4,5,T ingredient known as 'Agent Orange'. Burmah Oil was accused of paying its South African black workers starvation wages and the 1978 Bingham Report on sanction-busting by the oil companies noted that Castrol lubricants had been marketed in Rhodesia since the Unilateral Declaration of Independence in 1965. Three years later the newspapers published a private letter written on Number 10 paper from Denis to Nicholas Edwards, the secretary of state for Wales, asking that consideration of a planning application in Wales should be speeded up to help a business friend, a step strictly unacceptable for a prime minister's spouse to take unless in aid of charity. There had been discomfiture, too, much earlier when Burmah Oil was forced to appeal to Callaghan's government, which had been constantly attacked for inefficiency by Margaret Thatcher, for a loan of £282 million to avert disaster. Thereafter, we are told by *The Observer*, Denis had to spend eleven hours a day pruning Burmah's budget. Yet, because of the low profile required of him, Denis enjoys few of the outward trappings of the successful businessman. He must not appear rich, and it is rumoured that a stately Rolls-Royce that he bought some time ago for £15,000 languishes undriven in a garage, while he is seen these days in slower, more commonplace cars.

Speaking of Denis's work for Quinton Hazell, Ray Sollett, then chief executive director, said, 'Once a non-executive director like Denis was just a useful name on the writing paper, but Denis would never stand for that. The newspapers have got it all wrong. He's nobody's fool. When he's done his homework, and he *always* does his homework, he's formidable opposition. After nine years I like to think we are friends, but when I phone him for advice, he always tells me exactly what he thinks, and if I don't take it he's never the least offended.' Ray Sollett, who is also a director of Burmah Trading Ltd, is impressed by the way Denis plays his part in executive, business and social activities. 'If his diary allows it, he likes going round our factories; he's especially interested in plant and manufacturing processes. He'll always turn up at motor shows, if he can, and join us when we are entertaining guests.'

In January 1984 Denis accompanied Sollett to South Africa on business when the question of Burmah's wages to black workers was raised. 'Denis of course doesn't give interviews,' Sollet said, 'but I spoke on television pointing out that we paid between twenty per cent and sixty per cent more than our competitors. If we paid more we would have to employ fewer people.'

Travelling is still a joy for this inveterate globe-trotter, whether as businessman, consort or tourist.

'Sometimes he is recognised,' one of his fellow golfers told me. 'Only the other day people came up to him as we were about to leave the ferry, wanting his autograph. Now many a man would refuse to oblige in the circumstances. I mean it was only because of Margaret that he was asked. But he always signs for them; he never objects; and the reason is that he likes to serve the system. He doesn't like politics, but the constitution, the system of government are very important to him.'

When he's out on duty as consort Denis is usually a few steps behind Margaret, smiling but rarely speaking now unless specifically addressed. If he is a specially invited guest, however, Lord Home told me, Denis always does his homework. 'He went round a pig farm in Essex,' Lord Home said, 'and he had all the figures

203

ready, could talk about feeding stuffs, everything. He had read it all up before he went. I admire him for that.'

And the golfing friend tells of a visit to an African country, where the Thatchers were put up in a modern bungalow for a night. In the morning, he says, Margaret had hoped for a bath, but she soon came back into the bedroom. 'I've got news for you,' she said, 'the water's cold.' The Thatchers looked at each other, and as they looked the ceiling fell down. There was plaster and dust everywhere; but, this golfing friend says, they weren't angry, not at all, they sat down side by side on the bed and burst out laughing. 'It's that sort of marriage,' he told me. 'Very happy, a great success. They suit each other.' There was another prime ministerial trip, to the Commonwealth Conference in Lusaka, when Denis was the considerate man guiding Margaret the prime minister to bed when her companions and particularly Lord Carrington, who needs his sleep, were being stupefied by her lively talk far into the night. She was still sparkling while they grew heavy-lidded, longing for the chief to quit. 'Come on Margaret, time for bed,' said Denis, thinking of the other man, as his father had taught him. He will take just so much as a spouse and then no more, showing his muscles now and then, exerting his authority as a husband, though for the most part he is willing to take second place when the system demands it. Two contradictory stories of him were told by Simon Hoggart in *The Observer Review*. One describes a moment at a Downing Street reception when a special branch officer whispered in Denis's ear, 'The boss is back, sir,' and Denis adroitly used one hand to tip his gin and tonic into a pot plant and the other to greet his wife. The other is of a moment on an early morning flight to Scotland when Denis ordered a drink and his wife said, 'Isn't it a bit early for a gin and tonic?' and Denis said staunchly, 'It is never too early for a gin and tonic.'

Margaret cooks his breakfast every morning, while perhaps only eating an apple and a vitamin pill herself. Margaret occasionally chooses his clothes, which are always conventional, when time allows; but he runs her errands, to be exasperated sometimes when he feels people are failing to realise the importance of his wife's position.

But he never uses his own position as a husband to throw his weight around. Mark, less scrupulous, has been known to say to harassed shopkeepers, 'But don't you know who I am? I am the prime minister's son,' expecting instant priority as a result. Manners remain immensely important to Margaret and Denis, an attitude that is reflected in the organisational side of the Conservative Party. Phone the political office even in the midst of an election and your enquiries will be received with complete courtesy. Refusals of access will be couched in the politest terms. Handwritten letters have a special meaning for those who use secretaries. The personal touch is to be cultivated and Denis is proud of the fact that after prime ministerial visits to Chequers Margaret will write thank you letters to the staff in her own hand. When a shopkeeper in Hong Kong wrote to Denis to say a traveller's cheque with which Denis had paid for a shirt had not been approved, he recieved a handwritten apology by return with a National Westminster Bank cheque signed by Denis, which he now keeps framed in his shop window. 'Denis,' the golfing friend says, 'tries to make any party or reception at Number 10 a memorable occasion for the guests. He sees that no one is a wallflower. "They may only come once," he says, "and I want them to remember it as a special occasion, to take something away with them." ' When they arrive he holds out his hand, 'Denis Thatcher,' he announces, as if they didn't know, with the air of a man accustomed to introducing himself in the far corners of the earth where formal introductions are not always forthcoming. Throughout a party he will move restlessly about making sure nobody is left out. Usually he does not talk at any great length to anyone; profundities are not his style. Although unhappy with small talk, he conversationally skims the surface. He smokes untipped Piccadilly cigarettes and was rumoured to have used his influence to dilute a government campaign against smoking.

But after a meal at Number 10, Peter Ustinov painted a slightly different picture of Denis as host. 'He gave the impression of being completely aloof from political involvement and leading a life of his own. I might even say that he appeared to be attending the lunch just like any other guest rather than being at his own home. The meal was excellent.'

John Wells, author of the 'Dear Bill Letters' in *Private Eye*, was invited to drinks after a charitable performance of the farce *Anyone for Denis*, along with the rest of the cast. A generous gesture from two people who had watched themselves lampooned and satirised.

John Wells says that in an absent-minded moment Denis mistook the actor Nicholas Farrell, still dressed as inspector Eric Catchpole, for a real policeman. Always happy to congratulate where he feels congratulations are due, Denis complimented Farrell on the wonderful job the police were doing in Brixton and elsewhere when 'the fuzzy wuzzies are on the rampage. But when order is restored,' said Denis, 'and all is quiet, there won't be a television camera in sight, because the media is run by pinkos and marxists.' It was a remark in keeping with those sweeping and prejudiced generalisations which have cemented his entrenched right-wing image. He wittily acknowledged this image when he introduced a friend to the chairman of the BBC, George Howard, (later Lord Howard) with the words, 'Of course George thinks I am well to the right of Genghis Khan.' This throwaway line surely demonstrates a humorous side the public rarely sees, as does, 'when I'm not absolutely paralytic, I play a little golf.'

Mrs Thatcher will often kick off her shoes after dinner or a reception in the flat, and stand on the sofa to address the guests on what it means to live in a tied house. When the conversation is mainly political Denis will disappear into the small room he uses as an office to watch television, although he finds many of the programmes 'rubbish', and frequently falls asleep in a chair. On waking, he will return to the drawing-room to suggest that it is time for bed; after all, he will say, everyone has to go to work next morning.

The décor has been altered very little in Downing Street since the Thatchers came, although Margaret has changed the wallpaper in her study and brought in British furniture borrowed from the Victoria and Albert Museum to replace the French furniture of Callaghan's time. She has added portraits of Nelson, Wellington, and Priestley to those already hanging on the walls, and busts of Davy and Faraday and, of course, of Newton, with his Grantham associations. The Tate Gallery has lent her three Turners and she has borrowed from the Courtauld Institute Galleries portraits by Allan Ramsay and Sir Henry Raeburn and works by Roger Fry and the Bloomsbury Group for Chequers; but these choices do not reflect Denis's taste. Uneasy about making judgements because he feels he has little eye for paintings, Denis will say he likes works in the classical style, but dislikes 'modern art', a term which covers a far wider visual range than he probably realises. One of the major changes which Margaret made, supported by Denis, soon after moving in was to replace the Downing Street cutlery with Belton House silver borrowed from Lord Brownlow for use at official dinners.

Outside their drawing-room lies a stuffed black cat with a collar and bell round its neck, a present to bring the Thatchers luck during the Falklands Campaign, which they still treasure. Before it on the left stands Margaret's china cabinet full of the Crown Derby, some old, some new, which she collects; among it a piece depicting three soldiers in combat gear raising the flag on the Falklands. From time to time Denis presents his wife with new pieces of Crown Derby, always of the same pattern. Sometimes their guests dine off it. Margaret's taste is obvious in Number 10, clean lines, yellows and white, pale carpeting, a feeling of sunshine. In the entrance hall, before you reach the cabinet room, there are delicate water colours by John Piper, a Henry Moore sculpture. Everything is British, for the Thatchers always show the flag, believing that Britain will always be best given the will and opportunity to express herself.

In 1948 Margaret changed the décor of the drawing-room again, trying to lighten a room which Denis finds oppressively dark; the heavy chairs upholstered in darkish gold were discarded — not at the taxpayers' expense, Denis hastens to assure his friends. 'They will be used elsewhere.' The walls were painted a brownish-yellow, darker than cream, below the picture rail, white above it like the ceilings and fireplace. During the last stages of refurbishing only a Lowry painting remained, suggesting that perhaps it is a favourite; the others were rehung later. Denis leaves the décor to Margaret, trusting her taste. There is a junk room which can be used by the children if necessary, kept for Carol at first, who lived for several years in Australia and was rarely at Number 10, and a larger room with a bathroom for Mark, who has since removed himself to America. After the 1979 election both Thatcher children felt their lives had been made difficult by their mother's position. Carol, a qualified solicitor and journalist, decided she could make her way better in Australia where she would not be constantly referred to as Margaret Thatcher's daughter, and Mark, who tried to establish himself as a businessman in Britain, felt hounded by the press. When it was discovered that his name was high up on the IRA hit list he was provided with two security guards and Margaret persuaded him to live at Number 10, which she said would save taxpayer's money because he would be looked after by existing security arrangements. Denis, however, who has a certain fatalism about him, was unguarded in the early years of his wife's premiership. It is the press he fears, 'reptiles' he calls them, rather than the terrorists, and although he is now protected, Margaret does not seem to feel the same anxiety about his safety that she shows for her children's.

The Thatcher twins have certainly suffered more than any other prime minister's children from the attention of the newspapers, despite Carol's own professional status as a journalist. For example, 'Mrs T's twin trouble,' was the headline for Henry Porter's piece in *The Sunday Times* of May 27th 1984, which opened with the gambit, *The Thatcher twins do seem to be a bit of a trial to those who come in contact with them* and went on to describe Carol's 'carpeting' by the *Daily Telegraph* and Mark's supposed wish to return to England a few months after he had opted to leave to save his mother embarrassment.

Denis expected from the first to be a sitting duck for every 'fifth-rate journalist', and is rumoured to have alerted friends from his Mill Hill days not to talk to the press. Carol, as a journalist herself might be expected to cope and, after those five years in Australia, is making her way at home. Yet exasperation with her own kind is obvious in her book *Diary of an Election*, when she names them the 'media mob'. She has her father's penchant for slang. She lunches with 'fellow journos'. Her mother is 'back on the stump', or 'in cracking form'. Typists 'bash out' speeches at 'supersonic speed'. People 'bale out' of their responsibilities. At twenty-eight Carol told a *Sunday Times* interviewer that she did not see marriage and children fitting into her plans, and so far no Denis Thatcher has come along to change her mind. Her admiration and affection for her mother shines through the trendy prose in her *Diary of an Election*. She is on record as saying that *Private Eye's* 'Dear Bill' is 'spot on', but the play *Anyone for Denis* is not.

It is Mark, a friend says, whom Margaret misses more, for although deeply attached to Carol, she has always preferred the company of men to women. 'She really suffers,' I was told by a Thatcher friend, 'when there is a family reunion at Easter, for example, and Mark isn't there, simply because he feels hounded by the newspapers.' The first prime ministerial family crisis arose when Mark was lost in the Sahara with his French co-driver Charlotte Verney, during the Paris to Dakar car race. At first Denis, protective as usual of his wife, was cross when Carol pointed out that Mark had missed a check point. Typically optimistic, Denis played the incident down, but as the days passed and vague worry turned to deep, and for Margaret excruciating, anxiety, Denis's reassurances could not keep back Margaret's tears. Finally Denis flew out in their friend Sir Hector Laing's private plane to watch and, where possible, help the search operations. Afterwards Margaret commented in a television interview, 'I said to Denis *you must go*.' But it is doubtful that such a wide traveller and man of action needed much urging. When Mark was found, all good Tories in the nation heaved a sigh of relief, and when Carol read *Private Eye*'s version of events where Denis writes to 'Dear Bill' — 'The son and heir is chasing all over the desert with a bit of French fluff,' she commented, 'that is Dad to a tee.'

More damaging were the unsubstantiated reports that Mark, a poor examinee, falsely claimed to be a chartered accountant and that he was using his mother's name to promote his business interests. The second accusation peaked in March 1984 when *The Sunday Times* printed on its front page 'Denis Shares Mark's Oman Account'. The article stated that Denis was a co-signatory to the Barclay's account which was to be credited with the sum, rumoured to be less than £50,000, which was Mark's payment for his consultancy work, known in the trade as 'catering', in gaining an Oman contract for Cementation. The subject had surfaced two months earlier when *Observer* correspondents pointed out that Margaret and Denis were both in Oman in 1981 when Mark helped Cementation win the £300 million contract to build a university for the Sultanate of Oman. These are murky waters to stir. Parental love and pride can outweigh judgement, and prompt unwise words. But there are no witnesses to say such words were uttered, no proof that the Thatchers ever mentioned Mark's firm, Monteagle Marketing Ltd, which he runs with co-director and friend Stephen Tipping. Obviously since Mark is much abroad, a co-signatory was needed and who safer to choose than a father without a stake in the business but notable for his paternal loyalty? Inevitably doors are opened for prime ministers' children; everyone is interested to meet them; they carry kudos with them. The whole incident demonstrates again how much a consort (and his children) may be handicapped as well as helped by his partner's elevated public position. Mark, now immensely newsworthy, moves in wealthy circles in the United States with an oil millionaire's daughter as his current girl friend. Socially at least he has gained rather than lost because of his mother's position. For Carol the opposite is probably true. For a time her journalistic successes will often be attributed by some rivals to her mother's status, and her post on the *Daily Telegraph* to her father's friendship with the editor (purported to be 'Dear Bill' of the letters) despite the fact that she had previously qualified in Australia, partly in the hope of avoiding such suggestions.

Denis, armed with a clear conscience, manages to survive such traumas. His brand of patriotism makes him glad that Mark won a deal for Britain and undoubtedly inspired his support and possibly encouragement of his wife's actions at the time of the Falklands War. There are indeed observers who think that, although he is excellent at raising her spirits when she is down, he is possibly too encouraging when she is in one of her more manic moods. Sometimes he will say a little self-deprecatingly, 'You must remember I am a fan.' She is still for many men an attractive woman with sex appeal, inclined to raise strong emotions of either loyalty or dislike. A prime minister, in Lady Falkender's view — and she is a woman who does not lightly praise Tories — who looks younger and prettier now than when she took office.

At election time Denis is normally with Margaret, promoting his wife, spreading the Tory message; he is better at campaigning for a political cause than at arguing a political case. Perhaps because he has been a top person in his own field, he is more easily bored and exasperated than the female consorts who have gone before. His protectiveness towards Margaret is reminiscent of Elizabeth's nannying of Alec, but the days when he asked that the church bell should be stopped ringing are long past. His hesitant young wife has become the Iron Lady who can talk anyone or anything down. And somehow he has adjusted and kept his love for her. One of the keys to this success must be an absence of possessiveness, as he sees her surrounded sometimes far into the night by male colleagues, and another key must be that separateness which was in their marriage from the beginning. If she has to be away on some important occasion in his life she can remind him that he was at a party when the twins were born; he was in South Africa when Margaret was selected as prospective Conservative candidate for Finchley, and in Japan when she was appointed a junior minister in Macmillan's government. Wider perspectives and considerations decide the Thatchers' conduct. Jealousy is non-existent.

Denis's comparatively agreeable survival must also be due in part to his capacity to enjoy himself. He likes golf because it is fun. At the Tory conference in October 1982 he was gliding on the dance floor with the Brighton mayor's blonde, ex-beauty queen wife long after Margaret had retired to her suite. At another conference he was to be seen riding a bicycle cheerily along the sea front. He seems much freer than the spouses of previous prime ministers, apart from the curb on his tongue. He worries less about what he wears and laughs at himself if he makes a faux pas. He will go abroad more or less when he pleases, although he postponed one holiday when he found he was expected to attend a memorial for the Falklands Campaign, an event he would not have wanted to miss anyway. He arranges his own amusements at weekends without the resentment Mary Wilson felt. Although he cares little for dogs and horses, he probably makes the best of Balmoral, too, because of the fresh air and the well run house and sense of history and occasion.

The fact that he does not like his position and sympathises as a fellow *Private Eye* sufferer with Mary Wilson makes his support all the more remarkable. Although Margaret rarely asks him to fill a political breach, when the Cecil Parkinson affair blew up Denis went in his place at a moment's notice to open a new helicopter terminal at Blackpool Airport, although the commemorative plaque was inscribed with Parkinson's name rather than his own. He has told friends of an occasion when he opened an antiques fair and was asked afterwards what his fee was. Since he is comparatively rich through his own efforts, and goes to considerable lengths not to benefit financially in any way from his wife's position, he was horrified. 'We usually pay around five hundred pounds,' he was told. Later when brought a piece of china he had earlier admired, he forestalled any presentation by whipping out his cheque book and saying, 'How much?'

Sensibly helping charities that reflect his own interests, Denis is informally and happily involved in Operation Raleigh, an endeavour which appeals to the adventurous element in his nature. Travel under sail to distant places would have proved irresistible to him as a boy, so now he does what he can to give today's youth a chance to realise such ambitions. An enthusiastic sponsor, he was on the converted trawler *Sir Walter Raleigh* as it sailed up the Thames in September 1984 on a promotional trip. If everything goes as planned, this ship will transport four thousand young people across six continents over four years. 'Undoubtedly one of the finest examples of initiative and enterprise I have ever come across,' Denis told the *Standard* reporter on September 13th. 'There will be a wonderful opportunity for young people to face the challenge of a lifetime, and become stronger and better people through the experience.' Thus he joins hands with Prince Philip, Duke of Edinburgh, in his belief that tests of courage and endurance in the face of the elements will put backbone into the nation's youth, and, coupled with serious study — there are two science laboratories on the trawler — bring self-awareness, knowledge and inspiration. His great admiration for the leader, explorer Lieut-Col. Blashford Snell, is typical of a man who ranks courage high among human virtues.

In 1980 Denis became a member of the Lord's Taverners, proposed by Sir Harry Secombe and seconded by Hector Monro, an organisation he has on occasion described as 'great fun', and whose activities are entirely in keeping with his undiminished love of games. Since the club's formation in 1946, the number of Taverners has increased dramatically. The membership list now reads like a *Who's Who* of show celebrities. Chairman Terry Wogan was recently replaced by David Frost. Fourteen regional branches have been formed and so much money raised that in 1984 a minibus was presented to establishments for handicapped children every twenty-eight days. The funds come mainly from charity matches and that same year Nicholas Parsons and Omar Shariff opened the bowling for a Lord's Taverners' match in Monte Carlo. Celebrities, of course, pass on their enthusiasm to their colleagues, and the success of the organisation rests largely on the draw of the famous people who appear at the club's events. Cricket remains at the centre of the charity, but rugby matches, golf tournaments, boxing evenings, charity lunches and balls all increase revenue, which goes towards adventure playgrounds, grants for special projects usually connected with handicapped children, a steady stream of minibuses and, above all, youth cricket below first-class level.

Ted Cathie, the assistant treasurer, described Denis as 'a pretty loyal attendant'. Recently he was the member who presented a minibus to Brian Rix, chairman of the Friends of the Normansfield Hospital for Handicapped Children. 'He does whatever he's asked,' says Ted Cathie. 'His presence is a draw. He's taken part in some of our golf tournaments.'

Director Anthony Swainson goes further. 'His most important contribution has been the arranging of a dinner party at Number 10 hosted by Mrs Thatcher. We were launching our covenant scheme. I rang him up, asked for help. "Hold on a moment," he said, "I'll just speak to the boss." He thought I was going too far when I said we would charge £1,000 a head and a covenant of £1,000 a year thereafter for four years, but sixty came. We could have had many more. We were sold out.'

But Denis, unlike Audrey Callaghan, does not bring his spouse to the charitable events he supports. He slips away alone when he can, and Mr Swainson cites an occasion when he declined an invitation to a charity cricket match at Tunbridge Wells because he would be at Chequers. 'But he turned up after all, at five o'clock. He had driven himself over, and he stayed until eight watching the match, talking to people and signing autographs.'

'Loyalty, to me, is the one quality all men must have,' Denis told Kirstin Cubitt in 1970. 'I learnt this in the army; loyalty to the organisation, loyalty to the man you work for, that's the indispensable quality in life.'

But such a simple, admirable view, begs many questions. Supposing the boss is a rogue; the organisation exploits its workers; the general is sending his men to certain but avoidable death. Denis, who clearly does not mean *blind* loyalty, could resign, criticise, put in a damning report; but for the man lower down, who might find no alternative job were he to leave or risk the sack, the idea of total loyalty can have a bitter ring.

In Denis's life such loyalty has served him well, coupled with personal ambition. 'If I start something, by golly I mean to get to the top of the tree,' he told *The Times*. Despite moments of loneliness, those who think he moulders away his time in Number 10 while his wife carries on the business of government are mistaken. His desk is deep in letters which will be answered personally. His diary is full. Although sometimes he longs for peace, the habit of work remains; 'I tell Mark,' he once said, 'if you want to run two houses and two motor cars the only way you can do it is work.' Given such beliefs, it is surprising perhaps that he does not turn his thoughts and energies and compassion to the plight of the unemployed, especially to those who seem to have the drive but not the opportunity. He has been helped so much himself by a good start in life, loving parents, a family business to rejuvenate and later a degree of personal wealth not enjoyed by the other spouses in this book, which gives him the chance to escape abroad when he wishes.

Never tied down by children, he has been spared the rather patronising attitudes sometimes reserved for wives of the great, but he has not been accorded the chivalry and special consideration. In Canberra, left in the corner at a reception while the guests crowded round his wife, he was labelled 'wet' when he complained to an Australian farmer of his neglect, a misnomer for a man of proven physical courage, who has, in his opinion, overcome a lifetime of shyness to be a prime minister's consort. This complaint, though mild, does demonstrate once again how hard is the lot of prime minister's spouse; he or she must always take second place and cope with tiredness, jet-lag and abrupt changes of climate without the adrenalin of power charging the system.

At Mrs Indira Gandhi's funeral Denis was mistakenly asked to travel in a van with the leaders of the British Opposition parties, while Margaret was driven nearer the front of the cortège in a limousine. Parted from his spouse as surely no female partner would have been, he showed, in front of the television cameras, no embarrassment or discontent. The world saw a man without envy who would never follow the examples of those countless film actors whose marriages have collapsed as their wives became stars.

Denis is the first husband of a potential prime minister to have stayed the course; his survival, as we have seen, is partly due to his early acceptance of his wife's political ambition. Although it is difficult to draw a parallel because the men's circumstances were so different, Oriana Fallaci's acclaimed interviews in 1972 with Indira Gandhi and Golda Meir highlight tensions and sorrows in their marriages to which, despite his bravado, Denis cannot be a stranger.

Mrs Gandhi, fighting for the freedom of India, frequently forsook her husband to serve her father, Jawaharlal Nehru. When Feroze Gandhi, who found consolation with other women, was dead, she declared that she would not marry again. 'Why should I get married now that my life is so full?' Turned round another way this statement says, 'I have no time for a husband now that my life is so full.'

'He wanted me to stay at home and forget politics . . .' Mrs Meir says of her husband, a longing which has sometimes seized Denis, too. '. . . I made him suffer so much, so much. He took up a way of life which didn't suit him, because it was a kind of life I couldn't do without. It was a tragedy, a great tragedy.'

These women made their husbands feel redundant, unloved. Each spouse had to contend with a wife's overriding ambition to change the fate of a nation, and a growing appetite for power. Marital companionship was frequently denied them. Similarly, and like Mary Wilson, Denis is sometimes the lonely figure outside the action. Like Audrey Callaghan he has grown to see himself as dull and humdrum. Typically he speaks of his wife's cleverness in producing the desired boy and girl in one go, without pausing to think that he contributed to the event himself: biologically it is, after all, the male who decides the sex of a child. He has accepted totally, as many men would not, a second place.

But deep regrets surface from time to time; his last years, as he sees them, are often tinged with a sense of isolation; he expects to be 'in his box' by the end of his wife's second term of office. Speaking nostalgically to friends, he says, 'My idea of heaven is sitting in my garden on a warm June night with half a bottle of bubbly and my wife in a reasonably relaxed mood.'

Denis's position is unique; he is setting an example for others in his unobtrusive struggle to reconcile modern ideas of sexual equality with innate old-fashioned chivalry.

We saw him on television after the bomb explosion at the Grand Hotel, Brighton, in the early hours of October 12th during the Conservative Party's 1984 conference, dutifully standing behind Margaret while she announced that the conference would resume that day as planned. He was spectacleless, but quiet, fully dressed and composed. All good Tories, and many others, thanked God that Margaret had survived. Later she was to say that the following Sunday 'was a day I was not meant to see'. And Denis, who had also narrowly escaped death, was to comment in another of those throwaway lines which sometimes mask deeper feelings, 'Our bathroom was rather mangled.' He had been in bed when the bomb exploded, while his wife, assisted from time to time by an aide, wrote her conference speech. The shock, on which he did not comment, must have been considerable to a man of sixty-nine.

How much the curb on his tongue has been influenced by his wife we shall never know. One party aide has described it plainly as 'self-denial'. But the boyish noble ideal of self-sacrifice for the greater good remains. Kipling continues to strengthen resolve.

> If you can force your heart and nerve and sinew
> To serve your turn long after they are gone,
> And so hold on when there is nothing in you
> Except the Will which says to them: 'Hold on!'

Speaking again of her husband, whose unhappiness and death haunted her until the end, Golda Meir said, 'Anyway, his tragedy didn't come from the fact of not understanding me — he understood me very well. It came from the fact that he did understand me, and at the same time realised that he couldn't change me. In short, he knew I had no choice, that I had to be what I was. But he didn't approve, that's it. And who knows that he wasn't right.' But Denis Thatcher at rock bottom *does* approve — that is the saving grace — he believes implicitly that Margaret is leading Britain back to recovery. And yet, despite this approval, such a marriage cannot be without strife. Denis is no walkover. 'Like most of us, he has a temper,' one friend told me.

Husband rather than colleague, he has no axe to grind. If Margaret becomes, in Denis Healey's words, like 'Catherine the Great or the Dragon Empress presiding over the fall of the Manchu Dynasty in China', Denis is quite capable of saying, 'For Christ's sake, Margaret, shut up and relax!'

During her second term of office, fatalism, humour and a readiness to make jokes against established opinion keep him sane. Asked how he stays fit he will say, 'On gin and cigarettes'. His philosophy is very simple. Two days before his seventieth birthday he broke his silence in an interview with Carol. Speaking as consort, he said he was constantly asked 'Why do you do it?' His reply: 'For love and loyalty. God gives you a job . . . get out and do it.'

EPILOGUE

Audrey Callaghan thinks Mary Wilson was right when she said that there was no such thing as a prime minister's consort. 'The job is what you make of it. After all, Edward Heath did quite well without a wife.' True. But had Heath been married his wife would have been expected to play her part. All the spouses discussed in this book deserve high marks for trying. Only Elizabeth Home relished the job; only Mary Wilson had a fulltime secretary. Each grew up in a religious atmosphere of high endeavour and their lives and efforts reflected this. Three were the daughters of religious leaders whose voices were often heard from the pulpit. The ninth Duke of Devonshire had no official position within the church, but frequently took morning prayers or read the lesson.

Denis Thatcher found spiritual beliefs at a Nonconformist school, whose influence he believes to have been deep and lasting, but he was ecumenical enough to marry his first wife in a village church and his second in the Wesleyan Church. His *joie de vivre* has not been dimmed by the Calvinist shadow that sometimes stalks Mary Wilson.

Certainly the four women were conditioned in childhood to the idea that men took the helm, although Daniel Baldwin and Frank Moulton were influential in smaller spheres than the others. Undoubtedly Lady Dorothy and Elizabeth Home were helped by their youthful travels, becoming accustomed early to the change and excitement that Mary Wilson was to find so difficult. The Duchess of Devonshire, Mrs Alington and Mrs Moulton appear to have been stronger characters than Mrs Baldwin whose interests were more closely confined to the house, and if daughters are inclined to fashion their behaviour, albeit subconsciously, on their mothers' examples, this is significant. What is important is that every spouse was brought up with a belief in personal sacrifice for the greater good, which would ensure that each would later pick up the gauntlet and support the partner at the top. Undoubtedly Mary and Lady Dorothy did so with a degree of cynicism not experienced by the others. Elizabeth Home gave of herself most enthusiastically because she, above all, was a driving force behind her spouse's motivation. Lady Dorothy became more of a mentor than the others, not because she was the only one willing to offer advice, but because hers was the advice most often sought. Loyal enough to be forgiven the occasional snatched day at a point-to-point when she might have been expected in the House, she bore her responsibilities with a lightness of heart that eluded the others.

Denis Thatcher has weathered both the advantages and disadvantages of leadership in his own right; he is the breadwinner who has done so much to aid his spouse's climb to the top, only to find himself in second place. Fortunately a strong-willed mother and grandmother ensured that he accepted early that women could be both high-spirited and dominating. But he never expected to be outstripped by a woman, just as Mary never anticipated that her young husband would stray — once he had dropped his journalistic ambitions — from the more enclosed world of the academic. Mary and Denis seem to recognise in each other a mutual bewilderment; each is a little sorry for the other. It is no coincidence that *Private Eye*'s editor has singled them out for satire.

The influence of class, of schooling — still a divisive force today — has been a theme running through this book like the threads of scarlet and blue. Macmillan's dream of a classless society which once seemed so close to realisation has disappeared. Our present prime minister may be the daughter of a grocer married to a man devoid of snobbery, but under her government the polarisation of the classes, the gap between rich and poor, has become once again a major factor in politics, so that every consort's class background has taken on new significance. The cries of trade unionists for working-class solidarity across the world and the Tories' policy of encouraging the accumulation of wealth and therefore the *nouveaux riches* have only heightened a sense of class conflict which I have felt unable to ignore, believing that it impinges on many aspects of my subjects' lives and their contemporaries.

Each was well into middle age when power came within their partner's grasp. None sacrificed a career in playing prime minister's consort. For, although Mary Wilson felt deprived of time in which to write verse, such frustration can be inspiration's spur, such fame at one remove an incentive to publishers, and she has actually produced fewer poems since her husband's retirement.

No spouse really liked living in Number 10's flat, although Lady Home was uncritical, saying she 'was hardly ever there'. Mary Wilson's charitable and political works were linked most closely to her husband's position. She attended more official functions alone and addressed more meetings than the others simply as prime minister's spouse.

Students of religion will no doubt read into the characters and actions of these five very different people the influence of the various types of Christian education they received, whether or not they carried their beliefs with them into adulthood. The question tantalises: does a future leader choose a spouse, either consciously or unconsciously, most suitable for the job which will eventually come his or her way — a person of commitment, loyalty and altruism who will not divert attention away from the more ambitious partner, for no politician wishes to be upstaged? I think they do.

Mary Wilson, the most temperamental, the most tried, the least well-prepared has come out of the experience the most disillusioned with politics. You feel now that she still believes in the old socialist message, but not in the men and women who promote it. Like Lady Dorothy she has let people know that she has seen through the hypocrisies. The others remain stalwart behind their partners, not chic, not profound, but constant companions on trips across the world, remarkable for their loyalty, their endurance and their humility.

Now the Brighton bombing has added new and frightening dimensions, unknown to Lady Dorothy Macmillan. My five subjects have survived so far into old age or natural death; their stories have comparatively happy endings. Yet none will envy those who take their place in the future. None will recommend the post. Every married prime minister will be asking a spouse to sacrifice not only time, energy, privacy and peace, but possibly life itself.

BIBLIOGRAPHY

LADY DOROTHY MACMILLAN GBE

Boothby, Robert: *Fight to Live*, London 1947
Boothby, Robert: *My Yesterday, Your Tomorrow*, London 1962
Boothby, Robert: *Recollections of a Rebel*, London 1978
Burke's Peerage and Baronetage, London 1984
Channon, Chips: *The Diaries of Sir Henry Channon*, edited by R.A. James, London 1967
Devonshire, Duchess of: *The House, A Portrait of Chatsworth*, London 1982
Egremont, Lord: *Wyndham and Children First*. London 1968
Evans, Harold: *Downing Street Diary*, London 1981
Fisher, Nigel: *Harold Macmillan*, London 1984
Girouard, Mark: *Hardwick Hall*, London 1976
Hubbard, R.H.: *Rideau Hall, an Illustrated History of Government House Ottawa*, Montreal and London 1977
Hutchinson, George: *The Last Edwardian at Number Ten*, London 1980
Macmillan, Harold: *Winds of Change 1914–1939*, London 1966
Macmillan, Harold: *The Blast of War 1939–1945*, London 1967
Macmillan, Harold: *Tides of Fortune 1945–1955*, London 1969
Macmillan, Harold: *Riding the Storm 1956–1959*, London 1971
Nicolson, Harold: *Diaries 1930–1964*. London 1980
Pearson, John: *Stags and Serpents: The Story of the House of Cavendish and the Dukes of Devonshire*, London 1983
Sampson, Anthony: *A Study in Ambiguity*, London 1967
Waugh, Evelyn: *The Life of Ronald Knox*, London 1962

Interviews:
Ashcroft, Eileen: *Evening Standard*, 24th Nov 1958
King, Stella: *Evening News and Star*. 19th Oct 1962
Landen, Mavis: *Yorkshire Post*, 13th March 1958
'Portrait Gallery'; unsigned article: *Sunday Times*, 27th July 1958

'The New Hostess at No. 10' unsigned article: *Evening News*, 10th Jan 1957
Sharpley, Anne: *Evening Standard*, 10th Jan 1957

LADY HOME OF THE HIRSEL

Alington, C.A.: *A Dean's Apology*, London 1952
Alington, C.A.: *Eton Fables*, London 1921
Alington, C.A.: *An Eton Poetry Book*, London 1925
Alington, C.A.: *Fables and Fancies*, London 1943
Alington, C.A.: *In Shabby Streets*, London 1942
Alington, C.A.: *Things Ancient and Modern*, London 1936
Askith, Betty: *The Lytteltons: A Family Chronicle of the Nineteenth Century*, London 1975
Austen-Leigh, R.C. *Eton Guide* (revised by R.C. Martineau and T.P. Connor), Eton 1981
Dickie, John: *The Uncommon Commoner*, London 1964
Douglas-Home, William: *Mr Home Pronounced Hume: An Autobiography*, London 1974
Home, Lord: *The Way the Wind Blows*, London 1976
Home, Lord: *Letters to a Grandson*, London 1983

Interviews:
The Lady Home Collection of Scrapbooks, The Hirsel, Coldstream, Berwickshire

LADY WILSON OF RIEVAULX

Barnett, Joel: *Inside the Treasury*, London 1982
Crane, D.G.: *Fulbourn Chronicle 1901–1930*, Fulbourn 1983
Congregational Year Book, Nottingham 1946
Falkender (Williams) Marcia: *Inside Number 10*, London 1972
Falkender, Marcia: *Downing Street in Perspective*, London 1983
Haines, Joe: *The Politics of Power*, London 1977
Kay, Eric: *Pragmatic Premier*, London 1967
The Miltonian Centenary Issue 1871–1971, Grimsby 1972

Noel, Gerard Eyre: *Harold Wilson and the 'New Britain'*, London 1964

Roth, Andrew: *Sir Harold Wilson: Yorkshire Walter Mitty*, London 1977

Smith, Dudley: *Harold Wilson; A Critical Biography*, London 1964

Wells, John: *Masterpieces*, London 1982

Wilson, Mary: 'The Discreet Art of Making Small Talk', *The Times*, 16th Feb 1977

Wilson, Mary: *Selected Poems*, London 1970

Wilson, Mary: *New Poems*, London, 1977

Wilson, Mary: 'Some Childhood Memories', *Wentworth Milton Mount Magazine*, Grimsby 1978

Wilson, Mary: 'On Thirteen Years' Hard Labour', *Guardian* 10th May 1976

Interviews:

Coleman, Pamela: *Sunday Express Magazine*, 13th March 1983

Harris, Kenneth: *The Observer*, 9th June 1963

Harris, Kenneth: *The Observer*, 17th Jan 1965

Read, Sue: *Daily Mail*, 19th Oct 1979

Reynolds, Gillian: *Daily Telegraph*, 20th Oct 1979

Willis, Ted: *Woman's Own*, 22nd May 1976

Wilson, Lee: *Mail on Sunday*, 20th Feb 1983

Zec, Donald: *Daily Mail*, 5th June 1970

AUDREY CALLAGHAN

Abse, Leo: *Private Member*, London 1973

Barnett, Joel: *Inside the Treasury*, London 1982

Callaghan, Audrey: 'Leading Ladies', *Sunday Times* 8th Aug 1976

Callaghan, James: *A House Divided, The Dilemma of Northern Ireland*, London 1973

Kellner, Peter and Hitchens, Christopher: *Callaghan, The Road to Number Ten*, London 1976

Bibliography

Articles and Interviews:
Barrie, James: *Guardian*, 6th June 1970
Clare, John: *New York Times*, 6th April 1976
Coleman, Terry: *Guardian*, 6th July 1970
Toner, Michael: *Sunday Express*, 4th April 1976
Young, Hugo: *Sunday Times*, 1st Jan 1978

DENIS THATCHER MBE, TD

Aris, George: *The Fifth British Division 1939–1945*, London 1959
Cosgrave, Patrick: *Margaret Thatcher; A Tory and her Party*, London 1978
Fallaci, Oriana: *Interview with History*, London 1976
Gardiner, George: *Margaret Thatcher from Childhood to Leadership*, London 1978
Junor, Penny: *Margaret Thatcher, Wife, Mother and Politician*, London 1983
Mayer, Allan J.: *Madame Prime Minister: Margaret Thatcher and her Rise to Power*, New York 1979
Money, Ernle: *Margaret Thatcher: First Lady of the House*, London 1975
Murray, Tricia: *Margaret Thatcher*, London 1978
Nicholson, Lieut.-Col. C.W.L.: *The Canadians in Italy: The Official History of the Canadian Army in Italy in the Second World War Vol. 11*, Ottawa 1956
Scotney Castle, The National Trust, London 1982
Strickland, Margot: *The King Comes to Southwold*, Southwold 1984
Thatcher, Carol: *Diary of an Election: A Personal Account*, London 1983

Articles and Interviews:
Chester, Lewis: *Sunday Times*, 2nd Dec 1982
Corbett, Kirstin: *The Times*, 5th Oct 1970
Hoggart, Simon: *Observer Review*, 9th June 1983
Mailer, Norman: *Mail on Sunday*, 5th June 1983
Pile, Stephen: *Sunday Telegraph*, 4th May 1980
Porter, Henry: *Sunday Times*, 27th May 1984

'Supportive Consort at Number 10' (unsigned): *The Observer*, 29th May 1983

Thatcher, Carol: *Sunday Express*, 22nd Aug 1982; *Daily Telegraph*, 9th May 1985

Tyler, Rodney: *The Times*, 7th Feb 1985

Young, Hugo: BBC Radio 4, 12th May 1985

GENERAL BIBLIOGRAPHY

Barnes, Susan: *Behind the Image*, London 1974

Barrow, Andrew: *Gossip 1920–1970*, London 1978

Castle, The Rt Hon Barbara: *The Castle Diaries 1974–1976*, London 1980

Castle, The Rt Hon Barbara: *The Castle Diaries 1964–1970*, London 1984

Crosland, Susan (Barnes): *Tony Crosland*, London 1982

Crossman, Richard: *Diaries of a Cabinet Minister*, 1964–1966, London 1975

Crossman, Richard: *Backbench Diaries*, Edited by Janet Morgan, London 1981

Iremonger, Lucille: *The Fiery Chariot*, London 1970

Private Eye 1962–1984

Newspapers:
Daily Express, Daily Herald, Daily Mail, Daily Telegraph, Evening News, Evening Standard, Guardian, Mail on Sunday, New Statesman and Nation, The Observer, The Sketch, The Spectator, The Star, Sunday Express, Sunday Times, The Times, Yorkshire Post.

INDEX